PENGUIN BOOKS

EVERYTHING YOU PRETEND TO KNOW ABOUT FOOD
and are afraid someone will ask

Nancy Rommelmann is the co-author of the *New York Times* bestseller *The Real Real World*, based on the MTV series. A former caterer and baker, she is a contributing editor at *Los Angeles* magazine, a frequent contributor to *Bon Appétit*, and has written essays and features for *Buzz*, *bikini*, the *Los Angeles Times*, and *Living Fit*. She lives in Los Angeles with her seven-year-old daughter.

EVERYTHING YOU PRETEND TO KNOW ABOUT FOOD

and are afraid someone will ask

NANCY ROMMELMANN

PENGUIN BOOKS

PENGUIN BOOKS

Published by the Penguin Group
Penguin Putnam Inc., 375 Hudson Street,
New York, New York 10014, U.S.A.
Penguin Books Ltd, 27 Wrights Lane,
London W8 5TZ, England
Penguin Books Australia Ltd, Ringwood,
Victoria, Australia
Penguin Books Canada Ltd, 10 Alcorn Avenue,
Toronto, Ontario, Canada M4V 3B2
Penguin Books (N.Z.) Ltd, 182–190 Wairau Road,
Auckland 10, New Zealand

Penguin Books Ltd, Registered Offices:
Harmondsworth, Middlesex, England

First published in Penguin Books 1998

3 5 7 9 10 8 6 4

LIBRARY OF CONGRESS CATALOGING IN PUBLICATION DATA
Rommelmann, Nancy.
Everything you pretend to know about food and are afraid someone
will ask/Nancy Rommelmann.
p.   cm.
Includes bibliographical references (p.   ).
ISBN 0 14 02.6373 X (pbk.)
1. Food—Miscellanea.   I. Title.
TX355.R65   1998
641.3—dc21   97–36246

Printed in the United States of America
Set in Sabon
Designed by Claudyne Bedell

Thanks to my agent, Laura Dail; my editors at Viking Penguin, Laurie Walsh and Jane von Mehren; my friend Michelle Huneven, for graciously answering many a frantic food query; my mom, Kathy Hayes, for always adding another nickel of knowledge; and writers Laurie Colwin, Bert Greene, and M.F.K. Fisher, for arousing our somatic and cerebral appetites with enthusiasm, humor, and erudition.

CONTENTS

I was sitting in a Thai restaurant, trying to work up the nerve to order something besides the usual *saté,* when my friend slammed shut the menu and declared he was going to try some *larb*.

"What's larb?" I asked, conjuring up an unappetizing image of a brick of lard.

"I don't know," he answered, "but it sounds . . . good."

A salad of beef, lime juice, and chiles, larb *was* good, and I found myself feeling inordinately proud. Though my friend didn't have any idea of what he was in for, he was intrepid enough to investigate, damn the torpedoes and digestive tracts.

His confidence started me thinking about how timid we often are about what we eat; if we haven't heard of it (or our mothers didn't serve it), it is often relegated to a sort of gustatory limbo. We are more comfortable, somehow, ignoring cactus pads and honeycomb tripe than spending hours trying to figure out how to purchase and prepare them; squeamish that, if we do risk the effort, we may not like the result.

This disregard of the cornucopia of edible stuff available to us is an unfortunate reflection of a society fast losing its hold on the culinary reins, testament to an aggregate population more comfortable opening a can than reading about what goes into their mouths. (Do you really want to know what's inside that can of MacaroniOs?)

This was not the case one hundred years ago. Our rural ancestors surely knew what was for dinner; if they weren't growing it, their neighbors were. While urban dwellers may have had a wider selection of varied foodstuffs at their disposal, their cultural ties often dictated the menu. Hence, if your family was two generations off the boat from Italy, chances are you were still religiously eating gnocchi, while your German neighbors were feasting on spaetzle.

But times have changed. While our great-grandparents may not have had to decipher a foreign menu, they were also excluded from the culinary boom that is happening all around us, a boon that, granted, can be as confusing as it is rewarding.

So what can we do? Take an interpreter to the restaurant, an encyclopedia to the supermarket? How do we keep from looking like rubes, while at the same time eating like kings?

Some people choose to leave the esoteric to the gourmands, subscribing to a trickle-down theory of food awareness. If Mexican food is the season's cause célèbre, these folks may venture as far as a frozen enchilada. To them, it is more convenient (and less frightening) to taste a third-rate version of a new dish than risk venturing into a new culinary arena. For others, however, culinary diversification and a quest for better nutrition have prompted serious investigation.

This book is for all these people, in hopes a few questions about food, no matter how silly or arcane, will be answered.

This is not to say we should be obsessive about trying everything (hey, you still can't sell me on candied fruit), nor overly opinionated. (A pox on the next vegetarian who wanders into the barbecue shouting, "You're grilling dead cow!") But being informed and being obnoxious are two different matters. Knowing that gnocchi are potato dumplings and spaetzle are egg noodles never got on anyone's nerves.

In the end, I feel strongly that food should be a sensual experience, not an academic one. Still, a little knowledge can only make manifold the pleasures of the meal, and who knows? After perusing the following, you may just be the one informing others as to what's on the menu.

EVERYTHING YOU PRETEND TO KNOW ABOUT FOOD
and are afraid someone will ask

Meat and Game

There is poetry in a pork chop to a hungry man.
—PHILIP GIBBS, quoted in the *New York Times*, 1951

According to Waverely Root's glorious *Food*, "It is the universal experience that peoples everywhere, unless there are religious or cultural inhibitions, tend to eat as much meat as they can afford." In the United States, this means better than 115 pounds per person per year.

This is quite a bit more than the average citizen of the planet consumes. It is versatile, high in protein (20 to 25 grams per four-ounce serving of lean beef), and rich in B vitamins and zinc (both considered "brain food," a belief sustained by Buckminster Fuller's regimen of a raw steak each day). For many, meat is the centerpiece of a proper meal.

Unlike sugar and salt, meat is not one of those pesky ingredients that sneak into our diets surreptitiously. We eat meat aggressively, wantonly, attacking a classic Chateaubriand and a sloppy chili burger with equal gusto. And toward those who decry meat as murder, carnivores are tolerant. Perhaps because we know the voluptuous satisfaction that comes from biting into a buttery, broiled T-bone.

WHERE'S THE *T* IN A T-BONE STEAK?

A T-bone wears its eponymous T-shaped bone like a bow, on the top of the short loin cut. This small, flat bone (flat bones adjoin more tender cuts, whereas knobby or round bones indicate tougher sections) separates the small tenderloin section from the larger top loin. We can thank America's butchers for the T-bone steak; outside of the United States, the bone is usually removed and the cut given the generic name "sirloin." Too bad, as the T-bone's succulence proves the proverb "The nearer the bone, the sweeter the meat."

HOW DOES THE U.S. DEPARTMENT OF AGRICULTURE GRADE BEEF?

There are five grades of beef: Prime, Choice, Good, Standard, and Commercial. Contrary to what a fat-obsessed nation would like to believe, the higher the quality, the more choice fat there is in a piece of meat. Not extraneous gristle, not flaps of excess chub, but well-incorporated white fat that the USDA calls "marbling."

USDA Prime is the highest-quality meat available and comes from young, well-fed cattle. It is evenly marbled with fat, which makes it tender, juicy, and flavorful. Prime is harder to find and more expensive than the next grade of beef, the widely available *USDA Choice*. Choice contains less fat than Prime but enough interior marbling to guarantee a tender, tasty cut of meat. *USDA Good* lacks some of the fat and flavor of Choice meat and is often ground into hamburger. *USDA Standard* is quite lean, with decidedly less flavor than Good, and is not commonly found in supermarkets. *USDA Commercial* is used primarily by manufacturers for cold cuts, frankfurters, and sausage. It comes from older cows and is not suitable for home consumption.

Grading, however, is not always reflected in price. While you will always pay more for filet than chuck, supermarkets are well aware that consumers are trying to cut back on their fat intake; hence, a relatively low-fat, relatively flavorless minute steak may wind up costing, ounce for ounce, as much as a thick, juicy Spencer steak.

Additionally, the USDA has three *substandard* gradings for meat: *Utility, Cutter,* and *Canner.* These include sundry sections (neck bones, lower shanks) suitable for pet foods and bone meals.

IS LONDON BROIL AN ENGLISH CUT?

London broil, a section of *flank steak,* has no direct British link. However, the English do butcher their beef somewhat differently, cutting a larger flank section; hence, perhaps, the eponymous appropriation.

Whatever the country of origin, flank steaks are notoriously tough, and they benefit greatly from a few hours or overnight in a marinade. They are then broiled or grilled quickly, and are *always* cut on the diagonal, or against the grain, thereby slicing through the chewy connective tissue and making the rather tough cut infinitely less chewy.

DID NEW YORK STEAK ORIGINATE IN NEW YORK?

Ask a New Yorker, and he'll tell you *everything* originated in New York. Steak is no exception. That is, if you're talking about the aged, prime porterhouse they serve at Peter Luger's in Brooklyn. Or the beef tenderloin at Sammy's Roumanian in Manhattan. Or the rib eye from the fabled Delmonico's.

The fact is, there is no one New York steak but rather a coterie of well-prepared, choice cuts that go under the name "New York." The closest consensus (we're dealing with New Yorkers here) is that a New York steak is a shell steak or sirloin, cut one to one-and-a-half inches thick, with a rim of fat that gets crisp under the broiler. It is served medium-rare, with just its juices as an accompaniment. And good? You gotta ask?

WHY IS SOME MEAT TENDER AND SOME MEAT TOUGH?

The general rule on tenderness if is: The closer to the head or the hoof, the tougher the meat. Other factors that determine meat's tenderness include age and how active the steer was. The more active and older the animal, the more connective tissue will be built up and therefore the tougher the meat. In Japan, steers raised for Kobe beef are massaged daily to keep their muscles loose and pliant, yielding an incredibly tender meat. Tenderness, however, does not come cheap, with Kobe beef running upwards of one hundred dollars per pound.

WHAT'S THE MOST TENDER CUT OF MEAT? WHAT'S THE TOUGHEST?

The most tender cut usually available in America is a filet mignon. Literally translated as "dainty ribbon" or "little thread," filet mignon is a cut of the tenderloin, a boneless, elongated section that runs through the sirloin and the loin. Also called beef filet, the tapered tenderloin is butchered into three sections: Chateaubriand (from the center of the beef filet), tournedo (from the small end), and filet mignon (from the wide end). While it is extremely tender, it is not the most flavorful cut, as it relatively low in fat and does not benefit from being near a bone. It is best cooked very quickly, either by broiling, grilling, or sautéing.

The toughest sections of beef are near the head and feet: chuck (usually ground into hamburger) and shanks (edible only after slow, moist cooking).

WHAT IS AGED BEEF?

Aged beef is Prime beef that has been stored for several weeks at temperatures just above freezing. During this time, the connective tissues soften, and the meat "shrinks" slightly, concentrating the flavor. Aged meat has a deeper color, a more intense flavor, and cooks more quickly than non-aged beef. Before you try this at home, however, know that conditions must be optimal. Keeping meat in a home fridge, with its average temperature of forty degrees, for a couple of weeks will yield nothing but lethal bacteria.

THERE'S LAMB CHOP AND PORK CHOP. HOW COME NO BEEF CHOP?

There is. It's called a Porterhouse, or a T-bone, or top loin. All these sections come from the short loin of the steer. Because a cow is much larger than either a lamb or pig, the resulting cuts are bigger; a beef "chop," therefore, would weigh upwards of thirty pounds.

WHEN DOES VEAL BECOME BEEF?

At about three months. Veal are solely milk-fed, and their flesh is very white and tender. Three-to-six-month-old calves are called vealers, and though their meat is slightly pinker it is still very delicate. After six months, calves are young steers; after a year, they are considered cattle and are generally butchered, between the ages of eleven and sixteen months.

WHAT'S MEANT BY A MIXED GRILL?

A mixed grill is a dish of mixed, grilled meats comprised of (but not limited to) beef, lamb, and pork and usually including innards like kidneys and sweetbreads, as well as grilled tomatoes and mushrooms. It is said to be of English origin, though many an Argentinean meal features *parillada,* a sizzling platter of many grilled meats.

WHAT IS CHICKEN-FRIED STEAK?

Just about everyone knows what frying does for the taste of chicken. Meat eaters west of the Mississippi do the same for minute steaks (thin, boneless beefsteak that needs only about one minute of cooking per side). Pounded thin, dredged in seasoned flour, and pan fried in some kind of fat, the "chicken-fried" steak is heavenly stick-to-your-ribs fare, especially when served with milk gravy made with the pan juices and biscuits to sop up any errant calories.

HOW DID THE HAMBURGER GET ITS NAME?

If you guessed Hamburg, Germany, you're half right. In fact, the hamburger's earliest guise dates back to medieval times, when the Tartar peoples of the Baltic states ate their beef raw, chopped, and seasoned with salt, pepper, and onion. German ships began docking at Russian ports, and the Teutonic seamen devoured the raw meat, importing the idea back to their port city of Hamburg, where the original steak tartare became the Hamburg steak. The steaks were later subjected to broiling and, on a progressive march west, sandwiching. In the 1800s, German immigrants brought the Hamburg steak to the Ohio Valley. In 1904, the Hamburger Sandwich (this one fried) was launched at the Louisiana Exposition, and America's love affair with what would become a food synonymous with Americana was consummated.

IN NINETEENTH-CENTURY NOVELS, THE INFIRMED WERE FED "BEEF TEA." WHAT IS IT?

Beef tea is a broth intended for sick people who are having difficulty with solids. It is made by boiling lean, cubed meat in water for several hours. The resulting "tea" is defatted, strained, salted (or not), and served plain. Because of its restorative reputation, beef tea was fed with particular vigor to those with weakening ailments, such as the vapors and "thin blood."

As to its curative properties, beef tea seems to work for the same reasons as chicken soup: It's hydrating and easy on the system.

WHAT IS JERKY?

Jerky, a corruption of the Arawak Indian word *charqui*, is a food that has been cured and dried. We are most familiar with beef jerky (and its impoverished offspring, meat sticks wrapped in plastic), but any flesh food can be jerked. The Blackfeet Indians jerk elk, and jerk salmon is popular in Alaska.

While wood smoke and sunlight yield the tastiest jerky, this meat can also be made at home with good, defatted meat, a salt solution, and long-cooking in a very slow (175 to 200 degrees) oven.

WHAT DOES *AU JUS* MEAN?

Au jus (pronounced *o ju*, French for "in the gravy") is meat served solely with its own cooking juices. A primitive method for the modern, calorie-phobic cook, serving meat *au jus* is also appreciated by gourmands who've sworn off rich sauces like béarnaise (an herb-infused butter that rests like a crown on roasted meats). Remember, however, that meat must contain juice in order to produce *jus*. Prime rib is a prime example of a meat served *au jus*.

WHAT IS DAUBE?

Daube, which the writer Henri Bosco called "the greatest of all treasures," is a French stew made with beef, red wine, and vegetables. There are as many variations of and additions to daube as there are *grand-mères* in the kitchen, yet invariably the meat is slow-simmered about four hours, until the meat is succulent and thoroughly infused with the richness of the wine. Daube is served with noodles, potatoes, rice, or a big loaf of bread to drink up the winy sauce.

WHAT'S THE DIFFERENCE BETWEEN LAMB AND MUTTON?

About a year and a half. Lambs are slaughtered between three and twelve months of age, whereas mutton is the meat of a full-grown, two-year-old sheep. Lambs between one and two years are called yearling lambs.

The difference in flavor is pronounced. While lamb is prized for its creamy flavor and pale flesh, mutton is usually deep red and marbled, with a musky flavor and aroma. Predictably, the flavor of yearlings falls somewhere between the two.

If mutton is to be substituted for lamb, know that cooking times must be increased five to ten minutes per pound.

There's also baby lamb, or "hot-house" lamb, bottle-fed and marketed before nine weeks of age. As expected, the meat is extremely tender and the taste so delicate as to be inexpressible.

HOW DO YOU BUTTERFLY LAMB?

Butterflying involves the slitting open and spreading of food so that it resembles the wings of a butterfly. While it may also help to cook the food more quickly, butterflying is really a matter of aesthetics, not expediency.

Leg of lamb is most commonly butterflied. The process entails the trimming of all fat and fell (the membrane which covers the leg), removing the bone, and shaping the meat to look like a butterfly before it is grilled or broiled. In Italy, chicken that is butterflied and grilled is called *pollo alla diavolo,* or "chicken cooked the devil's way," perhaps because the spreading and roasting of the food resembles the treatment Satan accords sinners roasting on the racks of hell.

WHAT IS HAGGIS?

Haggis is a hearty pudding made by stuffing the belly of a sheep (or occasionally a pig) with boiled innards (such as the liver, heart, and lungs) chopped and mixed with seasonings and oatmeal. The mixture is stuffed into the stomach and boiled, until the oatmeal puffs and the pudding is thick. Although in his poem "To a Haggis" Robert Burns called this celebrated Scottish dish the "chieftain o' the puddin' race!" it sounds somewhat repulsive to the uninitiated. However, the taste is not unlike the giblet-rich stuffings so many look forward to on Thanksgiving.

DO THE FRENCH REALLY EAT HORSES?

Yes, and they're not the only ones. Horsemeat is still enjoyed in many European countries, including Germany and Yugoslavia. For millennia, horses were considered a source of meat. By the 1800s, however, most cultures had given up horseflesh, whether because horses were deemed more valuable as agricultural helpmates or because religious leaders proclaimed the meat unfit for human consumption.

France's affinity for horsemeat continues. Though it is purportedly healthful, it is not considered a delicacy. The dark-red meat is inexpensive, somewhat tough, oily, and not so much a dietary staple as a vestige of a gastronomic past.

WHAT'S THE DIFFERENCE BETWEEN RABBIT AND HARE?

Rabbits are smaller than hares, and their meat is all-white, as opposed to hares, whose meat is dark. Rabbits are born without fur and with their eyes closed, whereas hares are born furry and ready to run. These differences contribute to the impression that hares are wild rabbits; they are not. Both rabbits and hares can be bred in captivity.

Americans have been slow to incorporate rabbit and hare into their diet. (In Europe, rabbit is as common as chicken.) Perhaps it's the Easter Bunny correlation, or the fact that rabbits and hares are members of the rodent family. Either way, it's a shame, as rabbit is as versatile as chicken, with more protein and a richer taste.

I'VE SEEN BUFFALO BURGERS ON MENUS LATELY. WHY NOW?

It used to be you could get a buffalo burger only out West, where buffalo still roamed the range. The past decade, however, has seen a burgeoning number of cattle ranchers adding buffalo to their livestock and consequently to our diet.

Buffalo meat tastes a lot like beef, though it is slightly tougher and not as juicy. It is most often ground into burgers, slow-braised, or made into jerky.

WHAT'S "BEEFALO"?

Beefalo is a cross between bison, or buffalo, and cattle. A beefalo has rich, lean, dark-red meat and is prepared the same way as beef. The American market has been slow on the beefalo uptake, however, making it hard to find outside of specialty and mail-order markets.

This scarcity may also have something to do with America's revisionist romanticism of the Wild West. The images of slaughtered buffalo on the Western plains of yesteryear doesn't inspire appetite and makes the consumption of both buffalo and beefalo seem somehow sacriligious.

WHAT'S A RASHER OF BACON?

A rasher is a slice or a portion of bacon. This sixteenth-century term is still favored in England, where a side of ham or Canadian bacon is called a gammon (from the French word for ham, *jambon.*)

For the record, the fatty strips we call bacon are not bacon the world over. Most bacons contain more lean meat than ours and is sliced into rounds or rectangles, not ribbons. Familiar examples are dry, meaty Canadian bacon and salty, thin-sliced *pancetta,* from Italy. In France, they eat smoky *poitrine fumee* (or alternately, le lard), in Germany, extra-fatty *speck,* and in Austria (where they consume more pork per capita than any other country), the delicate *Kaiserfleisch.*

If you're counting on bacon and eggs while abroad, however, you may be in for a disappointment. Bacon is not considered breakfast fare in most countries but is eaten simply with bread and perhaps cheese, or added to stews or fried with potatoes or greens.

WHAT'S SUET?

Suet is the hard, fatty tissue around the kidneys of cattle and sheep. Removed and shredded, it is either used like lard (rendered pork fat), to make a flaky piecrust in recipes such as spotted Dick (a suet pastry filled with raisins and spices), or beaten, like butter, and used as the base for English steamed puddings rich in fruits and nuts.

WHAT IS HEAD CHEESE?

Head cheese, also called brawn, is described in *The Joy of Cooking* as "a well-liked, old-fashioned dish." The emphasis is on old-fashioned, when every part of a home-butchered animal was made use of.

Head cheese is a laborious, if straightforward, affair: The head of a calf, minus ears, eyes, and brains, is slowly simmered until the meat falls from the bones; then it is mixed with herbs and poured into a mold. The finished product is quite gelatinous, the result of all those boiling bones. For better or worse, there is no addition of cheese ("cheese" probably being a reference to the clabbered texture of the product). Commercial head cheese is often ringed in amber aspic, an attempt, perhaps, to dandify a rather plain food.

WHAT IS SCRAPPLE?

Scrapple is a sausage-like product made with the scraps (neck, feet, bones) of the pig. As in head cheese, these are boiled. The meat and the defatted cooking liquid is boiled again with cornmeal, and poured into a mold. After it has become firm, the scrapple is fried in butter or fat, and is usually served as breakfast fare.

WHAT IS RED-FLANNEL HASH?

Old-fashioned hash (from the French word *hacher,* to cut up)—meat, potatoes, and onions, cubed and cooked together in a skillet—becomes New England's red-flannel hash by the addition of beets.

If you fry up some good Virginia ham alongside, you can use the drippings to make *red-eye gravy,* ham fat with a cup of black coffee added to the skillet and stirred until all the ham bits that stuck to the pan are scraped into the whole.

WHAT IS NATURALLY RAISED MEAT?

Naturally raised meat comes from an animal that is raised without steroids, hormones, or antibiotics. Consumers' concerns about ingesting these substances are both immediate (there are claims that the meat is tasteless, akin to eating an artificially ripened tomato) and long-term (shot of steroids, anyone?).

Meat producers' use of these additives, ostensibly to promote growth and good health, has given birth to the natural-meat market. Though not readily available at most supermarkets, additive-free meat can usually be found at health food stores and specialty shops, and are always clearly marked as such. The taste of naturally raised meat is purportedly purer and stronger; in a word, meatier, and is certainly as healthful as chemically plumped meat.

IS IT PREFERABLE TO ROAST OR BRAISE A LARGE CUT OF MEAT?

Auguste Escoffier said, "One becomes a good roaster with a good deal of attention and observation and a little vocation." Perhaps this explains why competing schools of technique are forever vying for the title of "definitive."

The earliest roasting was, of course, done over an open fire. Today, most roasted food comes from the oven. The meat or poultry is placed in a pan, left uncovered (covering promotes steaming, definitely not what you want when you're going for crisp-on-the-outside, juicy-on-the-inside), and baked. But at what temperature? Many cooks roast meat and poultry on a rack (so juices accumulate in the pan, not around the meat) at 350 degrees Fahrenheit, allowing so many minutes per pound until done. Others insist that slow roasting for long periods yields juicier meat and, in the case of poultry, crisper skin. Some roast meat at a very high heat, then turn off the oven. Others roast at 500 degrees without a rack for a short amount of time, leaving the skin super-crisp and the meat exceptionally moist. While each method affords good results, the deciding factor is time and taste.

Braising involves slow, moist cooking and is used on larger, less tender cuts of meat, like shoulder or rump roast. After browning the meat in hot fat, the meat is partially covered with liquid (usually stock or water), covered, and allowed to braise in the oven at a moderately low temperature, 325 degrees, until tender.

Braising can also be done on the top of the stove, as in the case of pot roast or brisket, with the meat simmering several hours. But beware of letting the liquid come to a boil! Many a corned beef has been turned into a football by cooking the meat too quickly at too high heat. While long, slow cooking softens connective tissue, it also toughens muscle fiber. Proper braising requires striking a balance between the two.

Poultry

Poultry is to the kitchen what canvas is to the painter.
—JEAN-ANTHELME BRILLAT-SAVARIN,
The Physiology of Taste, 1825

If, as Grimod de la Reynière stipulated in *Almanach des Gourmands*, "the goose is a snappy brunette, with whom we get along very well," then the chicken is a well versed cosmopolitan, at home in every regional costume. (She is *kung po* in China, *saté* in Malaysia, *paprikás* in Hungary, Southern fried in the U.S. of A.)

She is flexible, reliable, our steadfast friend in any epicurean bind. When we don't know how to categorize the flavor of fowl, we compare it to chicken; felled by flu, we whimper for her soup; perplexed in a café, we go with the *poulet*.

She is essential. When Herbert Hoover's election literature pledged "a chicken in every pot," it was merely echoing Henry IV of France, who'd promised his subjects the same thing nearly four centuries earlier. And chicken goes back further than that: She has been part of our diet since 2000 B.C., when some wise soul in India domesticated a red jungle fowl.

A long-term relationship doesn't mean we know how to cook

her (chicken finger, anyone?) or even properly identify her, which truly does her disservice. In the face of such loyalty, the *least* we can do is identify her.

WHAT'S THE DIFFERENCE BETWEEN A FRYER AND A ROASTER?

A fryer, or *broiler,* is a chicken between six and eight weeks old, weighing between three and four-and-a-half pounds. Fryers are quite tender, but not especially meaty, and are best broiled, fried or poached. A *roaster* is between two and six months old and can reach a weight of up to eight pounds. Roasters' firm breasts and plump bodies make them perfect for roasting.

There are several other categories connoting chicken size. They include:

Rock Cornish game hen: The smallest hen available, these chickens are between five and six weeks old, weigh one to two pounds, and are prized as much for their tiny elegance as for their tenderness.

Capon: Neither cock nor hen, a capon is a caponized (castrated) male under six months. The removal of the sex organs causes the capons to grow lazy and fat, up to ten pounds. Their meat is succulent, plentiful, and mild.

Fowl: Also called a stewing hen, fowl can be up to a year old and weigh as much as seven pounds. These tough yet flavorful old birds benefit most from stewing, and they make a very rich stock.

WHAT IS A FREE-RANGE CHICKEN, AND WHY IS IT CONSIDERED SUPERIOR?

Gourmets claim free-range chickens, or birds that live free-roaming lives until they are killed, are tastier than mass-produced chickens, which spend their lives in cages until they are large enough to slaughter. The reason? Roaming chickens get a lot more air and exercise, thereby building up more muscle than their flabby, coop-bound cousins. But because they are killed at a relatively young age (two to three months), they don't develop enough muscle to make them tough. Ergo, they have a higher meat-to-bone ratio and, according to advocates, a happier life, which translates to a better-tasting afterlife.

IS THERE A NUTRITIONAL DIFFERENCE BETWEEN DARK MEAT AND LIGHT MEAT?

Dark meat (the leg, thigh, and back) has two to ten percent more calories than does light meat (the breast), depending on the bird; fryers are more caloric than roasters. Dark meat also has slightly less protein and about one third more fat. Both are low in cholesterol and supply comparable amounts of A and B vitamins and calcium.

WHAT'S THE BEST WAY TO FRY CHICKEN?

Culinary wars have been started over this seemingly innocuous question. Southerners may soak their chicken in buttermilk and pan-fry it in peanut oil. Northerners might use an egg-milk dip, roll the chicken in crumbs, and deep-fry it. In Maryland, they usually fry in butter. All these methods have purists shaking their skillets in protest.

Frying chicken is an empirical skill, and every good chicken-fryer has memories of burnt skin, bloody meat, bloated breasts, and deteriorated wings. Fortunately, most of these errors are still edible.

The simplest, most effective frying method may be to shake chicken pieces in a paper bag in which you've combined all-purpose flour, salt, and pepper. Let the pieces dry on a rack while you half-fill a heavy skillet with any flavorless oil (corn, peanut, safflower). Heat over a medium flame until hot but not smoking (375 degrees, or until a cube of bread fries golden in under 60 seconds). Quickly reshake the chicken pieces in the flour mix and place as many as will fit in the pan comfortably. Cover the pan, and let the chicken cook until golden brown on one side. Turn with tongs (never with a fork, which pierces the skin and lets the juices run out) and re-cover. Cook until browned on the other side. Lay cooked pieces on a paper bag to cool (placing hot chicken on paper towels steams the crispy skin), salt lightly, and try to wait at least ten minutes before eating, to let the interior juices of the chicken set and to avoid scalding your mouth.

DOES CHICKEN SOUP MERIT ITS CURE-ALL REPUTATION?

The short answer is: Yes, chicken soup earns its curative status. While the chicken *itself* may not harbor any proven panacean properties, its transformation to soup packs a restorative wallop. The technical reasons are many: Chicken soup is easy on a queasy stomach; hot liquids loosen mucus, helping to rid the body of infection; soup provides hydration, which people with a fever need.

Then there's the emotional side of the issue. Chicken soup, also known as "Jewish penicillin," is usually offered by someone, like your mother, who wants you to get better.

And the Jewish mother's secret to a soup that can't hurt and tastes sublime? A few chicken feet, added to the stock. Tradition dictates you remove the skin. Either singe the feet over a flame until the skin bubbles, and then pick it off; or plunge the feet into boiling water for a few seconds, and peel.

WHAT IS JERK CHICKEN?

Jerk chicken (and jerk beef, pork, and fish) hails from Jamaica. Not to be confused with jerky, jerking involves making a sauce of fiery *habañero* (also known as Scotch bonnet) chiles, onions, soy sauce, and spices, marinating the chicken, baking it in the oven, and finishing it on the grill. The flavor is complex and, depending on how heavy your pepper hand is, searingly hot. For this reason, jerked food is usually served with something to cool you down, like rice and peas (white rice cooked with kidney beans and coconut milk and, yes, more habeñero), a hush puppy, or a cool Jamaican beer. And plenty of napkins.

The work *jerk* comes from *charqui,* the Arawak Indian word for a food that has been cured and dried. Legend has it that when African ex-slaves settled in Jamaica, they combined the spices of the local Arawaks and their own African method of open-pit cooking, and jerk was born.

WHAT ARE BUFFALO CHICKEN WINGS?

Buffalo chicken wings are chicken wings doused with a tomato- and cayenne-based sauce, deep-fried, and served with hot sauce and blue cheese dressing for dipping. They were created in Buffalo, New York, in 1964, at Frank and Teresa's Anchor Bar & Restaurant, which still serves over a thousand pounds of wings a day.

WHAT'S A CONEY ISLAND CHICKEN?

A Coney Island chicken is a regional specialty of New York City and is better known as the hot dog.

DOES A TURKEY'S SIZE AND SEX AFFECT ITS FLAVOR?

Yes. Young turkeys (four to six pounds) of either sex are very tender and can be prepared like chicken. Larger hen, or female, turkeys can reach up to twenty pounds and are fatter and sweeter than toms, or males. Tom turkeys, between 16 and 40 pounds, are the big boys we buy over the holidays. Because they have been allowed to grow so large, they contain more muscle and less fat, and are not as juicy. Plus, they are also usually sold frozen, another strike against succulence.

WHAT DOES OSTRICH TASTE LIKE?

Touted as the "new red meat," ostrich began showing up in American markets in 1995. The meat is low in fat, and the flavor is mild, somewhere between beef and poultry—"red-meat chicken," as one diner proclaimed upon biting into her ostrich burger.

In 1996, ground ostrich cost a third as much as ground beef, but ostrich steaks were pricey, about ten dollars per pound, purchased, perhaps, more for their novelty than their flavor. A supermarket employee explained that they sold well initially, but interest flagged. It's doubtful the ostrich will become to American diets what the emu is to Australian, where the small, ostrichlike bird is a common comestible.

While the *Larousse Gastronomique* does not have much good to say about ostrich ("tough, rather flavorless meat"), it does report on the excellency of ostrich eggs: "They were fashionable in the nineteenth century but are not sold today. Since one ostrich egg weighs an average of 1.5 kilograms (3¼ pounds), it would be sufficient to prepare an omelette for eight to ten people." It also notes that the brains were considered a delicacy in the time of Nero.

WHAT IS PEKING DUCK?

Peking duck is a whole Long Island duckling, a descendent of the Beijing duck brought over from China in late 1700s. It is slaughtered and dressed with its head and neck intact. While few non-Asian cooks attempt this dish at home, the birds are readily available in Chinese restaurants and shops, and can usually be seen hanging from their feet in display windows.

In Peking duck, the plucked bird has air pumped into a small hole in its neck, inflating the space between the skin and the meat. The duck is trussed, glazed with honey, and hung to dry for twenty-four hours. It is then roasted, vertically, until the skin is brown and extremely crisp.

The duck is served with thin Chinese pancakes for rolling the rich meat and sweet, chewy skin and with hoisin sauce for dipping.

WHAT'S PRESSED DUCK?

A French specialty that involves removing the legs and breast of a duck, and pressing what remains in a special screw press called a duck press. While the breast meat sizzles in a wine reduction and the legs are grilled, the remaining duck is pressed of all its juices, which are combined with cognac, butter, and wine, and poured atop the prepared duck. The creation of a Rouen restaurateur named Méchenet; as the house specialty at the renowned La Tour d'Argent, in Paris, it is usually prepared tableside.

WHAT'S A GUINEA HEN?

A guinea hen is a small (three-quarters of a pound to four pounds) fowl native to Guinea, West Africa. It has been eaten for thousands of years (the Romans called it Carthage hen) and has been domesticated throughout most of the world. The guinea hen can be prepared like chicken, though it benefits most from slow, moist cooking (its meat is gamey and somewhat dry), and takes especially well to additions of fruits, such as apples and apricots.

IS SQUAB REALLY PIGEON?

The answer is yes. But before urban dwellers, forced to share every square inch of their city with millions of sooty, cooing "winged rats," experience paroxysms of disgust, they should understand squab is pigeon bred solely for eating purposes.

The dark, meaty bird usually weighs under a pound, making one squab per person the rule. It is eaten braised or sautéed and is traditionally accompanied by fresh peas.

WHY DON'T THEY SELL WILD GAME BIRDS, SUCH AS GROUSE AND PARTRIDGE, IN THE UNITED STATES?

Because it's illegal. If you shoot an indigenous wild game bird, you're welcome to eat it, but it can't be sold. What you buy at market will have been imported from Europe and were farm-raised. The varieties include grouse, partridge, pheasant, and wood pigeon, as well as dove, quail, and woodcock. They may not have the haunting, woody flavor of wild birds, but they come close.

WHAT'S THE DIFFERENCE BETWEEN *FOIE GRAS* AND *PÂTÉ DE FOIE GRAS*?

Foie gras is the liver of specially fattened geese and, to a lesser extent, ducks. The fowls are force-fed grains and grasses until their livers weigh about four pounds. (A normal goose liver weighs about four ounces). The flavor is exquisite, quite rich (Reverend Sydney Smith described heaven as "eating foie gras to the sound of trumpets"), and extremely expensive. One reason for the high cost is that the prized livers must be imported, as the force-feeding of geese is forbidden in the United States.

Foie gras is savored very simply, on buttered toast points, or added judiciously to other dishes.

Pâté de foie gras is a pâté made of foie gras mixed with bacon, butter, brandy, and, optimally, black truffles. The pâté is molded in a terrine, baked, and served with crusty bread.

If you're thinking, *sounds like chopped liver,* forget it. Pâté de foie gras is what chopped liver, made from chicken livers, would be if it were anointed by Athena. It is a food about which M. F. K. Fisher wrote, "I used to think, and perhaps still do, that I can never really have enough pâté de foie gras." If you're interest is piqued, know that the best pâté de foie gras comes from Strasbourg, in northeast France.

What are *schmaltz* and *gribenes*?

Schmaltz is a traditional Jewish food made from rendered poultry (chicken or goose) fat, and gribenes are the cracklings left over from making schmaltz. Room-temperature schmaltz, smooth and opaque, is a culinary staple in the kosher kitchen. It is used for frying, for spreading on bread and potatoes, mixing into chopped liver, or in any dish where religious dietary laws prohibit the eating of butter or lard.

Gribenes are chewy and savory and, if there are any left after snacking, are mixed into kasha, noodle pudding, and mashed potatoes.

Can you eat crow?

Most of us eat euphemistic crow on a regular basis. However, if you've somehow been spared the indelicate taste of this blackest of birds, you may follow this recipe, found in Cuniset-Carnot's *Vie aux Champs*: "Make a *pot-au-feu*. On the reversed lid of the pot, put a plucked crow. After five or six hours of gentle cooking, throw the crow on the fire and enjoy the pot-au-feu."

THREE

Fish and Shellfish

*Fish is held out to be one of the greatest
luxuries of the table, and not only necessary but
even indispensable at all dinners where there is any
pretense to excellence or fashion.*
—MRS. ISABELLA BEETON, *The Book of
Household Management*, 1861

While most of us fall with abandon for Neptune's bounty—swoon for the mighty bite of a swordfish steak and savor the metallic tickle of a sylphid oyster—the riches of the deep prove too mysterious for certain landlubbers, children especially, who scatter come Friday, fearing the cloudy eye and clacking claw and, most especially, those little fishies on the pizza.

A pity, as the sweetest of all flesh food is spawned in our oceans, our lakes, our rivers. But admiration for the sea and its denizens is more than a matter of taste; it's tradition. "From sea to shining sea" to *Moby-Dick* to tuna-on-white, our national identity is founded on an appreciation of and an affinity for our waters and what's below.

So don't be afraid. Jump in. It's the only way to learn.

Fish

HOW CAN YOU TELL IF FISH IS FRESH?

Fish markets are bound by honor to sell only fresh fish; they, in turn, must rely on their suppliers to deliver only fresh merchandise. It's a dicey process that can break down at many points along the way. Building a relationship with a reliable fish merchant who cares as much about reputation as sales is one way to ensure the fish you buy will be fresh.

Unless a fish is advertised as "thawed," you should buy fish that has been caught and killed within the last forty-eight hours. Fresh fish does not smell "fishy" but clean and sweet. Eyes should be bright and protuberant, not sunken, and scales secure. Poked with a finger, fresh fish should feel fleshy and firm, not flabby. You can also check the gills, which spoil more quickly than the rest of the fish. The more recently the fish was killed, the redder the gills will be. Fish that smells off and looks wan and limp and whose scales are falling off is past its prime and should be avoided.

Once you've gotten the fish home, it needs to be kept below forty degrees in the refrigerator. Top-quality seafood will last three to four days refrigerated, though it is best eaten as soon as possible. Fresh fish may, of course, be frozen, but because fish flesh is delicate, freezing compromises both flavor and texture.

DOES COOKING A WHOLE FISH WITH THE HEAD ON INCREASE ITS FLAVOR?

Yes. Leaving the head and tail on during cooking keeps the juices in the fish instead of leaking into the pan, and the savory bones add flavor. Cooking with head and tail on is also more healthful, as fish bones are high in nutrients such as calcium.

This doesn't mean you should take a whole fish and pop it in the oven, scales, guts and all. Most head and tail-on fish are purchased drawn, which means the fish has been scaled and gutted, and had its gills removed, but it is otherwise left intact. Drawn fish are just as flavorful as whole fish but are a lot less work.

WHAT'S THE SIMPLEST WAY TO PREPARE A FRESH FISH?

So you've just caught the largest trout in the lake, and you're ready to eat it as is. You will be doing yourself and your guests a favor if you curb your enthusiasm long enough to scale and gut it.

Using a fish scaler (a metal gizmo that works like a vegetable peeler) or the back of a chef's knife, rub the scales loose by working up toward the head. Then, with a very sharp knife, make a shallow slit in the belly of the fish, from just below the head to the top of the tail, being careful not to cut through the organs. Reach in and pull out the viscera; then rinse the body cavity well with cold water. If the fish is very fresh, it is not necessary to remove the gills, which are the first part of the fish to spoil. If you choose to remove them, make a slit beneath the head, reach in with a knife or scissors, and snip the gills. Remove them, rinse the fish again, dry well, and keep it cold until ready to cook.

WHAT SHOULD I DO IF I SWALLOW A FISH BONE?

If you swallow a bone, there's a simple remedy to dislodge it: Chew a piece of bread, and swallow. The bread should surround the bone and move it easily down your throat. This method is certainly preferable to the tweezer-and-flashlight "surgery" my brother performed on his new wife while honeymooning.

How can you tell if fish is done?

Because most fish flesh is delicate, it's ridiculously easy to over-cook. Paranoia about dryness often leads to a cooked-on-the-outside, slimy-on-the-inside dish fit only for the indiscriminate and the ravenous.

Fish should be cooked until it loses its opalescence and becomes opaque, except for the meat closest to the spine, which may retain a slight translucence. When poked, the flesh should feel firm but not hard. Like meat, fish continues to cook slightly after being removed from its heat source, so err on the side of underdone if you're not sure; you can always add fire, but you can't take it off.

While it's almost impossible to get an accurate temperature reading from filets, a whole fish should have an internal temperature of 140 degrees when properly cooked.

Are wild fish superior to farm-raised fish?

"Salmon are like men: too soft a life is not good for them." So said James de Coquet, the editor of *Le Figaro*, and the axiom may similarly be applied to farmed fish. Not only do wild fish get more exercise and develop firmer, tastier flesh than those on the farm, but their diet is much more varied than the diet of farm-raised fish, as is evident in their more complex flavor.

Proponents of aqua-farming rightfully argue that many once safe bodies of waters are now polluted and/or overfished, threatening certain species of fish with extinction. Considered in this light, aqua-farming may have meritorious long-term benefits, though extraordinary taste is not likely to be among them.

IS IT SAFE TO EAT RAW FISH?

With the exception of several rarely served species of potentially poisonous fish (like the Japanese blowfish, or fugu), raw fish, or sushi, is safe if the fish is fresh.

That's a medium-sized *if*. While Americans have fallen in love with sushi, they may not be able to discern whether what they're eating was caught the day or the week before. Anyone who's seen withered supermarket sushi knows it is not always sold with the strictest eye for freshness. Hence, it's best to eat sushi at a restaurant with a busy turnover, thereby assuring that the product has not been sitting around for several days.

Reputable sushi chefs have extremely rigid requirements regarding freshness and preparation, ensuring not only an appetizing meal but a safe one as well. In fact, the Japanese take extreme care in choosing sushi, often choosing fish that has been flash frozen to minus sixty degrees within minutes of its being caught, which rids the fish of both bacteria and parasites. If you are worried about raw fish, ask whether the fish has been flash frozen.

Even if the fish is not flash-frozen, the chances that it is parasite infested are low. Most larger, and potentially dangerous, parasites are removed during processing, before the fish ever gets to market. The process, called candling, involves running fish filets over a lighted conveyer belt, thereby illuminating any parasites, which are then removed.

In some cases, accidental ingestion of a parasite can cause intestinal distress or damage. This affliction can pose special hazards for pregnant women, who in this country are usually advised to abstain from eating raw fish until after giving birth.

WHAT IS THE DIFFERENCE BETWEEN PANFRYING, SAUTÉING, AND BLACKENING?

Though panfrying and sautéing are used synonymously, there are differences.

Strictly speaking, panfrying involves frying foods quickly in hot oil or butter over medium-high heat in a frying pan. Sturdier cuts of fish or shellfish such as catfish or softshell crabs take well to panfrying, as their flesh does not break down easily.

Sautéing uses less oil and is more appropriate for delicate fish, like sole, and for dishes where other ingredients are added to the cooking pan.

Blackening is a Creole method of cooking. The fish or meat is heavily coated with spices and fried in an extremely hot cast-iron skillet until the skin is blackened. This sears in the juices and causes the outside of the fish to become black and crunchy.

A word of warning: Do not attempt to panfry previously frozen fish, as the high levels of water left in the fish's thawed flesh will cause the fish to steam rather than fry.

WHAT IS IN A BOUILLABAISSE?

Bouillabaisse is the soul of Provençal cooking. A heady, cockle-warming soup made of fish, shellfish, potatoes, and tomatoes infused with saffron, Pernod, and garlic, bouillabaise is traditionally topped with a dollop of rust-colored rouille (homemade mayonnaise mixed with garlic, saffron, and other spices).

Traditionally, bouillabaisse (whose name comes from *bouillir,* to boil, and *abaisser,* to reduce) was made by Marseilles fishermen from the catch least suitable for market, namely the rascasse, or scorpion fish. Racasse are small and sharp, with venomous spines, yet their flavor is considered essential for an authentic Provençal bouillabaisse. As rascasse is generally unavailable outside of Marseilles, the rest of the world makes do with assorted small aquatic fare, such as snapper, sea bass, monkfish, halibut, and squid.

WHAT'S BOURRIDE?
Another Provençal fish soup, bourride eschews shellfish, and blends in aioli, the heavenly garlic-infused mayonnaise of Provence.

WHAT DOES *FUMET* MEAN?
Fumet, the French word for *aroma,* is a concentrated stock made of fish (or, less often, mushrooms) and is used as an addition to sauces, soups, and stocks. A concentrated stock made from meat or poultry is called a *fond,* meaning *bottom.*

WHAT'S FINNAN HADDIE?
Finnan haddie is cold-smoked haddock. In America, we usually eat finnan haddie in a cream-based chowder. But the British make a ritual of the fish, poaching it in a hot milk bath, adding pats of butter, and serving it with toast—a meal that does much to distance England from its maligned culinary reputation.

Craig Claiborne wrote in *The New York Times* that finnan haddie was the silver lining of a very dark smoke cloud. In the mid 1800s, in the town of Findan outside of Aberdeen, a fire started on the sawdust-strewn floor of a shed where freshly caught haddock was hung. The fishwife gave away the damaged fish, which were soon in demand. From then on, the sawdust was deliberately set afire, and finnan haddie was born. Learning that the fishwife, Mrs. Craig, was perhaps a distant relation, Mr. Claiborne, an ardent finnan haddie fan, wrote, "I was enchanted to learn of a possibility—however remote—that one of my ancestors 'invented' finnan haddie."

WHAT IS A GEFILTE FISH?

Gefilte fish is a fish dumpling of sorts, a traditional Jewish food eaten by Eastern European Jews during the Sabbath and holidays. While there are probably as many recipes for gefilte fish as there are Jewish mothers cooking them, the basic recipe calls for ground whitefish, pike, and carp to be mixed with matzoh meal and spices, formed into balls, and poached in simmering stock or water.

Properly made gefilte fish is light and fluffy. Beware canned gefilte, however, which tastes disturbingly like wet, compressed sawdust.

WHAT IS GRAVLAX?

Gravlax is a Swedish specialty that involves rubbing a salmon fillet with sugar and salt, wrapping it in fresh dill weed, and allowing it to cure for several days. During this time, the salmon becomes translucent and the meat meltingly tender.

The star of any Scandinavian fish buffet, gravlax is served thinly sliced, with a sweet mustard-dill sauce, and is often accompanied by: rollmops (herrings that have been rolled around an onion and pickled), maatjes herrings (fat, salt-cured female fish), and salt herrings that have been soaked in a vinegar solution and then bathed in sour cream.

ARE LOX AND SMOKED SALMON THE SAME THING?

Almost. They are both salmon that has been cured and smoked.

Lox is brine-cured, then smoked. It is generally saltier and slightly firmer than smoked salmon. Lox is what you usually eat on a bagel with cream cheese.

Smoked salmon, also called Nova, is cured with a salt and brown-sugar rub, then put in a wet brine before smoking. The flavor is less salty and the flesh slightly more delicate. It is usually more expensive than lox.

WHAT IS MAHIMAHI?

Mahimahi is a beautiful blue dolphin, native to Hawaiian waters (no, not Flipper, which was a porpoise), with fleshy, sweet meat. Because it quite perishable and does not travel well, mahimahi is more popular on the West Coast. On the East Coast, people eat bluefish instead, an ocean fish with a similar, if less delicate, taste.

WHY CAN'T YOU BUY BLUEFISH ON THE WEST COAST?

Bluefish, a rich, dark-meat fish caught off the Northeast Coast, is extremely oily and does not transport well. In a matter of days, its firm brown-and-white flesh takes on the taste of used motor oil. While there is no substitute, sturgeon or mahimahi comes close in flavor.

HOW CAN YOU TELL THE DIFFERENCE BETWEEN CAVIAR AND FISH ROE?

Caviar is eggs harvested from sturgeon in the Mediterranean and Caspian seas. The eggs, or berries, range in color from pale gray to black. There are three grades of caviar: *beluga,* which has the largest eggs, is rather mild, and sells for up to one thousand dollars for an eighteen-ounce tin; *ostera,* with smaller eggs, has a stronger flavor than beluga and sells for about half the price; *servuga,* tiny grayish-black eggs with a robust flavor, sell for three hundred dollars per eighteen-ounces; *malossol,* a Russian term for "lightly salted," does not necessarily indicate a type or size of caviar. However, tiny blackish eggs (with up to four percent added salt) often sell under the name malossol.

Though the USDA states that only imported sturgeon roe can be called caviar, American fish roe is often sold under the name.

Domestic fish roe usually comes from lumpfish, but it may also come from paddlefish, sturgeon, cod, salmon, and carp. Some of it is quite good, particularly sturgeon farmed in the Southeast, while other roe are inferior: dry, lusterless, overly salty. Be warned: inexpensive caviar is not be what you want to serve on New Year's Eve. However, if you crave the taste of beluga on your nightly baked potato with sour cream, by all means, try the $1.99 supermarket caviar. It'll give you a (faux) fix, for practically nothing.

Fine caviar eggs should be unbroken and "pop" when you bite into them. Once a tin of caviar is opened, it should be eaten within the week. Keep it in the coldest part of your refrigerator; it keeps best at 28 degrees Fahrenheit and will not freeze because of its high salt content. Caviar may be frozen, though you run the risk of having the eggs burst. But, if you have so much fresh caviar on hand that you need to freeze some, consider yourself blessed.

WHAT'S THE CLASSIEST WAY TO SERVE CAVIAR?
Purists keep it simple: lightly buttered toast points and iced vodka or champagne are the epicurean's sole accompaniments. Those less concerned with convention, or perhaps just hungrier, add chopped onion, chopped hard-cooked egg, and perhaps a few capers and lemon wedges. You should never use silver utensils when serving caviar, as they can impart a metallic taste.

FISH IS OFTEN SERVED WITH "DRAWN BUTTER." WHAT IS IT?
Drawn butter is clarified butter, or melted butter with the sediment poured off. Because it contains no sediment, drawn butter remains clear and is considered more elegant than plain melted butter.

To make drawn butter, melt unsalted butter over low heat,

skimming off any foam that develops. Remove from heat and let the butter stand several minutes. Skim off the clear liquid at the top, which is the clarified butter, and toss the milk solids at the bottom.

Clarified butter will keep two weeks or longer in the refrigerator and will look good as it's doing it (which cannot be said about refrigerated melted butter, which quickly separates into ice-floelike sheets atop liquid solids). To liquify refrigerated drawn butter, simply reheat.

How does lime juice "cook" fish?

The acidity of lime juice (and any acidic liquid, such as vinegar, wine, or lemon juice) has a tenderizing effect on the fibers of fish. While it does not actually raise the temperature of the fish, after six to twelve hours, it does penetrate the flesh (provided the pieces are small enough), causing it to soften and lose its "raw" translucence.

Seviche and pickled herring are two popular dishes that rely on acidic acids to do their "cooking."

Can fish be cooked in a dishwasher?

This scheme came about in the sixties, probably the result of some ad exec who was asked to come up with 99 novel ways to use an automatic dishwasher. The theory went: you wrap a fish in aluminum foil, set it on the top rack of the dishwasher, and let the machine run its cycle.

Although I've never tried it, I'm certain it would work. And while we're at it, we might throw a few pairs of panties in the machine, and the dog needs a bath, and . . . oh, the possibilities are endless.

Whatever happened to cod-liver oil?

The most vociferously loathed of all medicinals, administered by loving mothers and cruel disciplinarians for everything from colds to bad tempers, seems to have dropped from sight in the late twentieth century.

Or has it? When we take fish oil supplements that contain omega-3 long-chain fatty acids (which help to keep our arteries clear), we are actually swallowing an age-old remedy with a new name.

Is there any way to get rid of the smell of cooked fish?

Susan Loomis, author of *The Great American Seafood Cookbook*, claims fish odors are not caused by the fish themselves but the packaging. She suggests discarding it immediately, along with any fish remnants left over from the meal. If you can't get them out of the house and into the trash, "Freeze bones, shells and trimmings until garbage pickup day, then get rid of them."

Shellfish

What's the difference between Maine lobster and South African lobster?

Maine lobster, the species *Homarus americanus,* is almost identical to *Homarus gammarus,* lobster found in the waters off northern Europe. Both species have average weights of 1–2½ pounds, heavy tails and claws, and succulent meat.

South African lobster, or rock lobster, is *Homarus capensis,* which flourishes in the waters off Africa and Australia. These lobster are generally smaller and do not have claws, and their tail meat is somewhat less flavorful and less well textured.

None of these species should be confused with the spiny lobster (*Panulirus argus*), which is found in the tropical waters off the Caribbean, the southern Gulf of Mexico, and Brazil. These spiny lobsters have a long tail but no claws, and their meat is much like that of crayfish, with which they are often confused.

DOES A LOBSTER'S SIZE AFFECT ITS TASTE?

At a fish market in Martha's Vineyard, a gaggle of kids stared as a menacing thirteen-pound lobster fought the holding tank. With claws the size of dinner plates and a massive, thrashing tail, the creature looked like the irradiated antagonist of some Japanese sci-fi flick. Fantastic—but how would he taste? One would assume any lobster this humongous would be tough, the crustaceous equivalent of a spongy, overgrown zucchini.

Not so. Size is unimportant, as meat from a healthy lobster is always sweet and firm. A live lobster should smell clean, feel heavy for its size, and appear active, whether it's a *chicken* (1-pound), a *quarter* (at 1¼ pounds, a runaway bestseller), a *select* (1½–2½ pounders), or a *jumbo* (anything over 2½ pounds). Lobsters over ten pounds are rare, as they don't usually get a chance to grow that old and large. Yet the lobster industry also has regulations that ensure lobsters have a chance to grow large enough: in Maine, where most of America's lobsters are caught, it's illegal to net a lobster that measures less than five inches from its eyes to the end of its body.

DO LOBSTERS FEEL PAIN WHEN THEY'RE PLUNGED INTO BOILING WATER?

If you've ever watched a lobster spasm as it hits the boiling water, you have to assume the answer is yes. Some believe that severing the lobster's spinal cord by quickly plunging a knife between the head and abdomen before boiling is a more humane end, though others don't see the exponential difference between stabbing and boiling.

If you're having trouble tossing your dinner to its death, you can try the slow-kill method: stick the lobster(s) in the sink, and turn on both taps. As the sink fills, slowly turn off the cold tap. The logic is the lobster slowly becomes anesthetized and increasingly sluggish. You're still going to have to boil it—and right away!—only this time the lobster probably won't flail.

Another sympathetic gesture is submerging the lobster in wine, in order to get it drunk before its final plunge. This seems an unusually bizarre fate for the teetotaling crustacean and is a waste of good wine. It may be just as effective for the cook to have a glass, thus gathering the fortitude to proceed with supper.

WHY DO FISH MARKETS PUT RUBBER BANDS ON LIVE LOBSTERS' CLAWS?

It's not to protect the customer from the lobster but rather the lobsters from one another. Lobsters are carnivores, and one of their favorite foods is each other. Packed without bands, abnormally crowded into holding tanks, the lobsters would have a genocidal feast before they ever got to market.

WHICH IS PREFERABLE—A FEMALE LOBSTER OR A MALE?

Females generally have slightly more edible flesh per pound, and the meat is sweeter. They also contain the bright coral roe, which is quite rich and dense, though admittedly an acquired taste. (This feature should not be confused with the tomalley, or liver, the brackish green innards of both sexes.)

To determine whether your lobster is male or female, turn it over. On the underside, at the juncture between the tail and the body, there are two protrusions. If they are soft, the lobster is female; if they are rough, it is male.

WHAT IS A SHE-CRAB?

A she-crab is, of course, a female crab. Her entree into the lexicon is via a Georgia specialty, she-crab soup, a cream-based potage that uses both the crab's meat and eggs.

WHAT'S A SOFT-SHELL CRAB?

The soft-shell crab is a blue Atlantic crab that comes busting out of its shell (hence its nickname, "Buster") each spring. Fully molted, it is called a "Peeler" and is harvested, usually from Chesapeake Bay, where 95 percent of this country's soft-shell crabs spawn. The shells fall to the bottom of the sea, where they become part of the aquatic cycle, providing food and habitat for other ocean denizens.

Soft-shell crabs, usually available from April through September, average from four to seven inches across and are usually eaten deep-fried or sautéed. Make sure to eat what crab aficionados call the best part: the creamy yellow fat inside the body of the crab.

WHAT IS SURIMI?

Surimi is imitation crabmeat. Its skin is artificially reddened, its taste is ersatz and rather sweet, and everyone insists they hate it.

Then why has it become a ubiquitous sight at every fish store and supermarket in the country? Several reasons: it's cheap, very low in fat, and actually doesn't taste that bad. It doesn't taste like *crab,* but it does taste like fish, which it is, usually pollock that has been skinned and boned, minced, and made into a paste, mixed with sugar, salt, maybe a little crab juice, shaped, and dyed.

Supermarkets are required to label surimi "imitation crab" (or "imitation lobster": same stuff, different shape), but beware restaurants and delicatessens surreptitiously using surimi as a crab-salad extender.

WHAT'S THE DIFFERENCE BETWEEN PRAWNS AND SHRIMP?

While most people consider prawns and shrimp to be identical species, true prawns are larger, with lobsterlike claws. They are more common in Europe, most often harvested in the Dublin Bay and the Adriatic Sea, and rarely appear on American tables. Therefore, when buying prawns, you may assume you are actually getting large shrimp.

Of course, there are people who claim they can taste the difference, that prawns are more succulent than their shrimpy cousins. It's probably size delusion: a large shrimp (or prawn) delivers a bigger bite and consequently a bigger taste.

IS THERE AN EASY WAY TO PEEL SHRIMP?

The easiest way to peel a shrimp is to hold it in the middle, with its hump facing you, and tug off its tail with the other hand; this should remove about half of the shell. Flip the shrimp over and, using both thumbs, split the underside of the shell apart and slip off the rest of the shell. With a little practice, you should be able to peel a shrimp in about two seconds.

IS IT REALLY NECESSARY TO DEVEIN SHRIMP?

It depends on the shrimp. A shrimp's "vein" is its intestinal tract, the color and density of which depends on what it's been eating. Some shrimps, usually smaller ones, have a translucent or pale-orange tract. They may be deveined or not, as the vein will neither alter their taste or appearance. However, a dark, sandy tract, more common on large shrimp, is both unappetizing and unattractive and is best removed.

To devein shrimp, gently run a sharp knife down the vein on the outer side of the peeled shrimp, making sure not to cut all the way through. The vein will be exposed and can be removed with your fingers, or rinsed away under cold water.

How do they size shrimp?

Fresh shrimp is sized in five categories: *Jumbo* (10 shrimp per pound), *Large* (10–25 per pound), *Medium* (25–40 per pound), *Small* (40–60 per pound), and *Tiny* (over 60 per pound). Previously frozen shrimp are sized the same way, but buy fresh whenever possible. All flesh foods suffer from freezing, but fish and shellfish are particularly susceptible, as their flesh is delicate.

Individually Quick Frozen, or IQF, applies to frozen shrimp bought in bulk. The same size rules as above apply, for example 5 pounds of Jumbo IQFs yield about 50 shrimp.

What is a crawfish?

A crawfish, or crawdad, or mudbug, is a crustacean found in this country primarily in Louisiana and, to a lesser extent, the waters of the Northwest, where it is also called a crayfish. Crawfish look just like tiny lobsters (three to six inches down South; up to ten inches in the Northwest), and their meat is just as sweet. Their tails are good eating, as is the orange "fat" (the pancreas and the liver) used in signature Cajun dishes like *étouffée,* a spicy, roux-enriched stew enjoyed along the Louisiana bayou.

WHAT'S THE DIFFERENCE BETWEEN HARD AND SOFT-SHELL CLAMS?

While there are hundreds of varieties of hard and soft-shell clams up and down the American seaboard, we eat mostly four kinds: littlenecks, cherrystones, chowder clams (hard-shell), and razor clams (softshell).

Littlenecks, cherrystones, and chowder clams are communally known as quahogs, from the Narraganset word *poquaûhock,* or clam. Their sandy-gray, ovallike shells are between one and three inches across (littlenecks being the smallest, chowders the largest), and hard like stone. Smaller clams are eaten raw, steamed, fried, or sautéed, while the larger ones are used in stews and soups.

Razor clams, also called steamers, have narrow white shells (which are always full of sand, so rinse thoroughly), are between two and ten inches long, and are usually steamed and eaten with lemon-butter, or fried in crushed cracker crumbs and served with tartar sauce.

If possible, eat freshly shucked oysters and clams immediately. If they must be held, they may be stored on ice or rock salt (a nonedible salt that has the ability to hold in either cold or heat) in the refrigerator, for up to one hour.

WHY SHOULDN'T YOU EAT CLAMS IF THEIR SHELLS ARE OPEN?

Live clams (and oysters and mussels) have very good reflexes. When alert and healthy, a clam senses predators (including a human hand) and snaps shut to protect itself. One way to test a clam's vivacity is to tap it: if it closes, it's alive. If it doesn't, it means it's either dead, almost dead, or sick, and should not be eaten, as it may contain contaminants released upon expiration.

Likewise, a healthy clam should open when cooked, as the

muscle that causes the two shells to clamp relaxes when the clam dies. If this doesn't happen, it means the clam was not alive when it was cooked, and should be thrown away.

WHAT'S THE DIFFERENCE BETWEEN MANHATTAN AND NEW ENGLAND CLAM CHOWDER?

The only thing Manhattan and New England clam chowder have in common are clams—and maybe a few onions.

Cream-based clam chowder, a descendant of the seventeenth- and eighteenth-century *chaudières* (meaning "cauldrons") cooked up by French and Nova Scotian sailors, was embraced by New England cooks. It contains cream, potatoes, onions, clams and their juice, salt, and pepper. New England clam chowder is and always has been simple and warming and white.

In the late 1890s, Coney Island food stands (or Portuguese fishermen living on Rhode Island, or a New York fishmonger who supported the charlatans in Tammany Hall) began adding tomatoes and other vegetables, and Manhattan clam chowder was born.

New England was outraged. In 1939, Maine introduced a bill outlawing tomatoes in chowder, and one cookbook writer, Eleanor Early, insisted tomatoes and New England clam chowder should never be spoken of "in the same breath."

The next sixty years softened the scandal, and both soups are now commonly available throughout the country, though when one asks for clam chowder, one is likely to be served the cream version.

WHAT IS A GEODUCK?

Geoducks (pronounced "gooey-duck," from the Nisqualli Indian words for "dig deep") are native to the West Coast and are a kind of giant clam, with shells up to seven inches across and a meaty, foot-long neck that looks like an elephant's trunk sticking out from its shell. The inside flesh is eaten like other clams—raw, steamed, sautéed—while the neck can be cut into ringlets and fried.

IS THERE AN EASY WAY TO OPEN OYSTERS AND CLAMS?

If you find yourself in charge of shucking several dozen quahogs, a shucking or oyster knife with a 2½- 4-inch blade is essential. Scrub the oyster (or clam), hold it in a kitchen towel, and insert the tip of the knife into shell near the hinge. Twist ever so slightly, and work the knife around using a semicircular motion, being careful not to cut through the oyster and to keep the shell balanced so as not to lose the liquor (the salty liquid inside the shell). Slide the tip of the knife toward the back until you hit the hinge, and cut through the muscle. This will disengage the top shell. Remove it, and gently run the knife under the oyster to loosen it.

The National Fisheries Institute says one way to expedite clam-opening is to freeze them for fifteen to thirty minutes, or just until the shells separate.

WHEN IT IS SAFE TO EAT OYSTERS?

"What man would knowingly eat a bad oyster?" M. F. K. Fisher asked rhetorically in *Consider the Oyster*. "A bad oyster looks old and disagreeable in its shell, and it smells somewhat of copper and somewhat of rotten eggs."

In the days before reliable refrigeration, people were advised to eat oysters only with months containing an "R." This is no longer the case. True, there are fewer plump, fleshy oysters to be had during the summer months, when the oysters are spawning, but you may be assured that what are available are safe to eat.

Unless an oyster smells "off" (this is reason enough not to immediately drown the delicate bivalve in cocktail sauce), you may eat oysters with impunity the year round.

How do oysters form pearls?

A pearl is formed when a parasite or worm burrows into an oyster's flesh, carrying with it a minute amount of the mother of pearl that lines the oyster's inner shell. This mother of pearl begins to replicate itself within the oyster, forming a pearl around the parasite, which perishes within a pearlescent coffin. This process can take years, under the most optimum of conditions (warm waters, an absence of predators), after which time either the oyster is harvested and the pearl found, or the oyster perishes, its shell opens, and the pearl knows a new home, on the ocean floor.

What's billi-bi?

Billi-bi is a soup made of mussels, white wine, and cream. The chef of the Parisian restaurant Maxim's, Louis Barthe, is said to have named the soup in honor of a regular patron who loved it, American tin tycoon William B. Leeds (though there is also speculation it was named after the tycoon's son, a famous sportsman of the same name).

Pasta, Potatoes, and All Things on the Side

No man is lonely while eating spaghetti.
—ROBERT MORLEY

They are coquettish and substantial, simple and complex. They star or support with equanimity. And they never forfeit their national identities, even after centuries as expatriates.

They are our grains, starches, and tubers; our mainstays in lean times and our pleasures in plenitude. As any dieter knows, contemplating even a short period without them brings instantaneous cravings for mashed potatoes, fettuccine Alfredo, and kasha varnishkes.

These are foods we like, and like a lot, and as such should not be kept shrouded by an unrecognizable name or two. If our parents could learn the difference between macaroni and pasta, so can we learn to distinguish rice from risotto.

Pasta

WHAT IS THE DIFFERENCE BETWEEN FARFALLE, FETTUCINE, AND FUSILLI?

Pastas derive their names from their shapes. For instance, *farfalle*, Italian for *butterflies*, is shaped like an open-winged butterfly.

There are literally hundreds of pasta shapes. Among the most popular are:

Capelli d'angelo ("angel's hair"): the thinnest-strand pasta

Conchiglie ("seashells"): small oblong shells with a "scoop" to hold sauce

Fettucine ("little ribbons"): thin egg noodles

Fusilli ("corkscrews"): long corkscrew-shaped spirals

Lasagna ("cooking pot"): long, two-inch-wide egg noodles

Linguine ("little tongues"): thin, flat strands

Macaroni or *maccheróni* (dumplings): any short, stubby variety of pasta. In America, small tubular elbows.

Manicotti ("little muffs"): large tubes suitable for stuffing

Orecchiette ("little ears"): small, concave disks

Orzo ("barley"): rice-shaped pasta

Pappardelle: one-inch-wide egg noodles

Pastine ("little paste"): miniature pasta shapes, used mostly in soup

Penne ("quills"): short, diagonally cut tubes

Ravioli ("little turnips"): "pillows" of pasta filled with meat, cheese, or vegetables

Rotelli ("little rollers"): short spirals or wheel-shaped pasta

Rotini ("little wheels"): short corkscrews

Spaghetti ("little strings"): thin, round strands

Spaghettini ("very little strings"): thinner round strands

Tagliatelle ("cut-outs"): egg noodles; slightly wider than fettucine

Vermicelli ("little worms"): very thin strands

Ziti ("bridegrooms"): narrow tubes suitable for stuffing

With the exception of specialty pastas, which may add vegetables and/or herbs to pasta dough, pasta is made from hard durum wheat (semolina), salt, and in some cases eggs.

WHAT IS GNOCCHI?

Gnocchi (pronounced *nyo-kee* and derived from the German *Knödel,* or dumpling) are tiny dumplings that are occasionally made of semolina (hard durum wheat, the same grain pasta is made of), but more often from potatoes. Cooked potatoes are peeled and "dried" in a skillet for several moments to evaporate as much moisture as possible. They are then mashed, cooled, and mixed with egg, flour, and butter, and the resulting dough rolled into long, finger-thick ribbons. The ribbons are snipped into one-inch pieces and boiled, as pasta, for a few minutes, or until they float to the top of the cooking water.

Gnocchi is hearty enough to withstand sauces rich in mushrooms and game, but gnocchi is perhaps at its finest when drizzled in melted butter and dusted with freshly grated Parmesan.

WHY ARE CERTAIN SAUCES SERVED WITH CERTAIN PASTA?

The shaping and saucing of pasta is not serendipitous. Common sense tells you a thick, meaty sauce such as *ragù* (meat and tomato sauce), is not best served on *capellini,* a thin-strand pasta unable to properly transport the chunky sauce. Likewise, you would not serve a simple *àglio e òlio* (garlic and oil) on lasagne noodles, which would look obscenely underdressed in only a swipe of oil.

The rule is: the longer the strand, the thinner the sauce. Very thin sauces, like pesto, work best on a delicate pasta, such as angel's hair. Creamy sauces cling beautifully to noodle-shaped pasta, as the width provides a suitable base. More substantial sauces, such as those with bits of meat, seafood, or vegetables, are better served on pasta with ridges to accommodate the food. Tube pastas may be stuffed and sauced, and very small pasta put in broth or given a simple turn in butter and a sprinkling of herbs and/or grated cheese.

DOES ADDING SALT TO BOILING WATER HELP PASTA COOK FASTER? SHOULD YOU ADD OIL TO THE WATER?

While the addition of salt raises the boiling part very slightly (one degree for every teaspoon of salt added per quart of boiling water), thus allowing for brisker cooking, the main reason salt is added to pasta water is flavor. Try boiling some pasta without it and taste the difference.

Adding cooking oil to the water in an effort to keep pasta from sticking is a bad idea. The oil does not circulate through the boiling pasta, but instead floats on top, where it can do nothing to prevent sticking. Only when the pasta is drained does it come in contact with the oil, where it winds up coating the pasta. This not only inhibits the proper absorption of sauce but can also impart a slick taste.

The correct way to keep pasta from sticking is to keep it circulating. This means at least three quarts of water per pound of pasta, to which you add two tablespoons of salt. The water should come to a rolling boil before the pasta is added. Keep at a steady boil while the pasta cooks. Stir frequently to prevent sticking, and taste often to avoid overcooking.

WHAT DOES AL DENTE MEAN? HOW DO YOU KNOW WHEN PASTA IS COOKED?

Al dente means "to the tooth" and indicates that pasta should be cooked until tender but firm. Never rely on package directions for cooking times. Just keep checking—which means pulling out a strand of pasta and tasting—until the center of the pasta is no longer hard and floury, but the strand itself retains some firmness. Bear in mind that pasta keeps cooking slightly after it's been drained, so boiling pasta until soft means mushy pasta a few minutes later.

Fresh pasta cooks in a fraction of the time (usually the time it takes for the water to reboil) of dry pasta, and cooking times must be modified accordingly.

Corn

WHAT IS POLENTA?

Leave it to the Italians to make poetry of the prosaic. So fond are they of polenta that gastronomic organizations like the eighteenth-century P.P.P.P. Society (*Prima Patria, Poì Polenta,* "First homeland, then polenta!") have been founded to honor the humble grit.

Polenta is cornmeal, plain and simple. Yet unlike its Yankee counterpart, corn grits, polenta grits have a finer grain and are cooked very slowly, so that the resulting dish is creamy.

Polenta is eaten like hot cereal, with butter and syrup, or mixed with cheese, meat, and sauces. When cool, polenta becomes firm and can be sliced and sautéed, or layered and used as the basis for sweet and savory dishes.

Americans have been slow to welcome polenta and have basically ignored its northern Italian cousin, *polènta néra*, or buckwheat polenta, deeply colored and heartier than regular polenta, but prepared and eaten in much the same way.

WHAT ARE GRITS?

Grits are a food fondly embraced by many a Southerner and an utter bafflement to Yankees, who cannot understand why anyone would want runny Cream-of-Wheat-like substance served on the same plate as fried eggs. If you don't believe this, take a Northerner to breakfast down South and watch his reaction when the grits arrive at the table. ("I didn't order hot cereal," a diner was overheard telling a waitress in Savannah, Georgia. She pegged his New York accent and told him not to knock it till he'd tried it. He did, and after two bites declared the grits wallpaper paste masquerading as food.)

Very white or pale yellow, grits are large-grained cornmeal, boiled and served, usually at breakfast, with a pat of butter or a side of gravy. Quaker Oats alone sells more than a hundred million pounds of this Southern staple a year.

WHAT IS HOMINY?

Hominy is the anglicized Algonquin Indian word (*homen*) for dried corn. It can be bought either dry, coarsely broken (samp), ground (hominy grits), or ready-cooked in cans. The flavor is somewhat like sweet-starchy corn. It is eaten on its own, baked into breads, made into tortillas, and added to the Mexican pork stew called *pozole*.

The traditional Native-American way to eat hominy is to slow-cook the dried kernels in a water and wood-ash solution. The wood ash, leached from hardwood ashes, is alkaline and balances the amino acids in which the corn is lacking, resulting in a highly nutritious and complete food.

Rice

WHAT IS ARBORIO RICE?

Arborio is the name of an imported Italian rice used to make risotto. Short-grained and pearly, arborio has the capacity to absorb more liquid than other rice and therefore cooks up creamier.

Devotees get absolutely apoplectic about risotto, an Italian rice dish in which raw rice is first sautéed in oil and herbs, slow-cooked with boiling broth, and stirred constantly until the rice becomes a velvety mass. An equivalent can be made with regular white rice, and while the flavor may be matched, the consistency cannot be.

WHAT'S THE DIFFERENCE BETWEEN WHITE AND BROWN RICE?

All rice is created equal. When it comes from the field, "rough rice" has a hard outer hull. When this hull is removed, you have brown rice, which is still encased in several layers of bran. When that bran is milled and polished away, you are left with white rice, a product with substantially fewer vitamins and minerals than its brown brother.

Despite its nutritive paucity, 98 percent of the rice consumed in the world is white rice. One theory as to the reason has to do with status. Until the nineteenth century, white rice was labor intensive, since polishing was done by hand, and was considered a food of privilege. When mechanization brought white rice to the masses, brown rice was abandoned. After more than one hundred years of white rice, it's hard to go back to the complex taste and chewy texture of brown, even when we know it's good for us.

ARE THERE NUTRITIONAL AND TEXTURAL DIFFERENCES AMONG SHORT-, MEDIUM-, AND LONG-GRAINED RICES?

The length and width of the grain do not determine the nutritional value of rice as much as whether the rice has been denuded of its outer bran and germ. As these provide both nutrients and texture, the more processed the grain of rice, the fewer vitamins and less "chew" it will have. Because brown rice has its bran and germ intact, it is both more nutritious and chewier that white rice. (On the other end of the spectrum is instant rice, a precooked and dehydrated "time-saving" variety that costs about four times what you pay for plain white rice, and cooks up extremely bland and mushy.) In general, however, short-grained rice tends to be stickier than long-grained rice, whose grains usually stay dry and separate after cooking.

WHAT IS WILD RICE, AND CAN IT BE COOKED LIKE WHITE RICE?

Wild rice is not rice at all, but the seed of an aquatic grass, *Zizania aquatica,* that grows in shallow bodies of water in the central Northwest and Canada. Because it grows in paddies, like rice, early explorers to this continent took to calling it "wild rice" (or, in the case of the French, "crazy oats"), hence the misnomer.

Wild rice ranges in color from green to brown to red. The flavor is nutty, gamy, and intense. Because wild rice is so chewy, it is important to cook it thoroughly. It is boiled like white rice but for about twice as long, approximately forty-five to sixty minutes.

There is also cultivated wild rice, grown in paddies around the United States and widely available in supermarkets. Cultivated wild rice is almost black, not quite as flavorful, and cooks in about thirty minutes.

WHAT IS BASMATI RICE?

Translated as "the Queen of fragrance," basmati is a highly aromatic, long-grain rice from India and Pakistan. Because it is an aged rice, some of the moisture evaporates, resulting in a more concentrated aroma that, when the rice is cooked, fills the kitchen with a perfume redolent of tea and jasmine. It has a delicate yet nutty flavor and a fluffy texture, and is cooked and eaten like white rice.

WHY IS CHINESE RICE SO STICKY?

China's staple food is sticky because it is short grained and polished, and has a high gluten content, which means it absorbs more cooking water and consequently sticks together. A staple throughout Asia, where rice is eaten with every meal, sticky rice is not only the basis of the diet but a vehicle for other foods, too, much as we use a slice of bread as a means of transportation. Sticky rice is also easier to eat with chopsticks.

While there are many varieties of sticky rice, the sweetest and waxiest kinds are used to make sushi. The gelatinous quality of sushi rice, along with its unique preparation (the rice is soaked overnight before boiling), makes for an especially sticky product that holds its form when rolled.

Potatoes

WHY DO MASHED POTATOES SOMETIMES COME OUT LIKE GLUE?

Assuming you're using mature Idaho potatoes, there are two reasons: overbeating and the introduction of a cold liquid (like milk) to the hot potatoes.

Because overbeating stimulates the starch in potatoes (starch is what makes potatoes gummy), cooked potatoes should be mashed by hand (or with a ricer or food mill), not in an electric mixer, and never in the food processor or blender, where over-beating is almost a certainty. The trade-off for hand-mashing is you may have a few lumps. That's okay; that's how everyone knows they're homemade.

Adding cold milk to hot potatoes also adds to the glue factor, so have milk warmed, or at least at room temperature, before mashing into the hot potatoes.

IS THERE ANYTHING YOU CAN DO TO PREVENT CUT, UNCOOKED POTATOES FROM TURNING BLACK?

Yes. Keep the peeled potatoes in cold water until ready to use. Know that blackening, caused by oxidation, will not affect the flavor but may affect the color of the potatoes after they're cooked.

WHY ISN'T A RUSSET POTATO RED?

A dictionary definition of russet reads as follows: "Yellowish brown, light brown, or brownish red," which aptly describes most potatoes and especially America's favorite, the russet, or russet Burbank, named for its developer, Luther Burbank of Idaho. (Hence its other designation, the Idaho potato.)

WHAT'S THE DIFFERENCE BETWEEN A POTATO PANCAKE AND A LATKE?

Culture, and sometimes a little flour. Potato pancakes is a generic term for a dish enjoyed by every culture that eats potatoes. Latkes are of Jewish origin and are always eaten during Hanukkah, when foods fried in oil commemorate the miracle of the oil in the synagogue burning eight nights instead of one, during the triumph of the Maccabees over Antiochus of Syria, in the second century B.C.

While there are hundreds of recipes for potato pancakes, their

differences are infinitesimal. They are made of shredded potatoes, eggs, onion, salt, and occasionally a thickening ingredient,
either flour or, in the case of latkes, matzoh meal. Both mixtures
are formed into pancakes and fried in oil, butter, or chicken fat.
Both are served with applesauce and/or sour cream.

ARE A SWEET POTATO AND A YAM THE SAME THING?
The two varieties of sweet potatoes commonly found in supermarkets and farm stands would lead you to believe the answer
is yes. The sweet potato has brown-orange skin, gold flesh, and
a somewhat dry texture. The yam has darker, purplish skin,
deep-orange flesh, and a moist texture. Yet this "yam" is, in
fact, another variety of sweet potato.

True yams, *Dioscorea bulbifera*, belong to a family of climb-
ing plants that flourish in South and Central America, and the
West Indies. Their flesh is either white or yellow, and the flavor
mealy and extremely sweet, much sweeter than what we call a
yam. They are eaten as we eat yams, and can occasionally be
found in stores that carry Hispanic food products.

WHAT IS BUBBLE AND SQUEAK?
Bubble and squeak is a kind of hash, a British dish made by
combining mashed potatoes, cooked cabbage, and cooked beef.
The mixture is fried until crisp, during which time it makes quite
a noisome racket, hence its name.

All Things on the Side

WHAT IS COUSCOUS?
Couscous is semolina, or ground durum wheat, mixed with wa-
ter and formed into teeny-tiny pellets the size of raspberry seeds.
Larousse Gastronomique gives the meaning of the word as "a

Gallic version of *rac keskes,* which means crushed small." And while the French eat no more couscous than we do, couscous is a dietary staple in North Africa and parts of the Middle East.

Couscous has a delicate, pastalike flavor and a fluffy texture that readily absorbs sauces. Until several years ago, couscous required long steaming in a cumbersome three-tiered vessel called a *couscoussière*. Precooked couscous is now easily found on supermarket shelves, necessitating nothing more sophisticated than boiling water (or stock) in a pot with a lid.

WHAT IS FARINA?

Farina is a granular meal made from hard wheat. Known mostly in America as a breakfast cereal (and by the brand name Cream of Wheat), farina often brings back less-than-fond memories of cold winter mornings and hot, lumpy cereal.

That was farina's darkest hour. It is also used to make gnocchi, soufflés, and desserts, like the Greek custard-filled pastry *galactoboureko*.

Should you feel homesick for a toasty bowl of farina, *sans* lumps, simply stir continuously while cooking.

WHAT IS A TIMBALE?

Traditionally, a timbale resembles a small, crustless quiche: a rich custard mixed with meat, seafood, or vegetables that is poured into a mold and baked. A timbale is usually served sauced.

Currently, however, there are any number of timbale-shaped foods going by the name timbale. They are baked in small ramekins, needn't be custard based, and may encompass anything from caramelized apples to couscous.

FIVE

Vegetables and Fruits

There are many ways to love a vegetable. The most sensible way is to love it well-treated.

M. F. K. FISHER, *How to Cook a Wolf*, 1942

In the movie *Tin Men*, an aluminum-siding salesman tells of a religious experience he had at a smorgasbord. "They had corn, out of the ground. They had radishes, out of the ground. And you say to yourself, how can this be? With all these things coming out of the earth, there must be a God." Such awestruck appreciation is also acute in children, as any parent who's been bidden to pocket the seeds from a picnic watermelon, "so we can plant them when we get home," already knows.

As we get older, we either sow a garden and stare humbly as seeds and dirt and water make a meal, or we abandon the soil, buy frozen corn, and wonder why it doesn't taste as good as when we were kids. Hectic schedules and hydroponics can take some of the blame, but the truth is we give most vegetables short shrift, calling prepackaged lettuce "salad" and canned beans "roughage" in an effort to cheat our way to "five a day." Is it any wonder so many people claim they don't like vegetables?

The good news is, as the world gets smaller, our cornucopia

grows larger. While there may not be anything truly new under heaven, it's new to *us*. Case in point: jalepeños were a south-of-the-border curiosity ten years ago; now they're in Cheez Whiz. While it may not be crucial to our enlightenment to know if Scotch bonnet and habañero chiles are the same thing (they are), a little wisdom is a wondrous gift for the indentured palate, as vegetation once shrouded in mystery comes into the light.

Vegetables

ARE CHILES AND PEPPERS THE SAME THING?

Peppers and chiles are synonymous in many parts of the world, like Mexico, where all peppers are called *chiles*. Yet in America and much of Europe, only sweet peppers are "peppers," while fiery ones are chiles (that's chile with an e, not an i). Sweet or hot, they're all members of the capsicum family and play a featured role on the world's menu.

This wasn't always so. Chiles are one of the foods Columbus "discovered" in the Americas and hence have been part of most of the earth's cuisines for only five hundred years. Now cultivated on every continent, they are as at home in Hungarian cooking as African; as welcome in *kung pao* chicken as a chili dog.

WHAT IS THE DIFFERENCE BETWEEN A JALAPEÑO AND A SERRANO?

The state pepper of Texas, a jalapeño is a thick-skinned, medium-hot green chile about one and a half inches in length. In terms of heat, the jalapeño contains 2,500 to 5,000 Scoville units, a measure of hotness devised by pharmacologist Wilbur Scoville. (The higher the units, the hotter the chile.) Dried and smoked, jalepeños are called *chipotles*.

A serrano, meaning "mountain," is somewhat smaller and thinner, and at 10,000 to 23,000 Scoville units, considerably hotter.

Since their flavors are similar, jalepeños and serranos may be used interchangeably. Raw and roasted, they are ubiquitous in Mexican cooking—in salsas, guacamole, stews, and so on.

While there are over a thousand varieties of chiles, Americans basically eat the following, listed from scorching to timid.

Scotch bonnet: Also called habañero, meaning "from Havana," these are the world's hottest chile. Looking like tiny green or orange jack-o'-lanterns, they are fruity and intensely hot, containing 100,000 to 300,000 Scoville units, or 100 times the "heat" of a jalapeño. Grown in the Yucatán and the Caribbean, they give jerked food its flaming pungency.

Pequin: Tasting like a cayenne but much hotter (50,000 to 100,000 Scoville units), these one-inch, tapered, orange chiles are used dried.

Thai: Also called Santaka, these tiny peppers are thin-skinned and extremely hot (40,000 to 60,000 Scoville units), and are usually eaten whole. They are approximately three times hotter than a serrano.

Cayenne: Four to six inches long, bright red and thin, cayenne are most often dried and ground into powder or used in making hot sauce, like Tabasco. Raw, they are intensely hot and lend a fiery sweetness to salsas. They have a Scoville units rating of 30,000 to 50,000.

Hungarian: Also called yellow wax or banana pepper, these small, shiny, yellow peppers range from mild to medium-hot (5,000 to 20,000 Scoville units) and are often pickled.

Pasilla: A purplish-black chile that is used dried, the five-inch-long pasilla has the chewy-sweet taste of raisins (hence its name, "little raisin") and is the chile of choice for mole, the slow-cooked sauce from central Mexico that combines chiles, tomatoes, bitter chocolate, and spices, and is traditionally served with poultry or pork. At 1,000 to 1,500 Scoville units, they are mildly hot.

Poblano: Also called *ancho,* meaning "wide." A tapered, three-to-five-inch-long green-black chile with a smoky-sweet taste and a mild burn (1,000 to 1,500 Scoville units). Always used for *chiles rellenos* ("stuffed chiles").

New Mexican: Also called Anaheim, this four-to-six-inch-long, mild (500 to 1,000 Scoville units) green or red chile tastes like an earthy bell pepper.

Pimiento or *pimento:* Red and bulbous, pimientos are fleshy and sweet, very mild (500 Scoville units or less), and often roasted and bottled, or stuffed into green olives. Dried and ground into a powder, pimiento becomes paprika.

Peperoncini: Found on antipasti plates, peperoncini are small, fleshy green or red globes with little or no heat (100 Scoville units or less), they are best eaten pickled.

Bell pepper: Also called sweet peppers, bell peppers have no heat whatsoever (0 Scoville units); even their seeds are innocuous. Crunchy and with a high water content, they sweeten as they ripen from green to red. Like all other peppers, they contain high levels of vitamin C (120 units per globe) but are perhaps the only pepper mild enough to consume with an eye toward nutrition.

IS THERE ANY WAY TO REDUCE THE HEAT OF HOT PEPPERS?

We all remember our most hellacious chile mishap. Mine was watching my boyfriend bite into a tiny scarlet Santaka chile, nestled devilishly in a plate of Thai shrimp. He coughed and cried for ten minutes, while I remained jocular, patting him on the back and teasing him about his sensitive palate. This was right before I accidentally swallowed one of the infernal chiles. My guy was a gentleman: he handed me a rum punch and got the waitress to bring another napkin for me to weep into.

The rule is: the smaller the chile, the bigger the burn. A slice of bell pepper is a kiss on the cheek compared to a speck of habañero, which can blister your lip.

It's not the flesh that's so incendiary but what lurks inside. Capsaicin, the compound that gives chiles their heat, is found primarily in the ribs and the seeds; it's in the flesh as well, but at much lower levels. The way to avoid a chile's burn, therefore, is to seed it before cooking, making sure to use rubber gloves: capsaicin, often called the chile's "oils," can burn eyes and skin on contact (a condition known as "Hunan hand," in deference to the chile-rich cookery of Hunan, a province in southern China).

When dining out, know that cuisines that use a lot of hot peppers, like Mexican, Thai, and Indian, invariably provide a complementary food or beverage to cool you down. Starches such as rice and tortillas absorb chile oils from the mouth, while sour cream, yogurt, and milk neutralize the chile's oils and cool the burn. Sweet drinks, especially those with ice, can have a numbing effect, and their conflicting flavor can serve to distract from the pepper's punishment. Water and beer, however, offer little relief. Water doesn't cut the oils and offers nothing in the way of flavor, and beer's bubbles seem to intensify the pain rather than alleviate it.

How do you roast peppers, and why would you want to?

The easiest way to roast a pepper is to spear it with the tines of a fork and lay it on a rack over an open flame. Allow the pepper's skin to blister and blacken, making sure not to char the flesh below. (This can also be done under the broiler or with a small butane torch.) When the pepper is black all over, transfer it to a bowl, cover, and allow it to steam until cool enough to handle. (It may also be steamed in a closed plastic bag.) With your fingers or a paring knife, carefully peel the skin; then cut off the top and scoop out the seeds and ribs. Roasted peppers can be kept, refrigerated, for two to three days.

Very small chile peppers, such as serranos, may be roasted over high heat in a skillet, preferably cast-iron, until they are blackened. Skinning and seeding them can be an exercise in frustration. Instead, let them cool. Then chop them finely and use as is.

Roasting peppers brings out their sweetness and intensifies their natural smokiness. They make a vibrant condiment as is, and become velvety when puréed. Roasted, puréed peppers enrich soup and pasta, can be the basis for sauces, or can be used as a dip.

How much is a peck of peppers?

Literally, a peck is eight quarts (dry), yet the term is also used to indicate a large quantity. How many Peter picked is, of course, zero: One cannot pick pickled peppers.

Are tomatoes fruits or vegetables?

While we all seemed to learn in the third grade that tomatoes are actually a fruit, we somehow can't believe it, as tomatoes are used almost exclusively in savory dishes. A member of the nightshade family, the genus *Lycopersicon* only rarely find their way into sweet foods (Mystery Cake, which uses a can of tomato soup, notwithstanding), probably because tomatoes are not nearly as sweet as most fruits. Tangy, yes. Juicy, sure. But slice one atop cornflakes? No.

Having noted their status as a fruit, I would raise an equal argument that classification, like language, should be a flexible thing, determined not only by genus but also usage. So, the next time your child asks if a tomato is a fruit or a vegetable, why not equivocate and answer, "Both"?

WHAT IS THE BEST WAY TO SKIN TOMATOES?

Any kind of tomato may be skinned by cutting a small x in the bottom with a razor or very sharp knife and plunging the tomato into boiling water for fifteen seconds. The tomato should then be dunked in cold water, after which the skin should slip off easily.

Though many recipes calling for cooked tomatoes require that they be skinned first, know that the skin does not affect the flavor so much as the texture. If you don't mind chewy bits of tomato skin in your sauce, leave them on.

ARE SUN-DRIED TOMATOES REALLY DRIED IN THE SUN?

And is bread really baked in a hearth? Well, sure, but not in my house. While the exorbitant amounts we pay for chewy, tangy dried tomatoes would seem to indicate they are not only dried in the sun but the sun of some paradisiacal Mediterranean province where they are lovingly hand-turned by bare-breasted virgins, most commercial sun-dried tomatoes are dehydrated in electric vegetable dryers or very slow ovens.

DOES GARLIC TASTE DIFFERENT IF IT'S PRESSED RATHER THAN CHOPPED? SAUTÉED RATHER THAN BAKED?

Most cooks worth their salt don't care for garlic presses, considering them wasteful gizmos that leave most of the clove in the press. "Foodies have spat them out," decries *The Official Foodie Handbook*. "Cleaning a garlic press is impossible, involving pins and prods. And a bitter taste always comes through when garlic is pulped against metal."

The preferred method is to smash the bulb with the flat of a knife, remove the parchmentlike sheath, and then mince the crushed garlic. If you're picky, you can remove and discard the green center of the clove, which becomes fat and woody as herb ages and can impart a bitter taste.

The longer and slower you cook garlic (and onion), the sweeter it becomes, as its natural sugars develop during cooking. Therefore, a clove of garlic quickly sautéed retains a biting pungency, while forty cloves slow-baked in olive oil become creamy and caramel-sweet—and sublime, especially spread on Italian bread.

WHAT IS ELEPHANT GARLIC?

Elephant garlic, which looks like huge bulbs of garlic, is actually the wild ancestor of the cultivated leek. The flavor is mild, much more like leeks than garlic.

IS THERE ANY WAY TO KEEP FROM CRYING WHEN CHOPPING ONIONS?

Old wives' tales abound. There are claims that soaking whole, peeled onions in ice water before chopping takes away the sting, but most who've tried this method agree all you get are wet onions, which makes chopping messy and dangerous. Some cooks hold a piece of lemon under their nose (this will keep you distracted, at any rate), others a piece of toast between their teeth (to "catch" the fumes before they reach the eyes). Because the gaseous juices that waft up from the chopped onion are what sting the eyes, glasses can act as a barrier, and a well-ventilated room will prevent a buildup of fumes.

HOW DO YOU REMOVE THE SMELL OF ONIONS FROM YOUR HANDS?

George Washington may have proclaimed onions "the most favored food that grows!" but chances are he was not the one doing the chopping. Beloved on every continent, the onion (and the entire *Allium* family, which includes leeks, shallots, garlic, and chives) contains a redolent juice that lingers even longer on the fingers than it does on the tongue.

There are several ways to get rid of the smell. Rub your fingers with lemon juice and/or salt, or rub your hands against a stainless-steel bowl or spoon, which alchemizes the odor.

To get rid of onion or garlic on your breath, chew something rich in chlorophyll, like raw parsley (or cilantro, which neutralizes the offending odor), and drink an acidic liquid, such as lemonade or wine.

HOW CAN YOU PREVENT BEETS FROM "BLEEDING"?

A beet's throbbing redness is its vanity and virtue. Without it, it might as well be a turnip. However, the beet is also a most hemophilic vegetable, bleeding into and coloring everything it touches. In certain dishes, this is exactly the point (how wan borscht would be minus its vivid claret); other times, you need to stem the hemorrhage.

Should you want to keep the potato-and-beet salad white and red instead of mushy valentine pink, make sure you don't nick the beet's skin. And never peel a beet before cooking; merely trim the greens, leaving a one-inch stem, and gently scrub away any dirt. Boil (or steam, or bake) the beets, allow them to cool, then gently peel. (Tender-skinned baby beets needn't be peeled at all.)

If this fails, and you're left with a pot of beet-red cooking liquid, take a tip from one six-year-old: the juice from steamed beets makes dandy face paint.

WHAT ARE HARVARD BEETS?

Harvard beets are boiled, sliced beets dressed in a sweet, fruity vinaigrette, served hot or at room temperature. This much we know. How they got their name, however, is debatable. Harvard and Yale both claim the dish, but history tells us this dish is probably the invention of a seventeenth-century English tavern called Harwood. When one of its patrons, a Russian, emigrated to Boston and opened a restaurant, he either mispronounced the name of the Harwood beet dish as "Harvard," or saw fit to usurp a little eponymous celebrity from nearby Harvard College.

WHAT IS BELGIAN ENDIVE?

Belgian endive is the second growth of chicory, a curly, bitter lettuce. Legend has it endive was discovered by accident, when a Belgian gardener stored chicory roots in a cellar over the winter, and come spring found the roots had sprouted delicate, pale-green shoots, which we call endive leaves. While endive is most often braised in Europe, Americans eat endive as a salad, often dressed with a light vinaigrette, and topped with crumbled Roquefort and chopped walnuts.

WHAT IS BROCCOLI DI RAPE?

Broccoli di rape (also called broccoli rabe, bitter broccoli, and rapini) is not part of the broccoli family but is rather an Italian mustard green. It has long, deep-green stalks with tiny broccoli-like buds and even tinier yellow flowers. Crunchy and pleasantly bitter, it is usually sautéed (in olive oil and garlic, with maybe a little red pepper) and eaten on pasta, with poultry, or by itself.

WHAT IS CELERY ROOT?
Better known as celeriac, celery root is a knobby brown vegetable, the bulbous and hard root of certain varieties of celery. It tastes like strong celery, but it not at all stringy, and is peeled and chopped much like a beet. It is very popular in Europe, especially in France, where they eat celeriac *rémoulade* (shredded celery root dressed with mayonaisse-based rémoulade sauce) the way we eat coleslaw. It is also popular puréed and in soups.

WHAT ARE CARDOONS?
Cardoons, a member of the artichoke family, are eaten mostly in France, Italy, and Spain. Looking more like a broad, flat bunch of gray-green celery, the cardoons are trimmed of their tough, spiky outer ribs, then cooked in acidulated water (water to which a small amount of vinegar, lemon juice, or lime juice has been added), thus preventing discoloration of the vegetable. Like artichokes, they can be dipped in melted butter, fried or mashed, or sliced and served cold in a vinaigrette.

IS IT NECESSARY TO SOAK DRIED BEANS OVERNIGHT?
Countless thousands of words have been devoted to this debate. To summarize, there are three reasons to consider presoaking any type of dried beans that require long cooking: time, taste, and aftereffects. Pro-soakers claim that soaking cuts the time you need to cook beans in about half (true), the beans will cook up more tender (not necessarily), and presoaking prevents the flatulence associated with legumes. (Not true. Contrary to the

campfire ditty, the more beans you eat over time, the *less* discomfort you'll experience, as your system acclimates to the difficult process of digesting beans.) Of course, there are those to whom the entire point is moot, who agree with American journalist Don Marquis: "There will be no beans in the Almost Perfect State."

Should you choose to soak, the same quick-cooking results may be achieved with the quick-soak method: Place the beans in a cooking pot, cover with cold water by two inches, and bring to a boil. Remove the pot from the heat, cover it, and allow the beans to soak one hour. Change the water, and proceed with cooking. To ensure tender beans, make sure they are fresh and firm (old beans shrivel), and never salt the cooking water, which toughens the beans.

EGGPLANT IS NEITHER EGG NOR PLANT—IS IT?

Eggplant got its name through a series of misfortunes. The first were in the sixth century, in China, where newly cultivated eggplants were eaten raw. After causing much intestinal distress, they were named *ch'ieh-pzu,* meaning "poison"; the appellation has since been changed to *ch'ieh.* (The root validates the names: Eggplant is a member of the nightshade family, related to innocuous tomatoes and potatoes but also to deadly belladonna.) When eggplant reached the Mediterranean, a millennium later, it became known as *mala insana,* or "bad egg." By the time this much-maligned *fruit* reached France, it was named *l'aubergine,* but the English took the lead from the Italians, hence the name eggplant.

WHAT ARE FIDDLEHEAD FERNS?

Fiddlehead ferns are a reference to many edible ferns in the early stage of growth, when the tightly curled fern resembles the scrolled head of a violin. However, the most popular and most widely available fiddleheads are the fronds of the ostrich fern. The bright-green fiddleheads, crunchy and sweet and tasting like a cross between asparagus and green beans (and looking like a great, green centipede curled in on itself), are available for only two weeks in the spring; after that, they uncoil and become, well, ferns. They are best eaten raw, steamed, or sautéed.

What is a Jerusalem artichoke?

Jerusalem artichokes (also called sunchokes) are neither from Jerusalem nor are they artichokes. They are the tubers of a sunflower, or, in Italian, a *girasole,* from whence comes the corruption "Jerusalem."

Jerusalem artichokes are small and tan and knobby, looking somewhat like fresh ginger root, and taste like a sweet and nutty potato. They have their fans—naturalist Euell Gibbons favored them and proclaimed they had "as much food value as potatoes"—yet they are still a novelty on most American tables. They can be eaten raw, but are usually prepared like potatoes: fried, pureed or roasted.

What is jícama?

Jícama (pronounced *hee-ka-ma*) is a root vegetable that looks something like a very large radish with fibrous tan-and-white skin. Peeled, it is often eaten raw, in salads or as crudités, and its sweet-crisp, water chestnut-like taste does a stir-fry proud. It is also a popular component of Caribbean cooking.

What is kohlrabi?

Kohlrabi, or red cabbage, (from Kohl Rübe, German for "cabbage turnip") looks like a turnip that's been kept in a dark pantry too long, with green leaves sprouting all over its round red (or white, or green) body. Looks can be deceiving: This unattractive root vegetable, part of the cabbage family, has a clean, peppery taste and is eaten raw, cooked, or, at its apex, stuffed with veal and spices.

WHAT IS LAMB'S LETTUCE?

Lamb's lettuce, also known as corn salad and field lettuce, is a delicate lettuce with a sweet-nutty taste. The leaves are small, deep green, and cup-shaped, and don't keep very long. While the American market has only recently begun eating lamb's lettuce, it is a staple of European salads, where it is known as mâche.

WHAT IS MESCLUN?

Mesclun, also called mesclum, is a flexible combination of young greens such as arugula, oak-leaf lettuce, chervil, dandelion, and baby cress, and may also include herbs and edible flowers. A relatively recent (and immediately trendy) mix, mesclun is served as a salad, usually with a light and nutty vinaigrette.

WHAT ARE MORELS?

Morels are one of the world's most expensive wild mushrooms. The first mushrooms of spring, they have short, squat stems, conical, spongy heads, and a woodsy, meaty flavor. Because morels are a wild mushroom, they are hard to find fresh but are easily obtainable dried, and reconstitute beautifully. (Note: Never toss the water in which you've steeped dried mushrooms, as it is a delightful addition to sauces and stocks.) A little of this intense mushroom goes a long way: Six ounces of fresh or two ounces of dried morels will easily flavor a tureen of wild mushroom soup or a pasta sauce for eight.

SHOULD ALL MUSHROOMS BE WASHED BEFORE USING THEM?

Morels and other wild mushrooms (such as the golden, fluted chanterelle, tawny, big-capped cèpes, and spicy Japanese matsutakes) should never be peeled or washed before using, but wiped, if necessary, with a clean cloth or a soft-bristled mushroom-brush. Yes, brushing a mushroom clean can seem like a rather ridiculous chore, since mushrooms are already 90 percent water and a quick rinse doesn't really affect their taste that much. However, a wet mushroom is a slimy mushroom, and a slimy mushroom cannot be de-slimed.

WHAT'S THE DIFFERENCE BETWEEN WILD MUSHROOMS AND REGULAR MUSHROOMS?

How they are grown, and flavor. Wild mushrooms, such as morels, chanterelles, *trompettes-des-morts* (black, trumpet-shaped mushrooms), and cèpes (also called porcini) defy cultivation and must be foraged in damp, dung-rich forests and meadows. Other once-wild mushrooms, such as the teeny enoki (white-capped, with long, spindly stems), meaty Portobello, and anemonelike oyster mushroom, have all been successfully "tamed" and cultivated in recent years. Button mushrooms, the kind that come wrapped in plastic and sliced in cans, have long been cultivated and, while readily available and inexpensive, are not at the top of anyone's list in terms of flavor.

To the mind of a mushroom connoisseur, the longer a mushroom is cultivated, the more its ferocious flavor is compromised, until it is but a pale shadow of its former self. (Tennyson called the cultivated mushroom "the carrion of some woodland thing.") Is it not be better to have a perfect morel once a year than a mediocre shiitake every night? This quality-versus-quantity dilemma is for the diner to decide.

WHAT ARE TRUFFLES, AND WHY ARE THEY SO EXPENSIVE?

As a little girl, I knew truffles only as the three-tiered chocolates that were my mother's sweet indulgence. When I learned that specially trained hogs were used to hunt these confections that cost a zillion dollars a pound, I surmised that my mother was a gustatory pioneer, the culinary Amelia Earhart, boldly downing dainties rooted by pigs, and that we must be very rich. I did not know that truffles shared a name, though nothing else, with the world's most expensive subterranean fungi.

Found only in France and Italy (they defy cultivation) they are indeed hunted by hogs and hounds, specially trained to sniff them out from their burrows beneath live oaks.

Though the truffle is not much too look at (it is a small, irregular blob, usually dusted with mold), there is no end to the ways in which fresh truffles are eaten. White Italian truffles, from Piedmont, are enjoyed raw, or shaved over risotto, pasta, and eggs; France's black Périgord truffles are sautéed and used the same way, or mixed with foie gras. True voluptuaries have been known to sauté the truffles briefly in butter, splash them with cognac or marc, and eat them as is.

Indeed, the only limitation to truffle indulgence is the price: Fresh truffles can run over $500 per pound, making them the world's most expensive food. Dried truffles cost less and are acceptable, and truffle oil (white truffles steeped in best-quality olive oil) draws raves, but beware the canned truffle, a soggy impostor retaining none of the revered truffle's original taste or texture.

WHY ARE OLIVES DIFFERENT COLORS?

An olive's color indicates at what stage of ripeness it was picked. Young olives are green, becoming red, brown, and black the longer they're allowed to stay on the tree. Regardless of their age, all olives are bitter and must be cured before they are edible.

All olives, however, are not the same. The fruit of the evergreen tree *Oleo europaea,* there are over seven hundred varieties of olives grown worldwide, the bulk of them in the Mediterranean and California; exactly which type of olive depends on where and how it is cultivated, which in turn determines the olive's destiny.

Manzanilla olives, grown in central California, are picked when fat and green, brine-cured, and stuffed with pimento, whereas kalamata olives, from Greece, are ripened on the vine until they are deep purple, then cured in olive oil. Other popular olives include the reddish-brown nicoise from France, which are brine-cured, then steeped in oil; tiny, shriveled Moroccan black olives, which are dry-salt cured before being rubbed with olive oil, and bronze-green Calabreses from Italy, a plump brine-cured olive with a signature crack.

WHAT'S THE BEST WAY TO PIT AN OLIVE?

As a task, pitting olives is right up there with seeding grapes, something best avoided or relegated to an eager sous-chef or mooning teenager. If renowned bread baker and cookbook author Bernard Clayton says, "Authentic olive breads are made with unpitted olives," that should be good enough for the rest of us.

However, should you be worried about your dental crowns or are feeding a finicky eater, olives may be pitted with relative ease by squeezing the olive between your fingers, at which point the pit should pop out. This failing, the olive may be slightly crushed beneath the blade of a large kitchen knife, and the pit coaxed out with your fingers.

ISN'T THERE SOME PRECEDENT ABOUT EATING PEAS WITH A KNIFE?

A young M. F. K. Fisher may have eaten her grandmother's peas-and-cream with a spoon ("something we could never have done at home!"), while most of us coax our peas up the slope of a fork or, in desperation, spear them with its tines. It was Sir Walter Raleigh, however, who equated eating peas with a knife and the crash of civilization:

> *We could not lead a pleasant life,*
> *And 'twould be finished soon,*
> *If peas were eaten with a knife,*
> *And gravy with a spoon.*
> *Eat slowly; only men in rags,*
> *And gluttons old in sin,*
> *Mistake themselves for carpet bags,*
> *And tumble vituals in.*

Should you still be searching for (literary) license for your pea-eating, you may look to this nursery rhyme, attributed to "Anonymous":

> *I eat my peas with honey, I've done it all my life,*
> *It makes the peas taste funny, but it keeps them on my knife.*

WHAT'S THE BEST WAY TO KEEP SALAD GREENS FRESH?

You buy a head of lettuce and stick it in the fridge. Five days later, there's an algaelike mass in the bottom of the crisper. Another potential salad, gone to goo.

It's easier to avoid this problem than prevent it: Eat the greens within several days of purchase. If this isn't possible, wash the greens and dry them very well, either with a salad spinner or paper towels, wrap them in paper towels, and place in a plastic bag in which you've made several holes, to keep them well-ventilated. They should keep for seven to ten days.

Iceberg lettuce should be stored intact. When ready to use, slam the stem end of the lettuce on a counter; the conical core should slip right out. If you want to prepare it ahead of time, store as above, either in leaves or torn.

That's right, *torn*. Lettuce chopping is a major faux pas, the culinary equivalent of socks with sandals. Unless you're making tacos or slaw, tear lettuce into bite-size pieces. The one exception is a wedge of iceberg drenched in Russian or Roquefort dressing, an old-fashioned indulgence even current gourmands admit to.

WHAT IS YUCA?

Yuca (pronounced *yooka*), also known as cassava, is second only to the potato in world vegetable production. A staple in the Amazon (where it was first cultivated), Africa, Cuba, and Asia, yuca is a long, slender root vegetable with a thick, brown, barklike skin. Its white flesh looks like a cross between a coconut and a potato, and it is prepared like the latter: boiled, mashed, or fried.

Peeling can be a chore, as yuca are quite hard and chopping is messy, and their high-starch content (40 percent) can leave a white residue on counters and clothes. (Yuca is so starchy, in fact, that the Arawak Indians of the West Indies used yuca flour to bake bread, a product whose taste sixteenth-century Spanish explorers declared "not very good.") Boiled in a stew or soup, yuca tastes like a slightly sweet, waxy potato; in Jamaica, yuca is grated and used to make bammy, a popular bland bread eaten with fish and meat. But perhaps the tastiest way to enjoy yuca is fried, like French fries.

If you'd rather stick with potatoes but fear you're missing out on some exotic treat, relax. Chances are you've already tasted yuca: It's where we get tapioca.

WHAT ARE HEIRLOOM FRUITS AND VEGETABLES?

Heirloom fruits and vegetables are grown from seeds that have been handed down for at least three generations, and sometimes hundreds of years (not century-old seeds, of course, which would not germinate, but seeds from the plants of seeds from the plants your grandmother sowed). Reported to grow produce more nutritious and delicious than Johnny-come-lately seeds, heirloom seeds are equally prized for their historical significance.

Don't look for heirloom seeds at the local nursery, but through friends, at farmer's markets, and in catalogues that specialize in heirloom seeds, such as J. L. Hudson, P.O. Box 1058, Redwood City, CA 94064. You will pay for antiquity—certified heirloom seeds tend to be more expensive—but you will be growing the kind of produce our ancestors enjoyed, which, in a country where most tomatoes have the density of tennis balls, is a keen reward.

Fruit

WHAT'S AN ALLIGATOR PEAR?

An alligator pear is an avocado, whose name is a derivative of
the Nahuatl word *āhuacatl,* for "testicle," presumably a reference to the avocado's shape. When avocados were planted in
Florida in the 1830s, their bumpy green-and-black skins were
thought to resemble the local alligators, hence the name.

WHAT'S THE DIFFERENCE BETWEEN APPLE CIDER
AND APPLE JUICE?

Apple cider has many faces. In other parts of the world, apple
juice that's allowed to ferment and become alcoholic is called
cider. In America, we call that hard cider.

What we call cider is made from pressed apples whose juice
is left unfiltered and unpasteurized. It has a deeper, more complex taste than apple juice, which is strained, pasteurized, and
kept clear with preservatives. The taste of apple juice is decidedly childlike when compared with cider, but, like other highly
processed foods, it will last forever, something cider definitely
will not do. Cider's refrigerated shelf life is about two weeks,
after which time the plastic container it was bought in will begin
to swell like a bad liver. This expansion is caused by fermentation. You may drink the cider with impunity; know, however,
that it will taste more like cider spiked with baking soda than
the pint of Scrumpy's you had in London.

WHAT'S CITRON?

Citron is a large, lumpy, lemonlike fruit that grows in semitrop-
ical climates. The fruit itself is extremely sour and gives a very
small amount of tart juice. The thick peel is what's prized: It is

usually pickled, the oils removed (these are added to liqueurs), and then candied. Citron is eaten as is, or chopped and added to fruitcakes and coffee cakes, much to the chagrin of citron haters. (For some indeterminate reason, citron competes with lima beans and liver for the world's most loathsome food.)

How do you chop dates? They're so sticky!

If the dates are not pitted, pit them first by making a slice lengthwise and popping out the pit. Then oil the blade of a very sharp knife and chop away. Another method of chopping dates to be used in baked goods is to place the pitted dates in a food processor, sprinkle with a tablespoon or so of flour, and process quickly, turning the machine on and off until the dates are just chopped. Do not overprocess, or you'll wind up with date paste.

What's the difference between a huckleberry and a blueberry?

Almost never seen anymore (except in quaint bakeshops off the coast of New England in outrageously priced "fresh huckleberry pies"—probably made from blueberries, but who cares, you're on vacation), fresh huckleberries are so elusive as to be taking on the mythical proportions of their eponymous hero, Huckleberry Finn.

A huckleberry and a blueberry are of difference genera (*Gaylussacia* and *Vaccinium*, respectively), size, color (huckleberries are smaller and darker, almost black), and temperaments: Blueberries are easily cultivated and grown in many parts of the world, whereas huckleberries are wild and grow only in America. If you go berry picking and spy a low bush with dark, shiny fruit, and the berry reveals ten hard, tiny "seeds," you've found huckleberries. Pick as many as you can, and make a pie, the likes of which you will have never tasted before.

Blueberries you can pick up at the market.

WHAT IS A KEY LIME?

Key limes are small, hard, yellow limes with dark green flesh that yields copious amounts of sharp, flavorful juice. Alas, they are hard to find, either fresh or bottled. Once plentiful in the Florida Keys, they are no longer grown commercially in this country. That slice of Key lime pie you had at the diner last week, while tasty, was almost certainly made with regular lime juice, which is neither as tart nor as flavorful.

Key limes are still grown in this hemisphere in Mexico and the West Indies. (They are also common in Southeast Asia, where they were "discovered" by seventeenth-century British sailors, who were rationed the vitamin C–rich limes to prevent scurvy, hence the enduring nickname Limey.) If you do happen across a cache of Key limes, buy them all. The juice freezes beautifully, and your next Key lime pie/seviche/gin and tonic will be brighter for the addition.

WHAT IS LEMON CURD?

Lemon curd is a buttery, egg-rich English conserve, a tart, creamy custard used as a spread for bread or muffins and as a filling for tarts and cakes. Despite the curd reference, lemon curd is not coagulated but, when properly prepared, quite velvety. Also called lemon jelly and lemon cheese, it is made by cooking lemon juice with sugar, butter, and eggs.

WHAT ARE LITCHI NUTS?

A litchi (also called lychee) is not a nut at all but rather a fruit indigenous to China. It is small (about one and a half inches around), with dark-red, brittle skin and a fleshy, white interior. Fresh litchis are sold on the branch (this keeps them fresh longer), but their short summer season and lack of popularity make them hard to find outside of Chinese markets.

While canned litchis have become something of a culinary anachronism, anyone eating in Chinese restaurants in the sixties and seventies remembers them as those trembling, translucent orbs-in-syrup that followed the meal.

A close relation to the litchi in taste and texture, but with a hairy, bumpy shell, is the rambutan, from Malaysia.

WHAT IS THE DIFFERENCE BETWEEN A MANDARIN, A CLEMENTINE, AND A TANGERINE?

A mandarin is a *family* of fruits that includes clementines, tangerines, and satsumas. Indigenous to China but now cultivated worldwide, all are small citrus fruits with smooth, bright orange skin. Clementines are very sweet and seedless; satsumas are also seedless but can be quite sour. Tangerines, originally brought to America from Tangiers, are seeded and, while less sweet than a clementine, have the bonus of being a snap to peel, as the skin often "puffs" away from the fruit, making it easy to slip off in a piece.

Those mandarin orange sections that come in a can? They're tangerines minus their pith and pit.

WHAT'S AN UGLI FRUIT?

An Ugli fruit is the trademark name of a tangelo, a cross between a grapefruit and a tangerine. Grown in India and Jamaica (where it is also called hoogli fruit), it ranges in size from a navel orange to a huge grapefruit. Its greenish-yellow rind is thick and bumpy, and peels easily, revealing pale orange pulp that looks and smells like a sweet, juicy, highly perfumed orange.

CAN YOU TELL IF A MELON'S RIPE BY TAPPING ON IT?

Melon tapping is one of those things we do automatically, like lifting the hood of a stalled car. The question is, Do we know what we're looking for or, in the case of melons, listening for? A hollow sound indicates that the flesh is still firm, but this doesn't mean it's *ripe,* just not overripe. Squeezing isn't much help, either. We might want a honeydew with a little give, but we certainly don't want a pliant casaba.

A better way to choose melon is to look for firm, unblemished skin without dents or craters; melons with netted rinds, like cantaloupe, begin to fall in on themselves when overripe. You can also smell a melon, at the stem side, checking for a clean, sweet odor. With the exception of thick-skinned watermelon, no scent indicates an underripe melon, and a strong smell means one past its prime. Melons should also feel heavy for their size and never emit a "sloshing" sound, indicating that the flesh has broken down to the point of liquidity.

WHAT ARE PLANTAINS?

The first time I ate plantains, they had been made by a boyfriend's mother, who didn't like me. I didn't like her, either, but I liked the way she cooked, and, as they say, I licked the platter clean. Bound by kitchen pride and not affection, she fried me another batch of crispy-sweet *platanos*. Magnificent.

Before I got rid of the boyfriend, I got the recipe. Plantains, oil, and salt—that's it? Why wasn't everyone in America eating them? It turns out they were, just not in North America, which has been slow on the plantain uptake.

The plantain, which resembles a giant banana, grows abundantly in tropical climates, where they are a dietary staple. Plantains are larger than bananas and are never eaten raw, always cooked. While the peels are still green, the fruit is quite starchy and tough, and is added to stews or baked. As the plantain ripens, the skin turns yellow (and eventually black), and the fruit softens. The plantain is then fried or sautéed, and served alongside beans and rice and meat dishes, or broiled with brown sugar and made into a luscious dessert that cries out for a bed of vanilla ice cream.

CAN YOU EAT A HALLOWEEN PUMPKIN?

Once a jack-o'-lantern has scared the bejesus out of the neighborhood kids, it's ready for the compost heap, not the kitchen. But do buy a few extra pumpkins for eating. Small ones can be hollowed and baked like other winter squash, with a little brown sugar and butter; larger ones, especially sweet sugar pumpkins, are good for soups and stews. As for pie, know that the boiled, puréed flesh of fresh pumpkin is not as concentrated as canned pumpkin and will yield a pie with a more delicate, squashlike flavor.

WHAT IS A PRICKLY PEAR?

Also called cactus pear and Indian figs, prickly pears are the fruit of numerous cacti. They are egg-shaped, vary in color from green to salmon, and are covered with tiny, spinelike prickles that are almost invisible and can stay in your hands for days (trust me on this). The flesh is pomegranate-red, moist, and sweet. Peeled (use gloves), you may eat them as is or, as the Aztecs did, with a sprinkle of lime and salt.

YOU CAN EAT CACTUS?

Yes. The paddle-shaped pads of the prickly pear cactus are called nopals and are absolutely edible. However, they haven't caught on in a big way in America because they're hard to find and seem like an awful lot of work for something that tastes like okra. If, however, you find yourself in possession of a few nopals, remove the thorns, cook the pads in boiling water until tender, and slice or dice. Then have your guests try to guess what those green-on-the-outside, white-and-slimy on the inside cubes are in their salad.

WHAT'S A SUGARPLUM?

A sugarplum is an old-fashioned term for a holiday candy or cookie. While rarely used today, old sugarplum recipes include a sweetmeat with nuts, a candied sugarplum "tree" using a whole pineapple and maraschino cherries, and a butter cookie made with oats, coconuts, and chopped gumdrops.

But perhaps the proper answer to this question is, Sugarplums are whatever children tucked in for a long winter's nap imagine them to be.

WHAT'S A TAMARIND?

Also known as an Indian date, tamarind is a fruit used widely in Latin American, Indonesian, Indian, and Southeast Asian cuisines. Grown on thirty-foot-tall tamarind trees, the fruit is brown and pod-shaped, three to seven inches long, and with a sticky, sweet paste surrounding flat seeds. The paste, sweet and sour at once, is used in beverages, condiments (it's a major component of Worcestershire sauce), and chutneys.

SIX

Bread and Pizza

*The history of man from the beginning of time has been the
history of his struggle for his daily bread.*
—JOSUÉ DE CASTRO

Man cannot live by bread alone. But woman can.
—VICTORIA ESTERN

In the last twenty years, America has experienced a bread renaissance. When James Beard's classic *Beard on Bread* was published in 1973, he did not overstate the situation when he wrote,
"We are offered spongy, plasticized, tasteless breads, presliced,
doctored with nutrients and preservatives, and with about as
much gastronomic importance as cotton wool." Access to varied
ingredients, bread-baking machines, and an obsession with better health have raised the benchmark against which we judge
our loaves.

Not that abundance always goes down easily. As the people
who put white bread on the map, many Americans are still wary
of crumb, crust, and texture. (Why is stone-ground flour better?

What's a starter, and why spend three days making it? Why so many names for the bread that used to be called French?) While choice has spawned better taste and nutrition, it's also given rise to *pain de campagne* at eight bucks a pop, and fibrous clumps with enough hulls to crack a crown.

Want a worthy loaf every time? You can bake your own, which is simple enough, or apprise yourself of what's out there so that the next time you're asked to pick up some bread, you will select with confidence something other than balloon white (which, in its defense, makes a perfectly good grilled cheese sandwich).

Bread

WHAT IS YEAST, AND WHY DOES IT MAKE BREAD RISE?

Yeast, derived from the Sanskrit word *yas,* to seethe, is made up of single-cell, airborne fungi that, when activated, split the sugars found naturally in grains and cause the release of carbon dioxide. As the carbon dioxide bubbles expand, they are held in place by the naturally occurring gluten found in flours and grains, and developed further as the dough is kneaded and becomes elastic.

Waverley Root's *Food* quotes biochemist George Wald: "As living creatures, we are more like yeast than unlike it. Yeast and man have a common ancestor. Some of the ancestor's progeny became yeasts and some went the other way and became men, and these two journeys resulted in a change of only 53 nucleotides out of 312." And, like people, yeast needs a fairly secure environment in order to thrive. A little something to eat (preferably sugar, though yeast will get by on grains), a temperate climate (too much heat kills yeast; too little and yeast remains dormant), and a leisurely pace at which to grow. Well treated, a tiny amount of yeast will leaven an enormous amount of dough; neglect during any one step, however, and dough will not rise or will rise feebly, leaving bread at best misshapen, at worst, an inedible lump of solid gruel.

WHAT DOES IT MEAN TO "PROOF" YEAST?

While many bread recipes simply call for yeast to be mixed with flour and other ingredients and left to rise, what if the yeast is already dead? Proofing shows whether yeast cells are active. To do this, you *prove* the yeast is effective. The simplest way is to dissolve a packet of yeast granules (about two teaspoons) in one quarter cup of *warm* water (anything over 120 degrees instantaneously kills yeast cultures), to which you've added a teaspoon of sugar. Sugar is yeast's favorite food, and if yeast is living, it will begin to gobble up the sugar and bubble madly. If the mixture shows no sign of foaming within five minutes, the yeast is dead and has lost its leavening power.

To make sure yeast is active, manufacturers recommend using cake yeast within two weeks of purchase, or packaged yeast within one year (though I once came into possession of an industrial-sized jar of yeast and used it with success for four years). Store yeast in a cool, dry place (the refrigerator is ideal), and avoid opening and closing the container, as exposure to air robs yeast of its potency.

IS REGULAR YEAST BETTER THAN THE NEW QUICK-RISE?

Quick-rise yeast is genetically engineered to leaven dough faster and higher. But as any student of culture, be it yeast or civic, understands, producing more faster doesn't necessarily mean producing better.

Most bread doughs will not suffer for using quick-rise yeast, and for the baker, the time saved is beneficial. However, there are many breads whose flavor and texture are reliant on the time the dough takes to rise. A speedy sourdough, for instance, is an oxymoron, and a tasteless one at that, the comestible equivalent of Cliff Notes.

CAN BREWER'S YEAST BE SUBSTITUTED FOR BAKER'S YEAST?

No. Brewer's yeast, a high-protein yeast also known as nutritional yeast, is heat treated, which kills live yeast organisms. Though brewer's yeast may be added *sparingly* to some doughs for an additional vitamin boost, it will not leaven a loaf in any way, and tasting like a cross between almonds and wood ash, brewer's yeast is no one's favorite flavor.

IS THERE SUCH A THING AS HOMEMADE YEAST?

Wild yeast is colorless, microscopic, and in the air all around us (to say nothing of in our bodies). You can't harvest yeast per se, but you can attract it, by making a starter into which yeast will swarm and feed, creating a super-potent and long-lasting leavening agent.

HOW DO YOU MAKE A STARTER?

There are thousands of starters. Some are as simple as mixing flour and water, and waiting for fermentation to occur; others incorporate corn, hops, potatoes, yogurt, grapes, and/or salt, and require a great deal of straining and babying for anywhere from twenty-four hours to several weeks. Consult a bread-baking book for a simple starter or, better, ask a friend who bakes bread. Chances are they already have a starter sitting in the back of their fridge and will be delighted to share it with you. Be prepared, however, for a loving lecture on how this soupy liquid, which looks like library paste and smells like stale beer, is part of the original starter brought over on the *May-*

flower. Go ahead and smirk, but know that in five years, you, too, will be handing over a jelly jar of the beatified starter to a fledgling bread baker.

WHAT'S A SPONGE?

A sponge can be a synonym for a starter but is more often a mixture of an existing starter with flour and water. This sponge is allowed to ferment for a day or so, during which time it literary seethes and can become quite warm. (Go ahead, stick your finger in.) The lively mass is then mixed with flour and other ingredients, and baked into bread, usually a sourdough or a rye, both of which derive their tang from long fermentation.

Another method of imparting a mature flavor is to knead a *levain,* a small portion of dough from the previous dough, into a new loaf. This leavain imparts the specific taste and texture of a particular strain of yeast, and bequeaths the flavor to future generations of breads.

WAS SOURDOUGH INVENTED IN SAN FRANCISCO?

No. Sourdough is made with a starter that's allowed to ferment, and the fermenting of flour and water has been around since the Egyptians began baking bread, circa 2000 B.C.

However, because yeast spores are airborne, the place where bread is made affects its taste. San Francisco, on an inlet of the Pacific Ocean, feeds sourdough starter a particularly piquant strain of spore that gives the bread its distinctive sharpness. Bernard Clayton, perhaps the world's foremost authority on bread baking and author of the exhaustive *Bernard Clayton's Complete Book of Breads*, reports having no luck in preserving that unique Bay Area flavor. "Several times I have started with a bona fide sample brought out of San Francisco by me or by friends, but after it has been in my kitchen for a while it has become Bloomington [Indiana] sourdough bread, thanks to the billions of yeast spores floating freely in my kitchen that simply overpower the special fungi and bacteria that make San Francisco sourdough so special."

CAN BREAD BE MADE WITHOUT YEAST OR A STARTER?
Bread made with neither yeast nor starter will always be flat. However, for religious or dietary reasons, yeast and/or leavening of any kind must sometimes be avoided. Examples of unleavened bread include matzoh and nan, basic flour-and-water doughs, the former baked, the latter cooked on a hot griddle.

Other nonyeast breads include many thousands of quick breads leavened with baking powder and/or baking soda.

WHAT'S THE DIFFERENCE BETWEEN BAKING POWDER AND BAKING SODA?
Biscuits, pancakes, and quick breads such as banana bread do not rely on yeast for leavening, but instead on baking powder and/or baking soda.

Baking powder is sodium aluminum sulfate (and, in the case of double-acting baking powder, calcium acid phosphate) and sodium bicarbonate, better known as baking soda. Together, they contain the proper combination of acid and alkali to release the carbon dioxide that creates tiny air pockets in a neutral (neither alkali nor acid) dough or batter. Baking soda is an alkali that in itself does not leaven. However, combining it with an acid such as lemon juice, sour cream, or molasses generates enough carbon dioxide to leaven a mass of dough. Mixtures that require both baking powder and baking soda usually do so because one or more ingredients have tipped the acid-alkali balance, thus requiring more acid or alkali to ensure proper leavening.

WHY IS BAKING POWDER DOUBLE-ACTING?

Most baking powders are labeled "double-acting," because they leaven dough twice: once when it comes in contact with liquid, and again in the oven, when exposed to heat. This latter effect is achieved by adding a small amount of calcium acid phosphate (derived from either rocks or animal bones) to the existing baking soda/cream of tartar mixture. Cornstarch is also added to baking powder, to keep the mixture from absorbing moisture and losing potency.

HOW CAN YOU TELL IF BAKING POWDER OR SODA IS ACTIVE?

If you question the effectiveness of your baking powder or soda, mix a teaspoon into a half glass of hot water. It should bubble energetically.

CAN BAKING POWDER AND BAKING SODA BE USED INTERCHANGEABLY?

No. However, in a pinch, you can make your own baking powder, by combining a half teaspoon of baking soda plus one teaspoon of cream of tartar for every teaspoon of baking powder.

There is no substitute for baking soda.

WHAT IS GLUTEN?

Gluten is the protein found in flours and grains. Gluten is very absorbent and reacts with liquids to make dough elastic. In yeast breads, gluten releases the carbon dioxide needed for bread to rise and builds the molecular framework on which the carbon dioxide bubbles sit. A real workhorse, gluten is also a glutton for punishment, developing as dough is kneaded. It is also low in fat and calories, and adds volume and body.

The amount of gluten in flour depends on the kind of flour.

Hard wheat has a very high gluten-protein content (11–14 percent) and is ideal for the density that bread requires. Soft wheat produces a flour lower in gluten/protein (7–9 percent) and is therefore better used in delicate baking, as for cakes and cookies.

ALL-PURPOSE, UNBLEACHED, CAKE, PASTRY—THERE ARE TOO MANY KINDS OF FLOURS! WHAT ARE THE DIFFERENCES BETWEEN THEM, AND CAN THEY BE USED INTERCHANGEABLY?

The differences begin with the grain. For the sake of simplicity, let's look at wheat. Hard wheat, or winter wheat, is grown in cold climates and has a very high gluten-protein content that produces a dense product with good elasticity. The hardest wheat flour is durum, or semolina, which is usually made into pasta. The next hardest wheat is milled into bread flour, and a blend of hard wheats comprises unbleached flour. All-purpose flour is a blend of hard and soft wheat, which is grown in milder climates, and has lower gluten-protein content, which produces a more delicate product. Pastry flour is also made of soft wheat, as is cake flour, which has very little gluten-protein and makes for a very tender product.

Flours can be used interchangeably, but you must use common sense: You can't make an angel food cake with semolina, or pizza dough with pastry flour. The structure of the flours are simply too disparate to do the job properly. Think of flours as points on a protractor, with durum on the far left, all-purpose in the middle, and cake on the far right. When substituting, use a flour (or mix of flours) that falls within forty-five to fifty degrees of what the recipe requires. When in doubt, unbleached or all-purpose will suffice for almost all recipes.

IS WHOLE-WHEAT BREAD REALLY BETTER THAN WHITE BREAD?

In terms of nutrition, yes, whole wheat is "better" than white. Whereas white flour is robbed of its husk, germ, and endosperm before milling, whole-wheat flour is made of the entire wheat kernel, which is rich in vitamins and fiber. Stone-ground whole wheat, crushed between revolving one-ton stones, is even higher in fiber, and there's nothing like eating a lot of fiber to make a person feel virtuous.

However, there are a whole lot of people (many of them children) who cannot abide whole wheat. To them, whole wheat tastes like a cross between dust and straw, certainly not what they want nestled around peanut butter and jelly. It's a good idea to stop trying to convert these people to whole wheat. Good white bread is quite healthful, and its smooth, unfettered taste and texture often a better complement than nutty whole grains.

WHAT'S THE CORNELL FORMULA?

In the 1930s, Dr. Clive M. McCay of Cornell University developed a formula to enrich white bread. It consisted of one tablespoon soy flour, one tablespoon of dry milk, and one teaspoon of wheat germ to be added per cup of white flour. The additions added protein, calcium, and riboflavin, while not altering the flavor (try it). McCay's "Triple-Rich Formula" was a precursor to the more nutritionally balanced breads we eat today.

WHAT IS THE DIFFERENCE BETWEEN FRENCH AND ITALIAN BREAD?

Traditionally, both French and Italian breads are made with just four ingredients—flour, yeast, water, salt. French *boulangers* may add a pinch of ascorbic acid (which they believe helps in cell formation), while a baker in Napoli might incorporate a little olive oil. Dough for daily loaves is commonly shaped into slender loaves, French *baguettes* (meaning "wand" or "stick") being slightly longer and thinner than Italian *pane.* They are both baked in very hot (450 degrees) wood- or brick-burning ovens in which a pan of water has been allowed to create steam (alternately, the loaves are spritzed), ensuring a thick, crisp crust.

But technique tells only part of the story. The availability of ingredients (Italians tend to bake with harder wheat and semolina, which gives a chewier bread) and cultural and religious conventions influence the hundreds of breads baked on either side of the French-Italian border.

WHAT MAKES BAGELS SO CHEWY?

The way they are made. Bagels (from the German word *beugen,* to bend), like soft pretzels, undergo a two-step cooking procedure: The dough is first boiled, then baked. The initial waterbath gives the yeast dough a quick boost, puffing up the bagel and giving it a singular elasticity and chewiness, though not cooking it. That's done in the oven.

Unfortunately, many bagels available today forgo the waterbath and are basically rolls with holes. The holes, incidentally, are a holdover from centuries past, when bagel hawkers in eastern Europe (and, later, New York's Lower East Side) strung bagels onto long sticks for easy street selling.

WHAT ARE SCONES?

A scone, or *skon,* is a traditional Scottish biscuit made of oats or wheat flour, buttermilk, and perhaps a few currants. Like bagels, scones have been appropriated by flavorists in recent years and can now be found keeping company with fruits, cheeses, and nuts. Scones are occasionally cooked on the griddle but are more commonly cut into wedges, or farls (from an Old English word meaning "one quarter"), and baked. If the dough is baked in a large round, it is called a bannock, from the Gaelic *bannach,* or cake.

WHAT'S SHORT'NIN' BREAD?

Short'nin' bread puts a Southern spin on a Scottish standard. Traditional shortbread uses powdered sugar, which yields a meltingly tender crumb. The American version, made popular by a 1920s ditty, replaces the powdered sugar with brown sugar, making the bread more crunchy than crumbly, or "short," as doughs with a high percentage of fat (that is, short-ening) and a low liquid content are called.

IS FRENCH TOAST REALLY FRENCH?

Because traditional French bread contains no fat and goes stale very quickly, the French created *pain perdu* ("lost bread") as a way of using up leftover bread. Soaked in an egg-and-milk bat-ter and fried in butter, the lost bread eventually made its way across the Atlantic and found itself smothered in maple syrup, a distinctly American touch, as maple syrup is produced no-where but on North American soil.

That's not to say French toast isn't at home in other lands. In England, it's known as poor knights of Windsor and in Ger-many as *armer ritter* ("poor knight"). The etymology is as follows: An anachronistic distinction between nobility and commoners was whether they could afford dessert with their dinner. Though knights were considered gentry, they often could not afford expensive sweets, so they substituted what we call French toast, served with sugar, spirits, or jam.

WHAT ARE HUSH PUPPIES?

Hush puppies are deep-fried cornmeal fritters that accompany dishes requiring a lot of sopping, like gumbo, or come as part of those gargantuan platters featuring fried fish, fried potatoes, fried okra, fried you-name-it. It's known that the finger-shaped pups got their name when whoever was doing the frying threw a few to the dogs with the admonishment, "Hush, puppies," but whether the tosser was a New England fisherman, a Confederate soldier on the q.t. from the Yanks, or a cowboy named Cookie is a matter of regional debate.

HOW DID SALLY LUNN GETS ITS NAME?

There are at least three versions of how this sweet, egg-rich bread got its name. The first is that it's named for a baker who sold the breads on the streets of Bath, England, in the eighteenth century. The story goes that she sold her recipe (and the rights to her name) to a local bakery. The second is that it's a corruption of *solimeme,* a similar sweet egg bread from Alsace. The third that it comes from *le soleil et la lune,* French for "sun and moon."

Another woman's name that has wended its way into the bread world is Anna. Legend has it an irritable husband once shouted, "Anna, damn her!" or "Anna's damn bread!" when served his wife's distinctive loaf one time too many. His testiness gave name to anadama bread, a homey, yeast-risen loaf of cornmeal and molasses.

ARE ENGLISH MUFFINS ENGLISH?

While the English have taken more than their share of culinary hits ("In England there are sixty different religions, but one sauce," Voltaire once said), they are unrivaled when it comes to the sweet and savory dainties that accompany tea.

English muffins do hail from England, where they are referred to as simply muffins. Why a standard blend of flour, water, yeast, and salt becomes bread in France and a muffin in England has to do with the cooking. English muffin batter is rather thin and is cooked in rings (think of tuna cans with the tops and bottoms removed) on a hot griddle. The muffins are split (with fork or fingers, *never* a knife) and toasted again before eating, just as we enjoy the store-bought kind.

WHAT ARE CRUMPETS?

When Somerset Maugham wrote, "To eat well in England you should have breakfast three times a day," he may well have been thinking of crumpets, which are similar to English muffins in that they are cooked on a griddle, then toasted and slathered in butter. However, they are not baked in rings but are free form, as we make pancakes. (A smaller version of a crumpet, hailing from Yorkshire-Lancashire, is known as a pikelet.) Or perhaps Maugham was musing on the Hot Cross Buns of childhood verse, small, yeast-raised rolls containing currants and candied fruits, and marked with a sugar icing x.

WHAT IS A BEATEN BISCUIT?

Every Southern cookbook has a nostalgic tale of bygone Sundays listening to the *thwack! thwack!* of beaten biscuit dough being clobbered with an ax handle for no less than thirty minutes (longer, if company was coming). Thus the dough was stimulated beyond the breaking point, causing it to blister and bubble, after which it was cut into half-dollar-size rounds, baked, and served with a country ham. After reading a half dozen of these devoted testimonials, I tried my hand (and arm) on a batch. All I can say of the results is that I agree with Bill Neal, author of the sublime book on Southern baking, *Biscuits, Spoonbread and Sweet Potato Pie*: "Beaten biscuits are, like grits, very much a mystery to the uninitiated. . . . These chewy, unleavened morsels resemble more the hardtack produced by early European bakers for armies and navies than anything else."

Southern purists may shudder, but those longing for the taste of yesteryear can now turn to technology to achieve the "unique" texture of beaten biscuits: Instead of manual punishment, the dough may be whapped in the food processor for about thirty seconds, by which time it is supplicant enough to surrender to its fate.

WHY DO SOME BISCUITS TURN OUT LIGHT AND FLAKY AND OTHERS LIKE DOORSTOPS?

One of the kitchen's simplest recipes (to wit, flour, baking powder, salt, fat, and milk) can produce widely divergent results. Southerners are correct when they say it's the flour. Soft wheat flours milled in the South, like White Lily brand, have less gluten, which yields a lighter biscuit. Using lard instead of butter or Crisco will give a flakier biscuit. Baking at 450 to 500 degrees for eight to ten minutes gives the perfect proportion of crust to flake. (Such high temperatures can frighten amateur biscuit bakers, who either overbake or bake at a lower temperature, yielding a rather blah biscuit.)

None of these reasons, however, is as important as how biscuit dough is handled, which should be: as little as possible! Handling stimulates the gluten in flour, which, while crucial for a hearty rye, is death to the delicate biscuit. Ingredients should be stirred only briefly, dumped onto a floured surface, patted into shape, and cut with a floured biscuit cutter pushed straight down into the dough (twisting toughens the dough).

A very simple recipe for a dozen biscuits is:

2 cups flour (preferably soft wheat, like White Lily brand)
½ teaspoon salt
1 tablespoon baking powder
5 tablespoons shortening, lard, or butter, or a combination of these
1 cup milk or buttermilk

Mix the flour, salt, and baking powder. Cut in the fat, add the milk, and stir until just combined. Dump onto a floured surface, knead briefly (eight to ten strokes), cut with a biscuit cutter, place rounds on an ungreased cookie sheet, and bake in a pre-heated 450-degree oven until just browned, about eight minutes.

WHAT IS SPOON BREAD?

Spoon bread is a soufflélike pudding bread made with cornmeal and often served with rich, gravy-laden meats and roasts, or with rivers of melting butter.

Virginians claim spoon bread was invented in a Virginia kitchen when a creamy, egg-rich cornbread was accidentally left in the oven to slow-bake. The origins go back further than that, however, to Indian tribes of the Southeast, who slow-cooked corn grits into a thick porridge-bread called awendaw, which was eaten with a spoon, leading, perhaps, to the current appellation.

WHAT IS FRY BREAD?

Fry bread is a baking-powder leavened dough fried in oil. Also called Navajo bread, fry bread is very popular in the Native-

American community, where it is used as a base for Indian tacos (a big disc of fry bread topped with meat, beans, cheese, and condiments), or dusted with powdered sugar, like Italian *zeppole,* or drizzled with honey, like Mexican sopapillas.

Pizza

Growing up in New York, it was John's Pizzeria on Sundays. While my dad would wax nostalgic about eating a whole pie himself, my brother, Chris, and I would scarf down the best pizza in the city, the ultra-thin crust just the right side of burnt, a sauce that cried, *"Mangia, ragazzi!"* from beneath a judicious layer of melted mozzarella. Perfect.

But John's sold only by the pie, so by age twelve every schoolkid knew where to score a quick slice: Famous Ray's on Sixth Avenue (more cheese, but the same thin crust), Queen in Brooklyn (Chris's fave: corner slice, Sicilian), and Stromboli on St. Mark's Place (where we watched the downtown demimonde shift from hippie to punk).

Perhaps because New York is a walking town, they know how to serve food you can carry at a clip, pizza being the most popular. The first time I ordered pizza in Chicago, I was served a scoonerful of cheesy sauce that required a fork and six napkins. It tasted great, but it wasn't . . . pizza. (Little did I know how genuine Chicago deep-dish would look compared to the ghastly pizza that waited in L.A.; I find the mere memory of that first shrimp-and-mango-salsa slice frightening.)

WHAT IS THE DIFFERENCE BETWEEN NEW YORK-STYLE AND CHICAGO-STYLE PIZZA?

The main difference between New York and Chicago *pizze* (the plural of *pizza*) is the dimensions. Both use a yeast dough, tomatoes (or tomato sauce), and mozzarella, but New York-style pizza has a thin crust (a quarter inch thick) rolled into a circle (eighteen inches, for a large pie), and not so much tomato sauce that it's going to come squirting molten-red from beneath the melted cheese. The best New York pizza is still baked in coal-fired ovens built in the thirties and forties, ovens that can reach up to 750 degrees, which gives the crust patchy burns called "New York blisters." Chicago pizza rolls the dough thicker and lines large, rectangular jelly-roll pans with dough, building a two-inch rim and filling it with tomatoes and cheese, much as you would fill a pie shell. It cooks up soupier than New York-style pizza and is eaten with a knife and fork, which no self-respecting New Yorker (except my mother) would even consider using.

New York-style is more popular than Chicago-style (or deep-dish), and not only because it's been in this country longer. (The first American pizzeria was opened on Spring Street in New York City in 1905, whereas Chicago deep-dish premiered at Pizzeria Uno in 1943.) New York-style is easier to package, freeze, and deliver, all of which help buoy a $25 billion-a-year industry.

WHAT'S SICILIAN-STYLE PIZZA?

There are several types of Sicilian-style pizza popular in the United States. The first is similar to Chicago-deep dish, in that it has a thick crust and is baked in a large jelly-roll pan; however, it does not have as much filling, making it an ambulatory snack. Another type of Sicilian pizza is *sfincuini,* which has both a top and bottom crust; though the name sounds exotic, it actually translates to "pizza pie" (*pizza* meaning simply "pie," or "torte"). *Schiacciata,* dough baked simply with a wipe of olive oil and salt, is a delicious, flaky type of pizza more often served as a bread.

WHO IS MARGHERITA AND WHY DOES SHE HAVE A PIZZA NAMED AFTER HER?

Pizza toppings often carry colloquial or historical significance. Tomato, basil, and mozzarella pizza is named for Queen Margherita, of Savoy, who, in 1889, was well pleased with the simple green-red-and-white pizza (the colors of the national flag) served in her honor in the Capodimante palace in Naples. Pizza Liguria, an olive-and-anchovy pizza, is named for a village outside Genoa; and *scarpaccia,* a zucchini-and-onion pizza from Camaiore, translates roughly to "big old shoe." Tuscan food writer Wilma Pezzini explains: "It's meant to imply that this pizza should be as flat as possible, like the sole of a very old pair of shoes."

WHY DO YOU BAKE PIZZA IN A BRICK OVEN? CAN YOU DUPLICATE THE RESULTS AT HOME?

A friend recently ordered clay tiles for his oven so that he and his wife could make homemade pizza. But the dough kept shrinking back, no matter how hard they pulled it. In desperation, they wound up using their new tiles not to bake on, but to weight down the corners of their pizza dough.

Ingenious, if ineffective.

Coal-fired and wood-burning brick ovens, the kind used in many pizzerias, average temperatures over 550 degrees and bake the pizza directly atop the heat source, which gives a crisp crust. As the highest calibration on most home ovens is 500 degrees and tossing a fresh pizza on the oven floor is a less than savory prospect, home pizzamakers sometimes utilize clay baking tiles, pizza stones, or black steel pans to conduct extra heat. The crust is laid directly on these, resulting in a crisp crust.

Another option is individual tiles. Unglazed quarry tiles, about a half-inch thick (thinner ones crack, and thicker ones take too long to heat up), can be placed directly on the bottom of the oven, leaving a small space on all sides in order for the air to circulate. Slide the prepared pizza directly onto the hot tiles, making sure the dough is at room temperature (cold dough takes too long to heat up). Getting the baked pizza in and out can be tricky, so if you go the tile route, you may want to purchase a pizza peel, the long-handled wooden paddles you see pizza chefs sliding in and out of the oven. Or you can purchase a pizza stone, a large square that pops in and out of the oven easily; remember to heat the stone when you preheat the oven. You can also use a regular baking sheet, making sure to oil the sheet to prevent the pizza from sticking. A few minutes before the pizza is done, slide it off the pan directly onto the oven rack, which will crisp the bottom even further.

While none of these methods will give crust the signature woody aroma associated with great pizza, with the right dough and quality toppings the results will be very good.

IS THERE ANYTHING THAT SHOULDN'T BE PUT ON A PIZZA?

I tend to be a purist when it comes to pizza. To me, barbecued chicken and jalapeños mixed with tomato sauce and cheese on a soggy crust seems like a marketing strategy born from hunger.

However, as there are pizzas with blackberry jam and béchamel sauce and blue cheese being sold in more than 60,000 pizzerias across the country (and in twice as many supermarkets), popular opinion seems to be that anything goes. In his definitive book *The Ultimate Pizza*, Pasquale Bruno, Jr., reports that the world likes an eclectic pizza topping: "Eel and squid are favorite toppings in Japan. Australians like shrimp and pineapple on their pizza, while Mexicans go for ham and pineapple." In the States, the favorite is pepperoni, while the Italians tend to take theirs straight, with a thin layer of sauce and just a dusting of cheese.

Dessert

Bring on the dessert. I think I am about to die.
LAST WORDS OF BRILLAT-SAVARIN'S
GREAT-AUNT PIERETTE.

I have a litmus test for boyfriends, one directly linked to my obsessive need to bake. If I ask, "What's your favorite dessert?" and receive a waffly, "I don't care for sweets," I know the relationship is doomed. Oh, there's the occasional Lucullan, but more often than not, men are oblivious to sugar's siren call.

Or think they are. I recently read of a study where men's vital statistics were measured in response to various smells, among them rose, pine, perfume, and food. Pumpkin pie elicited the biggest blips. I have never known a guy not to gorge on warm chocolate-chip cookies, and I have received two proposals of marriage after feeding different sweethearts apple pie with a crumb topping. Still, when asked what kind of cake they'd like for their birthdays, they reply, to a man, "I don't like cake."

Makes a girl wonder. What primal misfire causes someone to disavow all foods based on nature's most aggressively adored substance, sugar? Does dessert apathy signal a dispassionate nature? A dyspeptic gene? After all, newborns smile when it's tapped on their tongues, children clamor for it incessantly, and all women respect the power of pastry. I can only surmise that we are closer to our primal hungers than are men. Or maybe they simply don't give their sweet tooths the plumbing they deserve. Whatever the cause, this chapter is dedicated to men, in the hope of whetting their appetites so that the next time some fetching girl asks what she can bake for them, they'll know what to say.

WHEN WAS CHOCOLATE DISCOVERED?

About 1000 B.C. History tells us the Aztecs drank a brew called *xocoatl*, meaning "bitter water," made from pulverized cocoa beans and water. When the Spaniards brought the beverage from the New World, *xocoatl* became *chocolātl*. It remained solely in beverage form until the 1800s, when the beans were mixed with cocoa butter, sugar, and other ingredients to produce what we know as chocolate.

WHAT'S THE DIFFERENCE BETWEEN BITTER CHOCOLATE, BITTERSWEET CHOCOLATE, AND MILK CHOCOLATE?

Bitter chocolate is made of cocoa "nibs" (shelled, roasted cocoa seeds) and cocoa butter (a vegetable fat). It is unsweetened and used mainly in baking, though occasionally as an addition to savory sauces, such as Mexican mole. Current recipes rarely refer to this product as "bitter chocolate" but rather as "unsweetened chocolate" or, very occasionally, "baking chocolate."

Bitter chocolate should not be confused with *bittersweet chocolate,* which has a higher fat content and added sugar (usually cane or beet). This type of sweetened chocolate ranges from very bittersweet to semisweet (the kind we use for chips) to very sweet.

Milk chocolate is made with powdered milk added and has a

mild flavor. It is usually eaten as is, though can be an ingredient in baking (the flavor will be less pronounced), or melted and used for dipping.

WHAT IS WHITE CHOCOLATE?

White chocolate is pure cocoa butter mixed with sugar, milk, and flavorings, like vanilla, but without added chocolate liquor (which adds both flavor and color). Its taste is quite sweet (according to some people, a little soapy) and not unlike a very mild milk chocolate. While it can occasionally be used in place of other chocolates (chips or chunks for cookies), the flavor will be less intense. White chocolate is also less resilient than dark, making it too stiff and heavy to whip into frosting, for instance. Melting white chocolate can also be problematic, as it can separate and pill if heated too quickly. If you want to use melted white chocolate (for dipping fresh strawberries, let's say), whisk a teaspoon of flavorless oil per cup of white chocolate as it melts. This will keep it from getting lumpy and give the chocolate a better sheen.

CAN I USE CHOCOLATES INTERCHANGEABLY WHEN COOKING?

Depending on the intensity of chocolate flavor desired, bittersweet and sweet chocolates may be used interchangeably. Milk chocolate, however, should not be substituted (or only in a pinch), as the flavor is far less sincere.

Unsweetened chocolate may be substituted for bittersweet chocolate or any sweet chocolate by adding four teaspoons of sugar to every ounce of unsweetened chocolate for every ounce of bittersweet needed.

To substitute cocoa for unsweetened chocolate, the rule is three tablespoons of cocoa and one tablespoon of fat (preferably butter, though margarine or shortening will do) for every ounce of unsweetened chocolate.

WHY DOES MELTED CHOCOLATE SOMETIMES "SEIZE"?

High heat and/or liquid can make chocolate tighten up, where-upon it becomes pebbly and unsuitable for anything but impromptu ice-cream topping. While remelting at a low temperature may restore chocolate to a liquid mass, it's better to avoid the problem. Always melt chocolate in a heavy-bottomed pan or a double boiler, over low heat, making sure no liquid (like a dash of vanilla, or a wet stirring spoon) gets in. If liquid is to be added to the chocolate, make sure there's at least one tablespoon for every ounce of chocolate, and that the liquid is warmed, if possible.

The microwave oven also melts chocolate beautifully. Place squares or chunks of chocolate in a microwave-safe bowl, and microwave, uncovered, for one minute. Take the bowl out, give it a stir, and zap for another minute, if necessary. Microwaving does not affect the taste or texture of chocolate.

HOW SHOULD CHOCOLATE BE STORED?

Chocolate will last in a cool, dry place for up to a year. If the temperature in your cupboard or climate averages above 75 degrees Fahrenheit, you may find that chocolate quickly develops blooms, white patches caused by the separation of cocoa butter rising to the surface. This chocolate is still edible, though should not be used for decorations, as it tends to crumble easily.

Though chocolate may be kept in the refrigerator (or freezer), it will take on the odors of other foods in time, so taste before using. Also, make sure to bring chocolate to room temperature before eating, as frozen bits of chocolate, while currently a popular addition to gourmet ice creams, always strike me as rather hard and tasteless.

WHO INVENTED CHOCOLATE-CHIP COOKIES?

A woman named Ruth Wakefield, who in the late 1920s became proprietress of an inn near a tollgate in Whitman, Massachusetts. She began adding chocolate bits to her butter cookies and called them Toll House Inn cookies. They were outrageously popular, and Nestlé agreed to supply Mrs. Wakefield with a lifetime supply of chocolate if they could publish her recipe on the back of their large chocolate bars. By 1939, Nestlé introduced morsels, thus eliminating the chore of hand-chopping the chocolate, and beginning America's everlasting love affair with chocolate-chip cookies.

They are not, however, the country's best-selling cookie. That honor goes to Oreo, five billion of which are consumed by snacking Americans every year.

WHAT IS GANACHE?

Ganache is a glossy blend of melted chocolate, heavy cream, and butter. It is insanely rich and smooth (*Death by Chocolate* author Marcel Desaulniers calls it "supernal food"), and is used as a frosting, filling, or sauce—for decorating or dipping, for licking off your fingers. And it's not hard to make: Heat one cup of heavy cream and two tablespoons of butter to boiling. Empty a twelve-ounce bag of chocolate morsels into a bowl. Pour hot cream over the mixture and stir until smooth. The ganache will harden as it cools but will never become stiff. Beautiful stuff.

IS CHOCOLATE BAD FOR YOU?

"Persons who drink chocolate regularly are conspicuous for un-failing health and immunity from the host of minor ailments which mar the enjoyment of life." This, according to Jean-Anthelme Brillat-Savarin, author of the classic *The Physiology of Taste*.

Okay, so you're thinking, He wrote this in 1825. Then how about this quote, from Maida Heatter's *Book of Great Chocolate Desserts*? "Chocolate is a quick-energy food that contains protein, carbohydrate, and fat. And the following vitamins and minerals: calcium, phosphorus, iron, sodium, potassium, and vitamin A. Plus thiamin, riboflavin, and niacin, which are B vitamins."

Still not convinced? Then know there is no conclusive evidence linking chocolate to acne; that chocolate has zero cholesterol; is converted into energy almost immediately; and soldiers from World War II to Desert Storm received Hershey bars in their rations. A 1979 *New York Times* article proclaimed: "The chocolate bar is an edible American flag, a security blanket for the distraught, a barometer of the nation's economic health." And while many of us subjugate our tastes to the latest health trend, almost everyone agrees that chocolate is eternally delicious. Indulge with impunity.

IS THERE A DIFFERENCE BETWEEN COCOA AND DUTCH-PROCESS COCOA?

Cocoa is simply unsweetened chocolate with most of the cocoa butter removed. Solidified and ground, it becomes cocoa.

Dutch-process cocoa differs slightly. It is an invention of Coenraad van Houten, who in 1828 discovered that adding alkali (a soluble mineral salt) to cocoa made it less bitter and gave it a richer color.

Both cocoa and Dutch-process cocoa may be used interchangeably, though richer results will be had with Dutch-process. Additionally, both can be used to make the drink we call cocoa, or hot chocolate, provided sugar is added along with milk. Know, however, that Dutch-process cocoa is more powdery and will not stir as easily into cold milk.

WHAT MAKES A CHEESECAKE "NEW YORK"?

New York cheesecake, an unctuous brick of a cake, was "invented" in New York by Jewish immigrants from eastern Europe. Who, exactly, gets the credit is still being contested. Reuben's Restaurant claims to have been the first to use cream cheese instead of cottage cheese, or pot cheese, and accused Lindy's Restaurant, which made the cheesecake world-famous, of stealing their recipe. Across the river, in Brooklyn, Junior's Delicatessen was making a reputation on their densely rich cheesecake—with a graham cracker instead of a cookie dough crust. They must be doing something right; *New York Cookbook* by Molly O'Neill reports that Junior's goes through "four tons of cream cheese a week."

Controversy aside, New York cheesecake uses cream cheese, eggs, sugar, and a little heavy cream in its filling. It is baked in a crust-lined springform pan and sometimes topped with a swipe of sweetened sour cream. Fruit-topped cheesecakes are also popular, but to purists it's gilding the lily.

Though there are many cream cheese-based desserts (such as *pashka,* a tower of cream cheese, fruits, and nuts eaten on the Russian Easter), the only other cheesecake of any celebrity is *torta di ricotta,* a ricotta-based "Italian-style" cheesecake that is crumbly rather than creamy.

DOES POUND CAKE REALLY WEIGH A POUND?

Originally, it weighed four pounds and called for a pound each of butter, sugar, eggs, and flour. In France, from whence it came, the cake is still called *quatre-quarts,* or "four quarts," a quart being equal to a pound. But a four-pound cake is a really large cake, over twice as big as most loaf pans. Still, if you'd like to try it, the formula works. However, the best pound cake I've ever eaten relies on measurements, not weight:

1¾ sticks butter, soft
1½ cups sugar
1½ cups flour
1½ teaspoons baking powder
¼ cup milk, at room temperature
4 large eggs, room temperature
2 teaspoons vanilla extract

Line a long loaf pan with the butter wrappers. Mix the butter and sugar by hand, and mix in the flour and the baking powder. Add the milk, then the eggs one at a time, beating only until blended. Add the vanilla. Bake in a preheated 350 degree oven for about one hour.

WHAT IS THE DIFFERENCE BETWEEN A TORTE AND A TART?

In Vienna, the home of the torte, they say, "A torte is a round cake, but not every round cake is a torte." That's because most round cakes use flour as a batter base, whereas tortes employ ground nuts or bread crumbs, and are often layered with butter cream, whipped cream, or jam. One famous example of a torte is the *linzertorte,* a rich ground-almond pastry filled with raspberry jam.

A tart, or tarte, is a pie with no top crust.

WHY DO YOU ADD LARD TO PIE CRUST?

Because it makes piecrust (and biscuits) extremely flaky. Made from rendered, clarified pork fat, lard has a higher fat and lower moisture content than either butter or shortening; it creates the best and most distinct layering, which causes flakiness. Lard also gives a subtle, nutlike taste (compared with shortening's neutrality) and does not burn (like butter). It's also cheap and keeps forever.

While lard's popularity has waned, with vegetarianism and worries about cholesterol, bakers (especially in the South) still rely on its unique properties to give both a light and crusty texture. Butter devotees may try using a mixture of both lard and butter in their crusts and biscuits, thereby gaining the former's flakiness and the latter's flavor.

WHAT DOES IT MEAN TO BAKE PIECRUST "BLIND"?

Blind baking is an English term that refers to baking a crust before it is filled. This is done either because the filling is not baked (as in Key lime pie), or because the filling is very wet and heavy, and would doom the crust to sogginess if it were not first crisped.

To blind bake, line a pie pan with dough, prick it well with a fork, lay over a piece of foil or wax paper, and fill it with raw rice, raw beans, or pie weights (tiny metal pellets manufactured specifically for this purpose), any of which will prevent the crust from puffing up. Bake the shell in a preheated 400-degree oven for ten minutes, remove the weights and paper, and bake five minutes longer, until the crust is lightly browned. The crust is then ready to be filled and baked.

The only difficulty you may have with blind baking is that the edges of the crust sometimes become overly browned. To avoid this problem, wrap the edges in strips of tinfoil after blind baking, fill, and bake as directed.

WHAT MAKES PASTRY SHORT?

A short pastry is a nonyeast pastry that has a high ratio of butter to flour. Short pastries bake up crumbly (think of shortbread) rather than chewy and tend to keep well, owing to their high fat content.

WHAT IS PUFF PASTE?

Puff paste, also called puff pastry, is the dough used in croissants, napoleons, and other flaky confections. In France, it's called *mille-feuille,* or "thousand-layer," because the pastry is comprised of hundreds of fragile layers. This feat is accomplished by incorporating butter into a *détrempe,* a dough made of flour, salt, water, and, yes, more butter. The détrempe is folded around cold butter and rolled, folded, and rolled, and again, creating a multi-tiered pastry that puffs up in the oven into many thin, fragile, buttery layers.

Puff pastry can be a lot of work to make at home but is easily found in the frozen food section of most supermarkets.

WHAT IS PHYLLO DOUGH?

Phyllo dough, sometimes marked "filo dough," is the Hellenic equivalent of puff pastry (see above). Phyllo, which translates to "leaf," is a tissue-thin pastry made of flour, salt, and water, and is so fine you can actually see through it. Turkish phyllo dough is known as *yufka* ("see-through"). It is used in making such Greek dishes as baklava (phyllo layered with nuts and honey) and *spanakopitta* (Greek spinach-and-cheese pie), as well as many strudels and hors d'oeuvres. With a little practice, phyllo is a handy and exquisite kitchen friend.

Phyllo is rarely made at home. Though it is readily available frozen at the supermarket, purchase it fresh if you can (it can be found in Middle Eastern specialty stores), as thawed phyllo sheets tend to stick together, at which point they become useless. Dried-out phyllo dough is likewise unusable, so make sure to keep a kitchen cloth or a damp paper towel atop the phyllo sheets when handling.

Working with phyllo dough is a matter of layering. Remove one sheet at a time, place it in whatever pan it will be baked in, brush it with butter, and repeat. (Most dishes that use phyllo require four or five of the 18- by 14-inch sheets per layer of filling.) Add a layer of filling, and repeat. If you should accidentally tear it, phyllo is easily patched with buttered fingers.

Unbaked phyllo dishes keep well (all that butter keeps things moist) and bake up dramatically beautiful even after months in the freezer.

WHAT IS *CLAFOUTIS*?

Though the recipe is old, clafoutis (kla-foo-tee) is currently enjoying something of a renaissance in America's restaurants, putting a French spin on what we call a cobbler. It's made by topping a layer of fresh fruit, most often cherries, with batter; when baked, bits of fruit poke through the top of the cake. It is often served with a dollop of crème fraîche alongside.

WHAT'S A FOOL?

A *fool,* an Old English word for a custard or clotted cream, is described in the *Oxford English Dictionary* as "a dish composed of fruit stewed, crushed, and mixed with milk, cream or custard." Though fools are no longer in fashion (except in the South, where people dote on fruit desserts), they are embarrassingly easy to make. Simply fold sweetened whipped cream into puréed stewed fruit or use ripe, uncooked fruit on which you've sprinkled a bit of sugar. The fool may be layered in a pretty serving bowl or spooned into individual ramekins. Fools are often served with a sweetened fruit sauce on the side.

WHAT'S A GRUNT?

A grunt is member of the spoon pie family, whose other members include slumps, cobblers, and pandowdies, which all combine fruit with a batter or biscuit dough. A grunt piles biscuit dough atop stewed fruit and is steamed rather than baked. A slump may be baked (often upside down) or steamed, the raw or cooked fruit being topped with biscuit dough or piecrust. A cobbler is more like a fruit stew with dumplings, as the biscuit dough is plopped onto the fruit, giving it the look of ancient cobblestones; hence the name. A pandowdy lays rolled piecrust atop the fruit, then breaks it up a bit; this process, known as "dowdying," allows the juices from the fruit to bubble through.

All of these American spoon pies (called such because they are soupier than regular pies) were especially popular in the eighteenth and nineteenth centuries, when the labors of farming required men to eat upwards of 6,000 calories per day, and women upwards of 4,000.

HOW IS GELATO DIFFERENT FROM ICE CREAM?

In *More Classic Italian Cooking*, Marcella Hazen rhapsodized about eating ice cream in Italy at an outdoor café: "There is perhaps no other pleasure we can take that is so kindly protective of those endangered attributes of happiness: indolence and well being." She was eating gelato, the intensely flavorful, superrich ice cream that is one of Italy's culinary coups.

While Italian ice cream uses the same basic ingredients as American, the final product is not churned and aerated to the extent that American ice cream is; nor is it stabilized with things like gelatin, which is added to slow the melting process. The result is a more velvety ice cream of incomparable richness.

Although the premium-ice-cream explosion of recent years has brought gelato to American freezers, there is nothing like ice cream from an Italian *gelateria* (found in Little Italys across the United States). Flavors like *gianduia* (chocolate-hazelnut) and *fica* (fig) verily shine, wetter and more seductive than their American counterparts.

WHAT IS *SEMIFREDDO*?

Semifreddo, which means "half-cold" in Italian, is a cream-based, chilled dessert. It begins as a simple custard, into which whipped cream and/or beaten egg whites are folded, creating a mousselike consistency that will not freeze as solid as ice cream. The semifreddo is frozen, though only for about eight hours, after which it is unmolded and sliced. It may be layered with crushed cookies, as in semifreddo's most famous incarnation, tortoni (layers of crumbled macaroons with whipped cream custard), or with fresh fruit.

ARE SHERBET AND SORBET THE SAME THING?

While many people think sorbet is simply a slick way of marketing sherbet, they are, in fact, two very different desserts. The reason is milk: Sherbet usually has it; sorbet never does.

Sherbet can be traced back to *sharbat,* a Persian drink made of sweetened fruit juice and water. When sharbat migrated to France, it became *sorbet* and was frozen; the Italians added a little cream and/or beaten egg white, and it became *sobretto*. American sherbet is usually closer to the last, a milk-based ice with a mild flavor (think: Creamsicle). In years past, however, sherbet's cream-ice hybrid has been largely abandoned for the richness of ice cream or the intensity of sorbet.

Sorbet delivers a much bigger flavor than sherbet simply because it is undiluted fruit, water, and, usually, sugar. It has more of a tang than sherbet, is less caloric, and comes in bracing flavors (cassis, kiwi, mango) that stimulate the eye as well as the palate.

WHAT IS GRANITA?

What we know as "Italian ice" is granita. It is like sorbet, in that it is made of fruit purée, water, and sugar. Granita, however, is not churned but frozen in a shallow pan and hand-crushed several times during the freezing process. The resulting clear, coarse, shardlike crystals are a dramatic departure from uniform sorbets, as refreshing as they are visually engaging.

WHAT IS *CRÈME ANGLAISE*?

Also called custard sauce, crème anglaise (English cream) is a dessert sauce consisting of egg yolks, sugar, cream, and flavorings, such as vanilla or brandy. It is served, hot or cold, alongside many plain cakes and is practically de rigueur with bread pudding. A variation of crème anglaise is what gives premium ice creams their eggy richness, and a spoonful atop sliced peaches is always welcome.

WHAT'S THE DIFFERENCE BETWEEN FROSTING AND ICING?

Often used interchangeably, frosting and icing are in fact different. Frosting tends to be thick and gooey, with a cream or butter base. It is slathered on cake layers, or applied in fluffy waves. Icing is thinner, sometimes with simply a sugar base, and creates a glaze on cakes and pastry, such as the kind you find on coffee cakes.

IS THERE ANY WAY TO RECYCLE FRUITCAKE?

Rumor has it there is only one fruitcake in the world, and that it is simply passed along each holiday season, in the spirit of questionable altruism. I've read of people using fruitcakes as doorstops and emergency brakes, and writer Russell Baker claims, "At age fifteen, [to have] dropped a small piece of fruitcake and shattered every bone in my right foot." This weighty claim stems from the fact that fruitcakes are deliberately aged, sometimes for ten years or more. Mold and vermin are kept at bay by dousing the heavyweight cake with liquor, which acts as a preservative and, it is said, a flavor enhancer.

Should you find yourself the recipient of a fruitcake and are loath to eat it, you may give it away the following Christmas and no one will be the wiser. Just be sure to keep it airtight. If someone in the family has actually opened the tin (which seems likely, judging from the number of holly-stenciled fruitcake tins that show up at every bake sale), you may slice the fruitcake thinly, spread it with cream cheese, and chase it with very strong coffee.

WHAT IS HALVAH?

Halvah is a Middle Eastern candy made from tahini (sesame seed paste) mixed with honey and sometimes flour and essences, like lemon or rosewater. Rolled in or studded with pistachios or left plain, halvah is extremely rich, like an oily piece of fudge. If you're having trouble finding halvah, try a Greek or Middle Eastern specialty store, where ounces of the thick confection are trimmed from a large tan block usually sitting in a place of prominence on the counter.

What's hard sauce?

Hard sauce is butter into which sugar, cream, lemon juice, and/or brandy has been beaten. It looks like tawny whipped butter and is served cold alongside hot puddings and cakes, such as gingerbread. Its name seems to imply that it is hard when it goes on, but it actually melts to a tantalizing slip-of-a-sauce once it hits the warm dessert.

What is mincemeat?

Mincemeat is a very old recipe devised to preserve meats. British in origin, mincemeat receipts of yore call for mixing chopped venison, rabbit, game birds, and/or tongues of neats (oxen) with alcohol and, for flavor, various fruits and spices. As refrigeration progressed, so did mincemeat's march into the twentieth century, so that today's mincemeat eschews most meat save for suet (the fatty membrane found on veal kidneys) in favor of dried fruits and nuts. Popular around the holidays, mincemeat can be baked into pies or eaten alongside savory meats.

Is there any mud in Mississippi mud pie?

Mississippi mud pie, a tooth-numbingly sweet chocolate dessert, apparently refers not to a region but to the pie's resemblance to rich Southern soil.

The first time I tasted Mississippi mud pie was outside Hartford, Connecticut, when a college friend's family took us out to dinner at the Chart House restaurant. The slice was about as big as a shoebox, with a crunchy Oreo cookie crust into which about a pint of coffee ice cream had been packed and the mass covered with gooey chocolate sauce. I was literally knocked out by it and slept all the way back to campus. Since then, I've had mud pies (as they are often called) made without ice cream, filled instead with a dense, fudgelike filling and topped with whipped cream. They've all been excessively delicious.

WHAT IS PANETTONE?

Panettone (pan-a-tone-ay), meaning "big bread," is a sweet, egg-rich yeast loaf, traditionally baked in coffee cans or tall panettone tins. Although studded with raisins and candied fruits, and occasionally glazed with powdered sugar icing, it is not a dessert so much as a rich bread. It is served with coffee and sometimes mascarpone cheese alongside, and is especially popular during the holidays.

WHAT IS TAPIOCA MADE OF?

My six-year-old says, "Fish eyeballs," but I say tapioca's a derivative of the cassava root, a starchy tuber grown in the West Indies. Tapioca is prepared by first boiling the cassava down to a paste, then pressing it through perforated plates to form the characteristic balls. It's not tapioca's shape, however, but its gelatinous (cooked) texture that's convinced generations of schoolchildren, both here and in France (where *le tapioca* is sometimes known as *le sagou* and obtained from the Asian sago palm), that the pudding they are eating once spied the mysteries of the deep.

WHAT IS TIRAMISU?

Tiramisu (teer-a-mee-su), which means "pick me up," is a Venetian dessert that gained popularity in American restaurants in the 1980s. Like that other recent dessert darling, créme brûlée (which now comes in such misguided flavors as corn), tiramisu's integrity has often been compromised by the addition of fruits, whipped cream, and what have you.

Traditional tiramisu, the kind enjoyed along the Grand Canal, consists of ladyfingers moistened with marsala and espresso, and layered with sweetened, egg yolk–enriched mascarpone cheese. The dessert is chilled, then given a top dusting of unsweetened cocoa powder. It is deceptively light, not too sweet, and lives up to its name, especially when accompanied by a cup of espresso.

WHAT'S A TRIFLE?

"Trifle: that time-honoured, excellent dish, so dear to the hearts of our elderly cousins and our maiden aunts." Thus did Col. A. Kenney-Herbert describe one of England's signature desserts in 1881, establishing trifle's gentile status even then.

An ornate affair, trifle is made by layering slices of sherry-soaked cake (genoise, pound, ladyfingers) with jam, custard, whipped cream, fresh fruits, and nuts in an elegant, cut-glass trifle bowl, so that each layer may be admired. While a mainstay in Britain, it has never been particularly popular in the States, reflecting, perhaps, a rapscallion attitude toward food as pomp. To wit, *The Joy of Cooking* calls trifle, "a good use for dry cake."

HOW LONG WILL WHIPPED CREAM STAY WHIPPED?

It's an old dilemma: Whip cream too soon, and it separates in the fridge; too late, and your guests are twiddling their thumbs. Then there's the caterer who insisted we whip cream by hand within five minutes of serving. This, while I was eight months pregnant and turning out a meal for thirty in a broom closet. Since that edifying experience, I have learned how to hold whipped cream for three hours, which will allow even the most harried hostess time to enjoy the courses preceding dessert.

When whipping cream, make sure everything is cold: the cream, the beaters, the bowl. Once the cream has formed soft peaks, add the sugar and any flavorings. Continue beating until well-peaked but not stiff; overbeat and you run the risk of turning your cream into butter. Pour the whipped cream into a cheesecloth-lined bowl and refrigerate until ready to use. The cream will lose some of its liquid, resulting in a slightly stiffer cream, but if you haven't overbeaten, the result will be sublime.

If this seems like altogether too much work, you may simply refrigerate the whipped cream in its bowl, making sure to give it a quick whisk by hand before serving.

Do not, repeat, do not resort to whipped cream stabilizers (made from gum arabic and the like), as they give whipped cream a slick, tongue-coating consistency.

Whipped cream in a canister is an acceptable option when making banana splits or going camping.

What is zabaglione?

Zabaglione (zah-bahl-yoh-nee), a foamy, rich, custardlike dessert, is considered by many to be the quintessential Italian *dolce.* Watching zabaglione (or *le sabayon,* as it is called in France) being made is a treat, and many restaurants still prepare it at table.

Making zabaglione involves whisking egg yolks and sugar, preferably in a copper bowl, over a very low flame until the mixture thickens. Sweet marsala wine is then added, and the whisking continues until the mixture becomes immensely frothy. The bowl is removed from the flame and the zabaglione served immediately, either in warmed glasses or as a covering for fresh berries.

IS THERE ANY WAY TO FLAMBÉ DESSERTS WITHOUT SCORCHING YOUR EYEBROWS?

The dramatic payoff of lighting food at table is often offset by the cook's fear of burns. A few cautionary hints: The best way to flambé, which involves briefly lighting a dish splashed with spirits, is to make sure both the food to be flambéed and the spirit itself are warm. Sweet dishes may be sprinkled with a bit of sugar before lighting (which seems to retard the flame), while savory foods should be skimmed of excess fat. When ready to flambé, tilt the pan away from you (and others), and light with a long wooden match near the edge of the pan. The small amount of spirits (usually a few tablespoons) should burn off within seconds.

Coffee and Tea

Coffee should be black as hell, strong as death,
and sweet as love.
—Turkish proverb

It makes some people hyper; others can't lift a lid without it. It keeps us company, and breaks the ice. It's cheap, it's easy, it's coffee, a morning constitutional for millions hoping, perhaps, to parlay on Scottish philosopher Sir James MacKintosh's contention that "the powers of a man's mind are directly proportional to the quantity of coffee he drinks."

When coffee arrived in Europe, in the late 1600s, it was immediately hailed for its positive cogitative effects. Voltaire drank fifty cups a day; Bach wrote the *Coffee Cantata* in reaction to a proclamation banning coffee for commoners, and Jean-Jacques Rousseau called for a cup on his deathbed. By the late 1700s, the London area alone boasted 2,000 boisterous coffeehouses, also called "penny universities," because a man might pick up more knowledge lingering over a one-penny cup of coffee, it was said, than during a month spent at school.

Yet not everyone praised coffee's popularity. In 1674, a Puritan pamphlet called *The Women's Petition Against Coffee* argued that coffeehouses (which excluded women) caused men to, "trifle away their time, scald their chops and spend their money, all for a little base, black, thick, nasty, bitter, stinking, nauseous puddle water."

Until recently, this fairly summed up many people's opinion of British coffee. American, too. "If this is coffee, please bring me some tea. If this is tea, please bring me some coffee," Abraham Lincoln is reported to have spoken over one such feeble cup.

The weary and pre-caffeinated face a similar quandry each morning, when they blearily try to discern the difference between a cappuccino and a latte.

Coffee

WHAT IS ESPRESSO?

Espresso, a strong coffee from Italy, is made from beans that have been long-roasted until they are almost black. These beans are ground very fine and cooked in an espresso pot (or machine), which forces steam at high pressure through the grounds. The resulting espresso, rich and bittersweet, is a deep blackish-brown, with a tiny dot of amber foam floating on top called *crèma*. Espresso is served in tiny cups, with sugar to taste, and sometimes a sliver of lemon peel.

There is debate about that peel. Some purists contend that the embellishment is not Italian, but an American whimsy, while others claim lemon (and orange) peel has long been offered, to counteract espresso's bitterness.

What is the difference between caffe latte and cappuccino?

Caffe latte (KAH-fay LAH-tay) is half espresso, half steamed milk. Cappuccino is one-third espresso, one-third steamed milk, and one-third steamed-milk foam. Named for its resemblance to the hooded, burnished habits of the Capuchin monks, cappuccino is considered a morning coffee in Italy.

Other popular coffeehouse coffees are:

Espresso ristrétto ("restricted"): A short (one-ounce) dose of espresso.

Lungo: Weaker ristrétto (made by forcing more steam through the *gruppo,* the strainer in the espresso maker that holds the grounds). Served in larger cups.

Espresso macchiato ("marked"): Espresso with a dollop of milk foam.

Latte macchiato: Caffe latte marked with a spot of espresso.

Any of the above may be ordered with a *doppio,* a double shot of espresso. You may also indicate how much milk you'd like by asking for *chiaro* ("clear," meaning *light*) or *scuro* ("dark"). Coffee-and-milk drinks are frequently served with a sprinkling of cinnamon, chocolate, or nutmeg on top.

Demitasse ("half-cup"): "Café nature" is France's answer to espresso. Made from darkly roasted beans, it is not quite as syrupy as espresso, yet it is drunk the same way: either black or with sugar and served in small cups.

Café au lait ("coffee with milk"): A French morning drink, half hot milk and half extra-strong coffee, served in wide cups ideal for dunking a piece of brioche.

Many coffeehouses also combine these coffees with chocolate flavorings of different sorts, prefacing the above drinks with *mocha* or *moka*. This should not, however, be confused with mocha Java.

WHAT'S MOCHA JAVA?

Mocha Java is a reference to a famous marriage of coffee beans. Until the eighteenth century, the city of Mukhā (Mocha), in Yemen, was the center of the world's coffee trade. The arid Arabian climate produced a rich, heavy coffee that blended beautifully with the milder coffees under cultivation in Indonesia, then called Java.

While many coffees call themselves mocha Java, few current blends contain beans from either region. Political turmoil in Mukhā (now called Al Mukaliā) has curtailed the exportation of coffee, and Javanese coffees come primarily from Sumatra. Still, when buying mocha Java, you can be certain that you are getting a blend of high-quality arabica beans.

WHAT ARE ARABICA BEANS?

Arabica beans are high-quality coffee beans grown at elevations between three thousand and six thousand feet throughout East Africa, Indonesia, parts of South America, Mexico, and Hawaii. Indigenous to Ethiopia, they are considered to be the finest coffee beans in the world and are broken down into two categories: *Brazils* and *Milds*. Brazils include almost all the coffee beans grown in Brazil, which makes up the bulk of mass-produced coffee. These beans are neither as rich nor as aromatic as Milds, the arabica beans that grown outside of Brazil.

Robusta beans hail from central Africa [the Congo]. Named because they are disease-resistant, they flourish at about two thousand feet and require less cultivation than high-ground arabicas. Robustas tend not to be as rich and complex as arabicas and often blend in some arabicas for flavor.

Liberica beans, another lowland grower native to Liberia and cultivated throughout Indonesia, are tough and not particularly tasty. They are often used in the making of instant coffee.

WHAT DETERMINES A COFFEE'S QUALITY?
Flavor, acidity, and body.

Flavor is of primary importance. Like wine, coffee comes with its own set of self-explanatory buzzwords: bitter, bland, briny, earthy, mellow, mild, soft, sour, sweet, spicy, tangy, wild, winy. Kona coffee, from Hawaii, might be described as having a mellow flavor and a soft aroma, whereas Ethiopian Yergacheffe has an earthy flavor and a wild, complex bouquet. Flavor is also determined by how long the beans are roasted. Lightly roasted coffee makes for subtle flavor without much bite, whereas long-roasting intensifies the flavor yet also makes it more bitter.

Acidity determines how sharp and spirited a coffee will be. Coffee beans with low acidity, like those from Venezuela, are smooth and mellow, whereas high-acid beans, like Ethiopian mocha, are considered winy, and jump in the mouth.

Body is the consistency of brewed coffee: thin and watery, or thick and syrupy. Body is also determined by how finely beans are ground. Coarsely ground coffee only has so much surface area with which to impart flavor, whereas coffee ground to a powder basically becomes one with the brewing water, creating a very rich, syrupy cup of coffee.

HOW FINE SHOULD COFFEE BEANS BE GROUND?

Many of us are familiar with the grinding machine in the supermarket, which asks us to specify how the coffee will be made and grinds the beans accordingly. The coarser the grind, the longer it takes for coffee to give up the essential oils that harbor its flavor. The fragrance of coarsely ground coffee, however, is stronger, as it loses little aroma to the air during the short grinding process.

Coarse-grind works well in percolators, where boiling water is repeatedly run through the grinds. Medium-ground coffee is good for drip, though a fine grind will yield more flavor. Extra-fine grind is used for espresso, and pulverized coffee (almost coffee powder) is used for Turkish coffee.

WHAT'S FRENCH ROAST?

French roast is a deep roast, though not the deepest. If 0 is raw and 100 is burnt, French roast is somewhere around 75.

Roasting and preparation determines the body of coffee. Light roasting (also called cinnamon) preserves the beans' delicacy and results in a mild coffee. Medium roasting yields the type of coffee most popular in America, hence medium roast's other name, American roast. Longer roasting breaks down the beans' acidity and replaces it with a bittersweet, caramel taste characteristic of dark roast, or French roast. Darkest roast (or Italian roast) cooks the beans until they are black, and is used in very strong, full-bodied coffees, like espresso.

WHAT IS CHICORY, AND WHY IS IT SOMETIMES ADDED TO COFFEE?

The chicory added to coffee is the root of the bitter green we use in salad. Dried, roasted, and ground, chicory root makes coffee darker, richer, and more bitter. In Louisiana, Creole chicory-flavored coffee is the rule.

Though it can be hard to find, chicory is worth seeking out, for flavor as well as economy: Two ounces of ground chicory added per pound of coffee acts as a coffee extender.

WHAT IS TURKISH COFFEE?

Turkish coffee is the black, grainy coffee drunk in Turkey, parts of the Middle East, and North Africa. Instead of water passing through ground coffee, pulverized coffee and water are boiled together in an *ibrik*, a small copper or brass pot with a long handle. The liquid is boiled three times, and occasionally flavored with a cardamom seed or cinnamon stick dropped into the boiling brew. After the third boil, the grounds are allowed to settle somewhat, though most usually pass right into the cup. It is taken black, with lots of sugar, and is very delicious.

It is, however, a huge departure from American coffee, and its sludgelike quality was commented upon by Mark Twain's provincials in *Innocents Abroad*: "Of all the unchristian beverages that have ever passed my lips, Turkish coffee is the worst. The cup is small, it is smeared with grounds; the coffee is black, thick, unsavory of smell and execrable taste. The bottom of the cup has a muddy sediment in it half an inch deep."

One's fortune, it is said, can be read in the sediment.

HOW IS COFFEE FLAVORED?

Flavored coffee was invented in the 1970s by American coffee conglomerates, which add artificial essences to instant coffees and sell them at abominably high prices. Flavored beans are usually sprayed with essences, sometimes artificial, sometimes not. If you've developed a taste for Kool-Aid–style coffees (those flavored with raspberry and the like), you can buy the artificial essences yourself and stir in a smidgen, or perhaps a teaspoon of jam.

Flavoring coffee naturally is easy and fast and does not leave a weird aftertaste. Try a drop of real vanilla, a shake of cinnamon, or a thimbleful of liquor to a cup of hot coffee. Or try making your own international coffee.

The Greeks and Swedes sometimes add cardamom seeds to the their coffee, whereas in Madagascar a vanilla pod is used. Mexican coffee often contains spices (cinnamon and nutmeg are popular), and Moroccan is sometimes served with salt and/or pepper. In Russia, coffee is served with a slice of lemon, and Brazil's afternoon drink, *cafezinho,* is basically a cup of brown sugar with coffee poured on top. All regional, all good.

The only provincial coffee I've ever read about that did not sound appealing comes from Greenland. As Harry Rolnick recounts in *The Complete Book of Coffee*, "Eggnog coffee" calls for a pot of coffee to be beaten "with four gulls eggs and some sugar." Then again, this is not unlike the campfire coffee of the American West, which stirs a beaten egg (and sometimes the shell) into the coffee grounds before brewing, on the theory that this takes out some of the bitterness.

HOW LONG DOES COFFEE STAY FRESH?

A food writer once asked a waiter when the coffee had been made. "This morning," he said. She ordered tea.

Long simmering does coffee a disservice. True, coffee grounds need a certain amount of time to steep in order for water to extract coffee's essence, yet continued cooking causes liquid to evaporate and the resulting coffee to turn sludgy and excessively bitter. In many ways, the answer to how long coffee stays fresh depends on how the coffee is prepared.

Most prone to overcooking are drip coffeemakers, their continual warming plate producing a burnt beverage that is the scourge of office workers everywhere. Percolator coffee should be drunk within one hour, as the continual circulation of water through the grounds can result in a very bitter brew. Coffee made in a press or plunger (also called a *cafetière*) is best drunk as soon as possible, as leftover coffee sitting atop cooked grounds can result only in excessive sediment. Espresso, which stays hot in its upper reservoir only ten minutes or so, should be drunk immediately, though the Italians are known to toss leftover sweetened espresso into a freezer pan, thus making a no-fuss granita.

SHOULD COFFEE BE GROUND RIGHT BEFORE BREWING?

The answer depends on how fussy you are. Coffee purists vehemently insist the answer is yes, that coffee loses flavor and aroma the longer it is exposed to air and therefore should be ground, in a coffee or spice grinder, immediately before brewing.

To others, this precaution seems excessive. "I am often asked if I buy coffee already ground and in tins," wrote Craig Claiborne in *The New York Times Food Encyclopedia*, "and the answer is yes." I agree. Good-quality coffee kept airtight yields a very satisfactory cup. Buy the beans whole, grind them at the market, and keep the ground coffee, tightly covered, in the freezer.

WHAT'S THE BEST WAY TO STORE COFFEE?

Ground or whole, coffee should be kept cool, preferably in the freezer, where it stays both fresh and dry. Refrigeration is not recommended, as the environment is too humid and can make the coffee (or beans) moist and soggy, causing them to spoil more quickly. Unopened cans of coffee may be kept in the pantry and used within a year for best taste. However, a friend recently found an unopened can of Chock Full o' Nuts coffee from the 1970s. We opened it and brewed a pot; it was weak, but tasted . . . like coffee.

WHAT IS INSTANT COFFEE?

Instant coffee has many guises. In Israel, they drink a brew called *botz,* basically boiling water poured over coffee grounds. It's instant, it's coffee, but it's certainly not the only option.

Instant started its long trek into our nervous systems at the turn of the century, when a chemist patented Red E coffee, a coffee powder made from the powdered deposits left in the pot after the coffee had been brewed. Today, instant coffee is manufactured from robusta and liberica beans. (High-quality arabicas are considered too refined; why turn gold into straw?) The beans are ground and brewed, and the water evaporated. The result is a soluble powder. Coffee oils are sometimes added, for aroma and color, though they don't add much in terms of flavor. Freeze-dried coffee is similar, except that it cools the brewed coffee and breaks the resulting slush into granules.

While some people don't mind instant coffee ("As long as it's hot and brown," my granddad used to say), others abhor it. *"¡Nescafé es no cafe!"* became a battle cry in Mexico, when that brand of instant coffee began to colonize Central America. And the recent U.S. espousal of coffeehouse coffee seems to indicate a departure of that old American standard, instant-with-creamer in a take-out cup. Perhaps we're learning that, what we gain in convenience, we sacrifice in flavor. Let's face it: Instant coffee tastes wan and thin, unless several extra spoonfuls are added, in which case the brew begins to look and taste like tar. It can also pack a nasty caffeine kick, as instant coffee averages one third as much caffeine per cup as brewed (about 130 milligrams per cup).

IS DECAFFEINATED COFFEE BETTER FOR YOU?

No, it just doesn't contain caffeine, an alkaloid that stimulates the nervous system.

Some people find the buzz they get from coffee pleasant and productive; others experience heart palpitations after two cups of espresso. Overall, however, caffeine is not considered harmful. And, while occasionally unpleasant, caffeine is, in fact, what keeps us drinking coffee. It's doubtful whether we'd bear the same universal allegiance to this brown beverage were it not for caffeine's vivifying effects.

One definitive caffeine story is retold by Claudia Roden, in her book *Coffee, A Connoisseur's Companion*: In eighteenth-century Sweden, "identical twin brothers were condemned to death for murder. King Gustav III commuted their sentences to life imprisonment on condition that one twin be given a large daily dose of tea and the other of coffee. The tea drinker died first at the age of eighty-three."

WHAT'S THE DIFFERENCE BETWEEN REGULAR DECAF AND WATER-PROCESS DECAF?

Caffeine is removed from coffee beans in one of two ways: chemically, or with water. The first method employs a solvent, usually methylene chloride or ethyl acetate. Unroasted coffee beans are steamed, then soaked in the solvent, until they release their caffeine. The beans are steamed again, to remove the solvent, and dried and roasted.

Water-process soaks the beans in very hot water, and the caffeine is removed by passing this water through charcoal filters. The decaffeinated water is used to reconstitute the beans.

Both methods also remove much of the coffee oils. Even though the oils are reprocessed into the decaffeinated beans and caffeine imparts no taste, coffee aficionados complain that removing the caffeine compromises the coffee beyond repair. Others feel a good-quality decaffeinated, especially a rich roast like espresso, is every bit as rich and delicious as the real thing. In matters of taste, let the tongue decide.

WHICH HAS MORE CAFFEINE, COFFEE OR TEA?

A pound of tea contains twice as much caffeine as a pound of coffee. However, a pound of tea makes about 160 cups; a pound of coffee, about forty. Therefore, a cup of brewed tea has about one quarter of the caffeine of a cup of coffee. (If you're doing your math and checking it twice, remember you must factor in the fluid ounces of the liquid.)

Caffeine is also present in minuscule amounts in chocolate, in some over-the-counter medications, and soft drinks. A can of cola has approximately as much caffeine as a cup of tea, and others types considerably more. (The highest caffeinated soft drink on the market is not a cola, however, but Mountain Dew, with fifty-five milograms per twelve-ounce can.)

WHAT'S A COFFEE KLATSCH?

A coffee klatsch is any social gathering where coffee is served. The term is derived from *Kaffeeklatsches* ("coffee and gossip"), the coffeehouses that sprang up in and around Berlin in the late eighteenth century, in flagrant disregard of Frederick the Great's ban on coffee. It seems the king felt coffee a corrupting luxury ("It is disgusting to note the increase in the quantity of coffee used by my subjects and the amount of money that goes out of

the country in consequence. . . . My people must drink beer.")
and sought to limit its consumption to the nobility. The edict
went so far as to appoint *Kaffeeriechers* (coffee smellers), spies
dispatched to the streets to sniff out offenders; this, despite the
fact that Frederick himself was a large imbiber of the brew,
boiling his beans not in water, but champagne. By the end of
the century, however, Frederick's edict was overruled, and Berlin was as awash in *Kaffeeklatsches* as its Viennese neighbor was
in *Konditoreisen* (pastry shops).

Tea

> *Tea is, without doubt, one of the most useful herbs
> ever introduced into this country. . . . It is exceedingly
> useful in many cases of sickness, and particularly after
> having partaken of any liquor to excess, or after
> extraordinary fatigue.*
> —ALEXIS SOYER, *The Modern Housewife, 1849*

> *Tea possesses an acid astringent quality, peculiar to
> most leaves and exterior barks of trees, and corrodes
> and paralyses the nerves.*
> —JESSE TORREY, *The Moral Instructor, 1819*

> *"Thank God for tea! What would the world
> do without tea?"*
> —REVEREND SYDNEY SMITH,
> *Lady Holland's Memoir, 1855.*

"This destruction of tea," wrote John Adams in 1773, following the uprising that was the Boston Tea Party, "is so bold, so daring, so firm, intrepid and inflexible . . . that I can't but consider it an epocha in history!" To be sure, Adams's words were politically motivated—the fledging colonists were straining for independence from the British and their incessant levies—yet there was also an issue of taste, for young America had developed an insatiable thirst for tea. (This, after early attempts to eat it, as described in Waverly Root and Richard de Rochement's *Eating in America*: "The leaves were cooked, salted, buttered and spread on bread, a habit which, understandably, did not last long.")

While we may have grown far more sophisticated in our tastes, enjoying potents made from flowers, herbs, roots, and barks, we are still most familiar (and perhaps most comfortable) with those paper pouches of crumbly brown leaves known generically as tea. While differentiating among teas may not be worth starting a revolution over, it will no doubt increase your enjoyment to find out what's in that little bag you're dunking.

WHERE DOES TEA COME FROM?

All teas come from the same plant, *Camellia sinensis*, and are native to China, though they are also cultivated in India, Indonesia, and the Middle East. The plants are tiny, with two leaves and one bud, and the best teas are harvested by hand. Taking tea from stem to cup involves the steaming, drying, roasting, and rolling of the leaves. The finest teas are made from the buds, or unbroken leaves, though most of the tea enjoyed in America is made from cut or broken leaves.

The major varieties of tea are:

Green: The most popular tea in China, green tea is made from leaves that are steamed, dried, and rolled. Green tea is graded according to the tea leaf's original shape and age, the choicest being the young, tender leaves. An example of young green tea is gunpowder, or pearl tea (*Zucha*), whose leaves are rolled into tiny balls. An older green tea is China's most popular tea, *meecha,* also called "precious eyebrow," because of the tea leaves' resemblance to a slender eyebrow. Hundreds of other varieties of green tea are sold simply under the name of the province in which they are made, such as Hunan.

Black: Black tea, which the Chinese refer to as *hongcha,* or "red tea," is not as prized as green tea. Unlike green tea, black tea is not steamed but dried. The leaves are then rolled and allowed to oxidize in a process called fermentation, during which the leaves turn from green to coppery red. Finally, the leaves are roasted, which turns them dark and imparts a deeper flavor.

Black tea is graded according to size, not quality. Extremely fine black teas from China, such as the delicate *Keemun*, are rare and expensive; pedestrian black teas, like pekoe, are not hard to find, but neither are they very good, often tasting rather ashy and bitter.

Black tea is also known as congou, a corruption of kong-hu, meaning "effort."

Oolong: In his book *The Tea Lover's Companion*, James Norwood Pratt notes that, "The typical Chinese restaurant-grade oolong provides no hint of what [oolong] can be." Top-grade oolong smells sweet and fresh, and tastes full and velvety. Produced primarily in China's Fujian province, oolong is a semifermented green tea. It is sold by quality, the best being made from both the leaves and bud of the tea plant. One fine oolong is *Formosa*, the former name of Taiwan, and the Portuguese word for "beautiful."

There are two less well-known types of Chinese tea:

White and yellow: These are very rare and quite expensive. Only new buds are used; these are gently steamed and then toasted, very lightly, in a large wok. Varieties include China white, *Shou Mei*, and *yinzhen* ("silver needles").

Pu-Er: Pu-Er, also called "Chinese penicillin," is an aged tea used primarily for medicinal purposes.

If you are interested in Chinese teas, a trip to Chinatown is a must. While the sheer number of teas can be intimidating, loose tea can be bought in minuscule amounts, so it won't cost much to experiment.

India produces as much tea per annum as does China. The most popular varieties are:

Assam: A deep, smoky black tea with a robust flavor, Assam is often used as the base for flavored teas.

Darjeeling: Grown in the foothills of the Himalayas, Darjeeling can be subtle and sweet. At its best, it's golden-red and fruity and is dubbed "the champagne of teas." However, with nearly 100 million pounds of faux Darjeeling sold each year, quality is iffy. To assure you are buying the real thing, look for the government-approved "Darjeeling" logo on the package.

Nilgiri: An everyday tea, Nilgiri is what is used to make *chai,* the spice-spiked, milky-sweet tea drunk in India from morning till might. Nilgiri is occasionally what we're buying when we purchase orange pekoe, though it's more likely the tea in our bags is from Sri Lanka (formerly Ceylon, where Sir Thomas Lipton made his tea plantation fortune).

WHAT IS ORANGE PEKOE?

Orange pekoe is neither a flavor nor a blend, but rather a reference to the smaller of the tea plants' leaves, whereas "pekoe" describes the medium-sized, coarser leaves. Orange is a reference to its golden color, and pekoe comes from the Chinese word *pa-ko,* meaning "white down," in reference to the soft filaments that cover the leaves. Most of the tea we drink in America is orange pekoe or an orange pekoe–black tea blend.

WHAT IS TANNIN?

Tannin is actually a misnomer, as it is not related in any way to tannic acid, the compound that gives red wine its astringent bite. The tannins found in tea are polyphenols, chemicals that provide tea its flavor and color. Green tea, which is not fermented, derives its pungent taste, but no color, from tannins. Fermented teas, such as black and oolong, undergo oxidization, during which time the tannins intensify the flavor and impart a deep, burnished color to the tea.

IS GREEN TEA AN EFFECTIVE DIET AID?

There are unconfirmed studies that show green tea helps decrease excess body fat. The theory is that the caffeine in green tea helps secrete adrenaline, which frees fatty acids from the fat cells.

Could be. Just as valid an explanation may be that drinking

hot liquids gives a sense of fullness, so you eat less. Caffeine is also a well-known appetite suppressant, in which case any non-caloric caffeinated beverage will do the trick. Green tea, however, contains less caffeine (about 20 milligrams per cup) than does oolong (40 milligrams) or black (60 milligrams), so you won't be as jittery.

WHAT CONSTITUTES HERBAL TEA?

Herb tea is an infusion made of herbs, greens, flowers, or roots. Herb teas are man's oldest medicines and are still used in abundance, whether casually (a little ginger infusion for a sore throat) or in earnest (the herbal remedies prescribed by Chinese doctors often contain twenty or more herbs). Making an herb tea is as simple as steeping the herb in hot water for five to ten minutes.

Some more popular herbal teas include:

Angelica: Brewed, it reportedly helps coughs and colic.

Chamomile: Made of tiny marigold-color chamomile flowers, this tea soothes the stomach and aids in relaxation.

Ginseng: This knobby Asian root is a reputed panacea for many ills, including fatigue, stress, impotence, and high blood pressure.

Lemon verbena: This sweet, lemony herb induces restful sleep and helps bring down a fever.

Peppermint: There is nothing better for nausea.

Rose hips: The fruit of the rose plant is high in vitamin C and is used to fight colds.

WHAT'S A TISANE?

Tisane, which comes from the Latin *ptisana* ("barley water"), is an herbal drink made by steeping any herb, flower, or spice in boiling water. Tisanes are synonymous with herbal teas and are used in the same way. Tisanes are particularly prized for their relaxation properties and often help people to sleep. A notably soothing tisane is an infusion of chamomile and ladies' slipper root, both of which are easily purchased at health food stores.

WHAT'S THE CORRECT WAY TO MAKE TEA?

Many Brits are repulsed by America's attachment to tea bags. While there is nothing criminal about plunking a tea bag into a cup of boiled water, neither is there anything noble in it.

Should you decide to make real tea, assemble a few things you may or may not have handy: a teapot, loose tea, and time. Measure loose tea either directly into a teapot or into a tea strainer. The rule is "one teaspoon per person and one for the pot," but you may add more or less, to taste. Bring six ounces of cold water (hot water can carry sediments from the pipe) per teaspoon of tea to a rolling boil (212 degrees Fahrenheit). Remove from the heat immediately (water that is allowed to boil too long loses its oxygen, resulting in a flat-tasting tea), and pour into the teapot. Allow to steep for between two and eight minutes, depending on the tea. Remember that the longer tea is steeped, the more intense the flavor, a wonderful boon for a rich oolong but a death knell to a delicate green tea.

If you wish to remove the caffeine from tea, pour off the water after thirty seconds, during which tea gives up 80 percent of its caffeine, pour fresh water over the tea leaves, and continue to steep.

HOW DO YOU MAKE SUN TEA?

It used to be that making iced tea entailed spilling boiling water into a glass jug containing a long metal spoon, which was supposed to conduct some of the heat so the jug wouldn't crack. Sometimes it worked; sometimes it didn't. These days, anyone over the age of four simply makes sun tea: Fill a glass container with cold water, add tea bags (about three to six per quart of water, depending on strength desired), and place in the sun for two to six hours. Add sugar to taste, shake well, and chill.

WHAT IS CAMBRIC?

Cambric is a weak tea drink fed to children and the infirm. Food writer M. F. K. Fisher recalls this nursery cup with fondness: "Cambric tea, as I drank it at lunchtime when I was little, was a privilege, and therefore lapped up like nectar." My own memories of the drink differ: I found the cambric spoon-fed to me by my doting Nana as insipid as pabulum.

In any case, making cambric is child's work. Place a few tablespoons of strong, fresh tea in a mug, fill with warm milk, and add sugar or honey to taste.

WHAT'S THAI TEA?

Thai tea is made from strong black tea, evaporated milk, and sugar. It is usually served chilled over crushed ice and is the best adult milkshake I know of. Beware, however, when ordering a Thai tea (or coffee) before dinner. Because it is incredibly caloric and filling, you may find yourself unable to eat more than a few mouthfuls of your *pad thai*.

NINE

Cocktails and Other Beverages

I think a man ought to get drunk at least twice a
year just on principle, so he won't let himself get
snotty about it.
—RAYMOND CHANDLER, *Selected Letters,*
ed. FRANK MCSHANE, *1981*

There are several ways to appreciate cocktail culture. One is to read authors who, by dint of having spent years investigating the subject, know a thing or two about inebriation. You might also peruse magazines, which have lately been banging the drum about the return of lounges, the kind of places where young and old mix-and-mingle over martinis, while the jukebox plays a selection of Rat Pack standards.

Perhaps the best way, however, is to get out there and do a little research yourself. Just as we judge a good Chinese restaurant by how many Chinese people eat there, a worthy bar will have a fair number of dedicated drinkers bellied up to the bar at all times. (Personal preference dictates whether you'll stop by the joint with the Open at 6 A.M. banner outside.) And there's a reason they choose to drink there: It's convivial, cheap, and probably close to home. Go ahead, look around your neighborhood. The likelihood is there are several bars you've never noticed before, and *someone* is keeping them in business. These same folks are probably ready to stand you a drink and spend a few minutes (or hours) bending your ear.

Now that you've made the pilgrimage, the only obstacle is, What to drink? Depending on the setting, it could be wine, beer, tequila, or an incendiary brew served in a wooden skull. Again, you might take your cue from the locals, or you can take a minute to peruse the following. Salut!

WHAT DOES *PROOF* MEAN?

Proof is a term used to indicate the amount of alcohol in liquor, wine, and other spirits. The amount of alcohol is equal to half the proof, e.g., a 120 proof bottle of bourbon contains 60 percent alcohol.

WHAT'S A JIGGER? WHAT'S A FIFTH?

A jigger is bar measurement equal to one and a half ounces. When a good bartender mixes a drink, he'll measure a jigger of spirit to the rim of a shotglass, rather than pouring it directly into the glass in which the cocktail is served. A *pony* (one ounce) fills a shotglass only two thirds of the way.

A *fifth* of spirits equals 25.6 ounces, four fifths of a quart or, alternately, one fifth of a gallon.

WHAT IS VODKA MADE FROM?

Russian vodka is made from fermented potatoes, which produce a colorless, odorless vodka. Outside of Russia and eastern Europe, vodka is made from corn, rye, or wheat, and is colorless and almost odorless.

Vodka is currently one of America's top-selling spirits, mixed endlessly with juice, soda, and other liquors. We pay top dollar (up to thirty dollars a fifth) for upscale vodkas, and hail flavored vodkas the way kids hoorah a new brand of pop.

This was not always the case. Forty years ago, the Cold War made vodka a marginal spirit, an interloper in a world of scotch, rye, and gin. It wasn't until after World War II that vodka crashed the party. "Smirnoff basically invented the screwdriver, as a way to sell their vodka," says Richard Anthony, a bartender at New York's Blue Mill Tavern in the 1950s. (Smirnoff also pushed the Bloody Mary, a drink created between world wars and originally called a Blood and Guts.) It wasn't vodka's taste so much that lured customers, says Anthony, but its lack thereof. "The main advantage to vodka was, you couldn't smell it on anyone's breath. You could have a three-martini lunch and no one would be the wiser."

WHAT IS THE DIFFERENCE BETWEEN DRY GIN AND SLOE GIN?

Dry gin is made by distilling grain spirits (made from barley, corn, rye) with juniper berries. The berries are suspended over the spirits, and the vapors waft up and absorb juniper's perfume. The resulting gin is colorless, with an aroma that one writer likened to "oriental flowers at dusk."

Sloe gin is made the same way, except that sloes, the tiny purple plums of the blackthorn shrub, are steeped in the gin for several months, coloring it a deep rose and giving it a bittersweet flavor. Sloe gin is most often enjoyed in a sloe gin fizz, which combines one jigger (one and a half ounces) of sloe gin, the juice of half a lemon, and a teaspoon of sugar. Shake well, strain into a highball glass, and fill with club soda.

Dry gin is enjoyed any number of ways, though its leap toward immortality was aided by a cocktail called the martini.

HOW DO YOU MAKE A MARTINI?

With gin. Though vodka martinis have their defenders, they never achieve the velvet iciness of a skillfully made gin martini.

A proper martini requires a deft hand. The gin must be extremely well chilled, which necessitates pouring it over a copious amount of ice (one recipe calls for gin, vermouth, "and five hundred pounds of ice"), taking care not to dilute the gin in any way. Then there's the vermouth question. 6:1 is the standard gin-vermouth ratio for a dry martini, though the Italians mix 4:1, which is called a medium, and Winston Churchill is reported to have measured his vermouth by simply glancing at the bottle. Both gin and vermouth are quickly swirled in an ice-filled bar shaker, then strained into a martini glass. Some add an olive (no pit or pimento, please); others prefer a twist of lemon peel, rubbed on the rim and hung gracefully over the lip. Adding a tiny cocktail onion makes a martini a *Gibson*; a dash of olive juice, and it becomes a *dirty martini*.

WHAT'S THE DIFFERENCE BETWEEN A COCKTAIL AND A COOLER?

There was a time, not so long ago, when grown-ups (read: anyone over age 21) drank cocktails, and acquiring a taste for scotch was considered a rite of passage.

These days, we tend to drink what are loosely called coolers: beer, wine mixed with designer water, maybe a gin and tonic. There's also a big market for premixed coolers in cans and bottles, usually fruit juices mixed with spirits. They're silly-looking and don't taste very good, but they seem to have found a market with people who've forgotten (or never learned) how to mix a drink.

Should you decide to host something as civil as a cocktail

party and need to brush up on bar skills, some fine hot-weather drinks include:

Fizz: A jigger of spirit mixed with a bit of fruit syrup or citrus juice, poured over ice, and topped with soda.

Highball: Spirits served over ice with soda, ginger ale, or cola.

Julep: Kentucky bourbon poured over crushed fresh mint and a bit of sugar, topped with soda.

Sour: Spirits mixed with lemon and sugar, mixed with juice, and garnished with bar fruit (lemon, orange, and/or maraschino cherry).

Collins: Spirits mixed with sugar, lemon or lime juice, and club soda.

In colder weather, offer the following:

On the rocks: Spirits poured over ice.

Cocktail: Spirits, straight or over ice, mixed 5:1 with vermouth and a dash of bitters.

Toddy: Spirits, such as brandy or rum, mixed with hot water, a little sugar, and perhaps some lemon and spices. Using milk instead of water makes this a *nog.*

And don't forget something to eat! A bag of chips and a plastic container of salsa is insufficient for guests whetting their appetite with real liquor. Set out a big wheel of cheese, a wagon of crackers, about thirty bowls of nuts and fruits. Or have it catered.

WHAT ARE BITTERS?

Bitters are a distillation of aromatic herbs, fruits, roots, and plants, and are used in minute amounts to enhance flavor, much as we add salt to food. Originally a medicine thought to counteract fever, one popular brand, Angostura, is made from cinnamon, cloves, mace, citrus peel, and prunes macerated in alcohol. A dash of bitters' bittersweet flavor is crucial in cocktails like an Old-Fashioned and a Manhattan.

Bitters are said to also stimulate the appetite, and to aid in digestion.

WHAT'S THE DIFFERENCE BETWEEN WHISKEY, BOURBON, AND RYE?

In the beginning, the spirits we drank were made from whatever grew locally. In Russia, potatoes begat vodka; in Scotland, barely bore Scotch. In America, our indigenous waves of grain, corn, and rye produced whiskey, bourbon, and rye respectively.

While recipes at different distilleries vary, whiskey is generally a fermented mash of grain, usually wheat. Straight whiskey is heavy and full-bodied, owing to a long aging process (generally two to twelve years). Bourbon is typically made of about 60 percent corn (the remainder is rye and barley malt) and aged in charred oak barrels, giving bourbon its signature burnished hue. Sour mash bourbon is more prized than sweet mash, in that it is aged longer. In order to earn its name, rye must be made from at least 51 percent rye, the rest being corn and barley malt. Straight ryes come from a single distiller, while blended ryes are made up of ryes from different distilleries.

WHAT'S A BLENDED WHISKEY?

A blended whiskey (or scotch) is one that contains at least 20 percent by volume of 100 proof straight whiskey, mixed with neutral spirits (alcohol distilled from any raw material). Because neutral spirits are rough stuff (190 proof), they manage to raise the proof of the whiskey while at the same time "diluting" the flavor. The result: a stronger, less refined drink that costs less but works well for mixed whiskey drinks, like a whiskey sour (one ounce of lemon juice, one teaspoon of sugar, one jigger of whiskey. Shake over ice and strain into a cocktail glass). For sipping, however, go with the costlier straight whiskey.

ARE BRANDY AND ARMAGNAC THE SAME THING?

Brandy, from the Dutch word *brandwijn* ("burned wine"), is a distillate of fruit—grapes, apples, berries, peaches. However, just as there is no one wine, there is no one brandy. Brandy changes its name as it changes regions, fruits, and duration of distillation.

Armagnac is made from grapes produced in the Bordeaux region of France. It is somewhat drier than cognac, made from grapes in and around Cognac, in western France, and considered the finest brandy in the world (see below). Calvados is made from apples; it is strong yet subtle, with a clear finish. *Spanish brandy* is distilled from Spanish sherry and is rather sweet, as is *Greek brandy,* with its resin-rich undertone.

Brandy is usually taken as a *disgestif,* after a meal or as a nightcap. It is also a favorite of skiers and cold-weather nuts, who believe brandy, whether bought at the bar or trekked up-mountain by a Saint Bernard, possesses warming powers. This is not so. Brandy (indeed, all alcohol) causes the blood vessels to dilate, tricking the body into thinking it's warmer, when in fact the body immediately compensates by stimulating perspiration, thus releasing heat from the body.

WHY ARE SOME COGNACS MARKED V.S.O.P.?

True cognac, the finest of all brandies, is made in the Charente region of France, 250 miles southwest of Paris. Charente's most celebrated town is Cognac, where local grapes are pressed to make a precious sour wine, aged long and slow in Limousin oak barrels. As the cognac ripens, it takes on the flavor of the wood, developing a silken sting and inimitable bouquet that has been called "a ministering angel without wings yet visible."

Since vintners are no longer legally allowed to specify whether a cognac is over seven years old (twenty years is considered a very old cognac, though seventy-year-old casks have been reported), they've instituted a system of initials: V = Very, S = Superior, O = Old, P = Pale, F = Fine and E = Extra. A cognac labeled V.S.O.P., for instance, is a Very Superior Old Pale, at least five years old, and made with grapes from the Charente region. If the bottle also says *fine Champagne*, some of the grapes are from the nearby vineyards of Champagne, whereas a bottle that states *grand fine Champagne* is made exclusively from grapes of that region.

The stars on a bottle of cognac used to be purely decorative but now also denote age: one star, aged three years; two stars, aged at least four years; three stars, aged at least five years.

You can trust the system (it's enforced by the French government, sticklers for quality on everything from wine to butter), or test the cognac yourself: Thoroughly wet a snifter with cognac and empty it (preferably by drinking). A good quality cognac will leave its aroma in the glass for up to several days.

ARE SHERRY, PORT, AND MARSALA THE SAME THING?

Sherry (from Spain), Marsala (from Sicily), and port (from Portugal) are all fortified wines, which means brandy or some other spirit has been added to increase the wine's richness and alcohol content. Fortified wines are distilled to different levels of sweetness, known as *dry* and *sweet*. Dry, they are served as aperitifs and used for flavoring savory dishes (especially seafood) and sauces, much as we use white wine. Sweet fortified wines are served as dessert wines, and, in the case of Marsala, in flavoring tiramisu and zabaglione.

WHAT IS ABSINTHE?

After reading about Paris in the twenties, the question many Americans ask is: Where can I get my hands on some absinthe? Unfortunately, you can't, at least not in this country. The very potent (136 proof), anise-flavored liqueur, made of wormwood and aromatic herbs, was, apparently, considered aphrodisiac and habit-forming, and was banned in the early 1900s.

No longer made with wormwood, absinthe is still worth seeking out, if only for its aesthetic dance: When mixed with water, it changes from emerald green to pink to pearly white. Should you obtain a bottle, here or abroad, and fancy a bit of the expatriate experience, you might try Ernest Hemingway's "death in the afternoon," published in *Esquire Drink Book*: "Pour 1 jigger of absinthe into a champagne glass. Add iced champagne until it attains the proper opalescent milkiness. Drink 3 to 5 of these slowly."

WHAT'S A CORDIAL?

Cordial (from the Latin *cordis*, "of the heart") is another name for liqueur. Also called ratafias, cordials are sweet alcoholic beverages made from fruits, herbs, flowers, or spices mixed with a spirit, such as brandy or rum. Fine cordials are sweet and clean; cheap ones are artificially flavored and taste like cough syrup. Some fine cordials include Drambuie (Scotch whisky flavored with honey and herbs), and Grand Marnier, a mixture of curaçao (brandy mixed with oranges from the island of Curaçao) and cognac.

Cordials are very occasionally nonalcoholic, as is the case with *grenadine,* the pomegranate syrup that flavors and colors a Shirley Temple, and *gomme,* a simple syrup used to sweeten drinks.

WHAT IS GRAPPA?

I have a Welsh friend who owns a bar. As expected, he is well inured to the powers of the grape. When the New York Knicks won their division, my brother treated him to a bottle of grappa, which my friend declared the most incendiary liquor on earth. He also claimed it gave him a wallop of a hangover. I disagree. Good grappa *is* fiery, yet it's a bright, lucid fire, a silver arrow with a smooth burn. And it's never given me a big head.

I have heard grappa described at the Italian version of marc, which is true, as they are both distilled from the skins, seeds, and pulp left over from wine making. They are both colorless and potent (120 proof). Whereas marc often goes on to become fruit-infused eau-de-vie ("water of life"), grappa is left alone to age in wood barrels, where it takes on the subtle, earthy flavor of oak, birch, or juniper.

Grappa is drunk straight, at room temperature, in tiny glasses, and the contrast between brands is astounding. (I was once involved in a grappa tasting, and not one of the twelve we sampled tasted alike.) Grappa can also be used in the kitchen, baked into a chocolate grappa torte, and used to spike fruit compotes and puddings.

WHAT IS MEAD?

Mead is a drink that dates back to Biblical times but was most common during the Middle Ages. It is a blend of honey and water and a little yeast, fermented and mixed with various herbs. While Americans have never taken to mead in a big way, it is available here—imported from England and Ireland.

WHAT IS MOONSHINE?

I had real moonshine once, in college. It tasted like sour mash and was eerily potent: After three shots, I could no longer hold up my head and sat slumped against a wall as the revelry went on around me.

Having since read about moonshine, I'm surprised anyone was left standing. Traditionally brewed in backwoods stills from corn, water, sugar, and yeast, hooch or poteen, as moonshine is also called, can also contain a host of other additives, like hog feed (for flavor) and formaldehyde (for kick), and is often heated over a manure-stoked fire. While there's no reason to become alarmist—all liquor is fermented somewhere, the most prized often in small batches at home—it's something to think about the next time some yokel asks, "What's your poison?"

WHAT'S A SHRUB?

A shrub, from the Arab word *sharāb* ("drink"), is a sweet and tart refreshment served to keep cool in hot weather. Most popular in Colonial America, there is no definitive recipe, though a shrub almost always calls for juice, sugar, and white vinegar. These ingredients are mixed with soda water (or not) and served over ice. One very good shrub is made from chopped fresh ginger, lemon juice, and sugar. Mixed with soda water and poured over ice, it goes down easy on a hot day.

There are also alcoholic shrubs. One recipe calls for macerating citrus fruits in rum or brandy for several days. The resulting liquor is poured off and mixed with citrus juice (one cup per quart of liquor), two cups of sugar, and four cups of water. The mixture is simmered, bottled, and kept in a cool, dark place for a month or longer. The resulting shrub syrup is served over ice.

WHAT'S SYLLABUB?

Syllabub is an Old English drink of milk or cream flavored with wine or hard cider, and sweetened with sugar and spices. The mixture is whisked until frothy, whereupon it is drunk like a nog, or until it is custardlike, whereupon it is served as dessert.

A hot syllabub is called a *posset*.

WHAT IS WASSAIL?

Wassail comes from the Norse *ves heill,* "be in good health," as well as the similar *wes hel,* an Old English term meaning "good wishes." Over the centuries, however, it has come to mean any drink with which one make a toast offered on festive occasions. (Toasting, however, predates wassail by at least 1,500 years, the Greeks having started the practice in the sixth century B.C., as a way of assuring guests the wine was not poisoned.)

Loosely, any drink used to make a toast is a wassail, though heated, alcoholic beverages, like eggnog and grog (often hot apple cider or tea mixed with spices and liquor), are most often designated "wassail." One traditional wassail comes from Scandinavia and calls for beer or wine to be sweetened with sugar and flavored with spices. The mixture is simmered several hours with clove-studded apples, poured into a wassail (punch) bowl, and ladled into cups. It is traditional for the host or hostess to offer the first toast; if it is "Wassail!" the appropriate response is "Drink hail!"

WHERE DOES THE TERM "86" COME FROM?

The Dictionary of American Slang states the numerical expression was started by lunch counter cooks, "to inform waiters they were out of a specific dish." Two other explanations, however, offer a better idea of how the code moved into the barroom. The West Coast version calls on Section 86 of the California beverage code, which prohibits serving alcohol to the intoxicated. The New York version stems from the subway, when the old Second Avenue El train made its last stop at 86th Street, and the conductor announced that everyone had to get out. Bartenders apparently appropriated the phrase and used it to throw out drunks.

WHAT IS THE DIFFERENCE BETWEEN BEER, ALE, AND LAGER?

Beer has become a kind of umbrella phrase covering brews such as lager, ale, porter, and stout. The difference has less to do with what beer's made of, than in what proportions.

Beer, which came into being almost 8,000 years ago, was originally brewed from barley and water, with a little piece of bread added to induce fermentation. To the Egyptians and the Greeks, it was a God-given drink, and beer was christened *cerevisia*, after Ceres, the goddess of grains. Malted barley (barley made to sprout by heat) was added in the sixteenth century by the British, which resulted in a pale drink called ale. Hops were added shortly thereafter, and the brew was called beer.

Ale (4 to 5 percent alcohol), rich in hops and slightly bitter, is still the most popular type of beer in England, whereas America prefers the lighter and drier *lager* (3.6 percent alcohol), and, to a lesser extent, *malt liquor*, which is sugar-enriched and quite alcoholic (5 to 9 percent). *India pale ale* (5 percent alcohol) is a somewhat stronger ale, and *porter* a darker, heavier lager. *Stout* (6 percent alcohol) is an extremely dark and rich beer of the British Isles, made with roasted barley malt and a great deal of hops, and aged for a year in oak barrels. There is also *triple stout*, a hair-of-the-dog milkshake for grown-ups, and *bock*, a sweet, dark German beer.

British pubs often combine beers with each other or other beverages. Half-and-half is half stout and half ale; shandygaff, half ale or porter and half ginger ale; and Black Velvet, half stout and half champagne.

WHAT'S THE PROPER TEMPERATURE TO SERVE BEER?

Depends on which side of the Atlantic you're on. More than one Yank has been shocked to tip his first pub beer, only to find it kiddie-pool warm.

The Brits are under the impression that the flavor of ale and stout is squelched by anything under 55 degrees Fahrenheit, and they're probably right. Americans, however, like their lager ice cold. Anyone who's ever accidentally left a beer in the freezer, however, knows you don't want beer *too* cold, as it becomes cloudy and the flavor indistinct, and since beer is 90 percent water, it does freeze. Drinkers who like their beer cold should chill it to about 42 degrees, the temperature inside most American refrigerators.

WHICH STAYS COLDER—BEER IN A BOTTLE OR BEER IN A CAN?

While an aluminum can is a good conductor of cold and therefore chills beer very quickly, it's also very thin, which means the beer loses its chill just as quickly, especially when held in a body-temperature hand. Glass may take a little longer to cool, but its thickness keeps the beer inside cold a lot longer.

IS THERE ANY TRUTH TO THE "BEER AFTER WINE IS FINE, WINE AFTER BEER IS QUEER" RULE?

Mixing liquors isn't the problem; it's the decision to switch to something stronger. Here's a scenario: It's one in the morning, and the party is winding down. On the way to fetch your coat, you spy a bottle of bourbon. You've been sipping wine all evening, but it's been ages since you've had bourbon, so you pour yourself a belt and, since it's the final drink of the evening, a healthy one. And you drink it. At about 3:30 in the morning, you regret it. Whether you're sick during the night or not, you feel lousy in the morning, and tell your spouse or your own sallow mug, "Don't ever let me mix liquors again."

So there is some truth in the "beer after wine" proclamation, in that beer has a lower alcohol content than wine. The rule, then, is to go softer as the evening progresses, not harder.

Is there any way to cure a hangover?

Of course not. If you drink too much, you will suffer as your body struggles to purge itself of the liquor.

However, that doesn't mean there is no relief. First, try not to drink on an empty stomach. Post-revelry, eat something, drink as much water as you can, and toss in a few aspirin while you're at it. In the morning, some people like to eat a big, greasy breakfast, on the supposition that eggs-and-toast-and-butter-with-a-tomato-juice-chaser calms a queasy stomach. Others believe in coffee, though that usually compounds the headache and sour stomach. A cold shower helps (and will probably make you smell better), as do a few more aspirin. Menudo, a spicy Mexican soup made from pork stomach, is supposed to cure hangovers, but if it did, it would be sitting on the druggist's shelf next to the Alka-Seltzer. Having another drink only seems to delay the hangover, which, for the truly suffering, sometimes seems a sensible alternative. Unless you have another day to lose, forgo the temptation.

WHAT IS COLA MADE FROM?

Cola is mostly sugar, water, and caramel color, though it also contains caffeine and theobromine, both derived from the kola nut. Both caffeine and theobromine are also present in the cocoa bean, thus linking two of America's favored foods: cola and chocolate.

WHAT'S AN EGG CREAM?

The source of much confusion, because it contains neither egg nor cream, the egg cream was invented on New York's Lower East Side in the early 1900s. A combination of milk, seltzer, and Fox's U-Bet chocolate syrup (which was, and still is, manufactured in the Bronxville section of New York) it is easy to make and very refreshing. However, you need a seltzer siphon to achieve the correct degree of foaminess.

1/2 cup milk
1/4 cup seltzer
2 tablespoons chocolate syrup, preferably Fox's U-Bet

Place milk in a 12-ounce glass. Shoot in the seltzer until the milky foam reaches the top of the glass. Gently stir in the chocolate syrup with a long spoon, taking care not to disturb the meringuelike top. Makes one drink.

WHAT IS MINERAL WATER?

Mineral water is mineral-rich water tapped from a natural spring (Vittel) or high in some yon alp (Evian). Containing up to dozens of different minerals (such as iron, magnesium, and potassium), some mineral waters are flat or still (Calistoga), while others contain naturally occurring gases (Perrier, San Pelligrino), making them a bubbling mineral water. *Sparkling waters* are mineral waters that have been artificially carbonated.

WHAT IS ORGEAT?

Orgeat is a syrup made from almonds and rosewater (or orange-flower water), used in alcoholic drinks such as mai-tais and scorpions and to flavor coffee drinks. It may also be used in cooking when a sweet almond taste is desired.

WHO INVENTED ROOT BEER?

Root beer was the invention of Philadelphia pharmacist Charles Hires. In the mid-1800s, he mixed up an elixir containing extracts of roots, barks, and herbs (including sarsaparilla, wild cherry, spruce, and ginger), fermented them with a little sugar and yeast, and created a mildly alcoholic drink that was naturally effervescent.

These days, root beer is nonalcoholic, flavored with sugar, water, caramel coloring, and artificial and natural flavorings, including some of what went into Hires's original brew.

Birch beer, which tastes like a lighter, sweeter root beer, is a nonalcoholic soda flavored with an extract of birch bark.

ARE SELTZER, SODA WATER, AND CLUB SODA ALL THE SAME THING?

Seltzer takes its name from a naturally effervescing water found in the town of Nieder Selters, Germany. In the late eighteenth century, they figured out how to inject carbon dioxide into water, by way of a small carbon dioxide cartridge. Today, seltzer is available precarbonated in plastic bottles or, less frequently, in heavy blue or green glass bottles with a metal spigot that shoots out the seltzer at high pressure.

Soda water differs from seltzer in that it contains a minuscule amount of bicarbonate of soda, which helps to neutralize stomach acid but does not affect the taste. It is synonymous with club soda and carbonated water.

Wine

A man will be eloquent if you give him good wine.
—RALPH WALDO EMERSON, *Representative Man*, 1850

One of the disadvantages of wine is that it makes man mistake words for thoughts.
—DR. SAMUEL JOHNSON, q. in *The Life of Samuel Johnson*, by James Boswell, 1791

Way back in the seventies, there was an impostor's code for recognizing fine wine: the five Châteaus. Like employing the acronym HOMES to remember the Great Lakes (Huron, Ontario, Michigan, Erie, Superior), insecure hosts memorized Château Haut Brion, Château Margaux, Château Lafite Rothschild, Château Mouton Rothschild, and Château Latour as if their social standing depended on it. For this, they (and their guests) were rewarded with good, often outstanding wine. Then a cad named California came on the scene and threw a wrench into the whole lovely, ordered scheme of things.

Of course, true oenophiles have been drinking wine from all

over the world forever and ever, not caring if it came from Wee-hawken, if it tasted good. (Which it probably wouldn't, New Jersey not being known for its vineyards. But neither is Massachusetts, which turned out some pretty decent Cabernets last year.) And therein lies the secret of fine wine: Do you like the way it tastes? Don't drive yourself batty worrying about what Hugh Johnson or your father-in-law thinks; what do *you* think? While there are no shortcuts in an area as subjective as taste, there isn't any harm in arming yourself with a few facts before raiding the liquor cabinet.

WHY DO YOU LET WINE BREATHE?

Airing wine lets it absorb oxygen, allowing the flavor to expand and soften. This is especially important in red wines, whose bouquet becomes more redolent and complex after a few hours of aeration. Simply opening the bottle is not enough; very little air, after all, can circulate in through the tiny bottleneck.

All wine should be decanted, preferably several hours before serving, to allow its bouquet to ripen and its flavor to reach its full potential. The exception to this rule are very old or rare wines, whose reaction to hours of breathing is unknown. While these wines, too, should be decanted, they must be monitored more closely, to determine when they cease developing character and begin to dissipate themselves into the air.

Wines that are overexposed to air will taste flat and stale.

WHAT'S THE BEST WAY TO DECANT WINE?

In addition to allowing wine to breathe, decanting gets rid of sediment, which can make wine bitter. If you don't decant, each time you tip the bottle, the sediment gets remixed into the wine. While white wines rarely contain sediment, red wines almost always do.

To decant properly, you need a light source (a candle or a flashlight) set on a tabletop. Place the open wine bottle on one side of the light and the decanter on the other. Begin pouring the wine into the decanter with a slow and steady hand, making sure that the light shines through the wine bottle. When you are about three quarters of the way through, begin to look for the sediment, which will creep up in the shape of an arrow. When the sediment begins to filter into the neck of the bottle, stop pouring. You'll probably be left with an ounce of wine left in the bottle, which should be thrown away.

Not only will your wine be muck-free; it will now be able to get the air it needs to breathe.

WHY DO SOME WINES COME IN LONG, SLENDER BOTTLES AND OTHERS IN SHORT, ROUND ONES? WHY ARE SOME BOTTLES GREEN AND OTHERS CLEAR?

Different regions use different bottles. Bordeaux uses bottles with high shoulders, whereas Burgundy wine comes in bottles with sloped shoulders. Wine from the Rhine comes in long, slender bottles and Chianti in bulbous ones. Indented bottoms are intended to allow sediment to settle, and high shoulders act as a sediment barrier. Both are good ideas that work only with a very steady hand, and even then not so well.

Wine bottles are dark to keep light from filtering through; dark green and brown are best. Wine in clear bottles is meant to be drunk quickly, as light accelerates fermentation, a process that requires ideal conditions and time. A carefully aged Châteu Neuf-de-Pape is one thing; sitting a bottle of this year's white Zinfandel in the sun, in hopes of it aging, will yield nothing but hot, flat wine.

ARE THERE EXCEPTIONS TO THE "RED WINE WITH MEAT, WHITE WINE WITH FISH" RULE?

Yes, and you get to choose them. The red flesh with red/white flesh with white aphorism is there only as a marker, not a hard-and-fast rule. If you like Chenin Blanc with your rib eye, honey, you go ahead and drink it.

Of course, not everybody thinks it's an ideal match, which is understandable. Chenin Blanc is a delicate lass, while a rib eye is something of a bloody brute. This comparison is what is meant by marrying wine with food. You have to think: Do these characters belong together? Will they bring out the best in each other? You wouldn't serve a Chianti with angel food cake (well, maybe you would, but don't serve it to anyone else), as the heavy, tannin-rich flavor of the wine would simply bulldoze the delicacy of the dessert.

There are several schools of thought on the subject. Some prefer to keep tastes of a family, marrying a dry, light wine with delicate food (e.g., Frascati with fish). Others prefer finding a balance, pairing a slightly sweet wine with savory or salty foods (e.g., port with pork roast, sake with sushi). The second school of thought strikes me as a bit more complex, the mingling of tastes an exciting challenge.

Choosing what wine goes with what comes down to common sense, personal taste, and at least a smidgen of sagacity about wine and food. Do not, however, be intimidated to try something radical if you think it might be good. It just might.

WHAT IS THE BEST WAY TO STORE WINE?

Two words will tell you why wine needs to be babied: It's alive. Treat it well, and it will thrive. Mistreat it, and you've shortened its lifespan and your own enjoyment.

These rules for storing full bottles of corked wine are pretty simple.

- KEEP WINE ON ITS SIDE. Wine bottles should be kept horizontal to ensure that the wine stays in contact with the cork and keeps it moist. When a cork dries out, it shrinks and allows oxygen into the bottle. And while several hours of breathing help many wines, days (or months) of oxidation mean death to all.

- KEEP WINE AT A CONSTANT TEMPERATURE OF BETWEEN 42 AND 65 DEGREES FAHRENHEIT. The ideal temperature is 50 degrees, which gives white wine a proper serving chill, while allowing reds to slowly yet steadily mature. Don't allow the temperature to fluctuate quickly. While a slow rise or dip in temperature will not hurt wine, quick changes in temperature will age it prematurely. For this reason, the kitchen is not an ideal place to keep wine.

- KEEP WINE BOTTLES DRY. Excessive humidity will not only rot your cork but will also mold your label, your only indication to what's inside the bottle.

- AVOID KEEPING WINE IN DIRECT SUNLIGHT. Ultraviolet rays can pierce even the darkest of bottles, accelerating the wine's aging process. Tangentially, don't buy wine that's been sitting in a brightly lit store.

- TRY NOT TO LET THE WINE VIBRATE. This may sound like an unnecessary admonishment for anyone living east of the San Andreas fault, but many people, such as apartment dwellers, wind up storing wine above a washing machine or behind an oft-slammed door. Movement disturbs and distributes sediment and loosens corks, both of which affect the integrity of the wine.

Working on the assumption that most people will never invest in something as rigorous as a wine cellar, a cupboard (preferably one insulated against vibration) is a sensible solution. Or you might procure several Styrofoam or cardboard wine boxes with separation inserts. Kept in a cool, dark, still place, they make satisfactory shelving.

SHOULD WINE BE SERVED CHILLED?

To chill or not to chill depends on three factors: the wine, the weather, and personal preference. While chilling inhibits the flavor of most full-bodied wines (which means almost all reds), it makes fruity wines, such as Gamays and Zinfandels, more lively.

In hot weather, wine served at room temperature (60 degrees Fahrenheit) can seem rather flabby. Chilled wines should be served at about 44 degrees or perhaps a few degrees cooler, depending on the weather and personal preference.

The fastest way to chill wine is to plunge it into a bucket of icy water, which will bring a bottle of 65-degree wine down to 55 degrees in eight minutes (as opposed to an hour in the fridge).

WHAT IS THE DIFFERENCE BETWEEN A BORDEAUX AND A BURGUNDY?

There have literally been millions of pages devoted to oenology (the study of wine). Here's 500 words' worth.

Different wines are made from different grapes, different grapes grow in different regions, and variables such as soil and climate account for the final product as much as pressing and fermentation. Some wines are made from one grape, some from a blend. Some have better reputations than others, yet there are always new wines aging in the wings.

Below is a summary of some of the wines we drink most, beginning with the whites:

Chardonnay: The leading white grape, Chardonnay wines are rich, fruity, and dry. Chardonnays come from Burgundy, but they are also grown in California, Italy, Spain, Australia, New Zealand, Bulgaria, and Brazil. Chardonnays are blended into many wines, including champagnes and white Burgundies.

Chenin Blanc: Chenin Blanc grapes are grown in France's Loire Valley and in California. The flavor is intense, slightly sweet, and acidic. It is the basis for Vouvray and for California Chablis and champagnes.

Gewürztraminer: Grown in Alsace, Germany, and California, Gewürztraminer is a heady, floral grape. The wines it produces are crisp, dry, and spicy (*Gewürz* is German for "spice"). Gewürztraminer is a powerful wine and will bulldoze over some food (and some people).

Pinot Grigio: Cultivated in Alsace, Italy, Oregon, and California, Pinot Grigio (and its cousin, Pinot Gris) is crisp and light, with a hint of fruit. A delicate and easy wine.

Riesling: A native of Germany since the Middle Ages (and maybe longer), Riesling is among the world's great whites. It is now cultivated in many regions, including Austria, Yugoslavia, Chile, California, and the Pacific Northwest. Rieslings are delicate, sweet, and complex, with a long finish or what the French call *la caudalie* (from the Latin *cauda,* "a tail").

Sauvignon Blanc, Fumé Blanc: A great white from Bordeaux, Sauvignon Blanc can be very dry or lightly sweet. Now cultivated from Russia to New Zealand to California, the flavors of Sauvignon Blanc differ radically, from grassy and acidic (New Zealand) to light and herby (California). Sauvignon Blanc is often blended with other wines and is the basis for sweet Sauternes.

White Zinfandel: Just when rosé became passé, white Zinfandel came on the scene. It is a blush wine, or a wine from red grapes whose juice runs clear, but it is fermented with the skins for two or three days, until it takes on a slightly pink tinge. White Zinfandel is sweet and smells (and looks) like pale raspberries, with a slightly acidic under-taste. Not a terribly sophisticated wine, it does have its fans, particularly when it is chilled on a hot day.

Red wines:

Barolo: A robust, earthy red from the Piedmont region of Italy.

Cabernet Sauvignon: Red wine's most successful grape, Cabernet Sauvignon is fruity, intense, muscular, and the base for most of the world's great wines, including Château Margaux, Château Lafite Rothschild, Château Mouton Rothschild, and Château Latour. This Bordeaux native, now cultivated wherever wine grapes grow, forms the foundation of California's wine industry.

Chianti: A dry, bold wine from Tuscany, Chianti is easily recognizable as the wine in the straw-covered bottles.

Gamay (Beaujolais): A fruity, woodsy wine tasting of berries and herbs, Gamay grapes are cultivated in Burgundy and the Napa Valley.

Merlot: A softer version of Cabernet Sauvignon, also from Bordeaux (and now California), Merlot tastes of plums and berries, with a very slight woody undertone.

Pinot Noir: A spicy, rich red grape that produces French Burgundies, Pinot Noir is now cultivated in Australia, California, and the Pacific Northwest. Pinot Noir make some of the world's best reds, including those from the area of Burgundy known as Côte d'Or ("slope of gold"), like Chambertin, Romanée-Conti and Corton.

Rioja: A robust, "chewy" table wine from Spain, Riojas prove a little too rustic for some, though others find their big, soft taste the perfect complement to meat and game.

Rosé: White Zinfandel (see above) is America's most popular rosé. Others include Mateus and Lancers, from Portugal, and *rosados* from Spain. These sweet, pink wines taste of raspberry or strawberry, with a slightly astringent undertone.

Syrah/Shiraz: A grape from France's Rhône region, Syrah tastes of pepper and plums, and has gained popularity in recent years as its cultivation has expanded to the States and Australia, where it is known as Shiraz and is that country's most popular wine.

Zinfandel: Once dubbed "California's mystery grape" in an effort to propound the theory that California had an indigenous grape, the spicy, bold Zinfandel has since been traced to Italy. Zinfandel's big, bold taste benefits from long aging; when young, it tends to be a bit blunt.

What does *VARIETAL* mean?

A varietal is an American term meaning a wine, such as a Sauvignon Blanc, that is made from at least 75 percent of the grape named on the label. Before you feel misled, know this is not always a bad thing. Just as a painter will mix colors to achieve a desired hue, some wines benefit from a little blending. Château Neuf-de-Pape, for instance, is a blend of as many as thirteen different varieties.

What does *VINTAGE* mean, and how do you know if it's a good one?

Vintage does not in any way indicate the quality of wine, only the year in which it was harvested. (Legally, in order for a winery to use the term *vintage,* 95 percent of the grapes in that particular wine must have been harvested during that year.) Obviously, this information does not tell you anything about the wine. While one vineyard's vintage 1995 Cabernet Sauvignon may be outstanding, another's may be merely so-so.

What is a split of champagne?

A split of champagne is six ounces, less than one quarter of a standard champagne bottle, 27 ounces. A magnum is equal to two bottles (55 ounces). Larger-sized bottles are named for Biblical kings: Jeroboam, four bottles (108 ounces); Rehoboam, six bottles (162 ounces); Methuselah, eight bottles (216.4 ounces); Salmanazar, twelve bottles (324.5 ounces); Balthazar, sixteen bottles (432.7 ounces); and Nebuchadnezzar, twenty bottles (541 ounces).

Wine bottles are sized differently. A single bottle of wine is usually 25.4 ounces; a magnum, equal to two bottles, 50.7 ounces. A double magnum is 101.4 ounces, a Jeroboam 152 ounces, and an imperial, 203 ounces.

WHAT DO THE TERMS *BRUT* AND *EXTRA SEC* MEAN?

These terms refer to the dryness of champagne. Brut is extremely dry, very good on its own or with just a bit of something savory (like caviar or smoked salmon). It is the champagne for special occasions. Extra sec (extra dry) is just slightly sweeter, good with a meal or when serving brut to a crowd becomes prohibitively expensive. Sec and demi-Sec are sweeter still, some say too sweet. They are, however, easily mixed into the brunch cocktail known as mimosa, half champagne and half fresh orange juice.

Crémant does not indicate a champagne's level of sweetness but rather its carbon dioxide pressure. Crémants' slight sparkle and light sweetness make them an ideal champagne to serve with dessert, when a more insistent fizz would confuse the palate.

WHAT'S THE DIFFERENCE BETWEEN CHAMPAGNE AND SPARKLING WINE?

By international agreement, only sparkling wines from the region of Champagne, in France, may be called *champagne*. Therefore, sparkling wines from France are called crémants or *vins mousseux;* from Italy, *Spumante;* from Germany, *Sekt.* They will usually indicate on their label *"méthode champenoise,"* meaning the wine has been subjected to the same method of production as champagne from Champagne.

IF CHAMPAGNE IS ONLY PRODUCED IN CHAMPAGNE, WHY IS THERE SUCH A THING AS AMERICAN CHAMPAGNE?

Because America refuses to respect the agreement that allows only sparkling wine from the region of Champagne to be called champagne, America produces sparkling wines called champagne. The name, however, doesn't have any effect on the quality. Like any wine from any region, champagne depends on the grape and the integrity with which it is produced. Some American champagnes are wonderful, and some are lousy.

How long can you keep an opened bottle of wine?

Because an open bottle of wine will become dull and flat-tasting within twenty-four hours, the best way to store unconsumed wine is to decant it into a smaller bottle (to reduce the amount of oxygen it comes in contact with) and store it in the refrigerator. This leftover is best drunk within a week (make sure to bring a red back to room temperature), although it may be used for cooking for several weeks or, in the case of white wine, up to a month. Make sure, however, to smell it before using. Wine that has turned will smell distinctly of vinegar or strong sherry.

What's the proper way to open a bottle of wine?

While wine bottles have used corks (made from the outer bark of an oak) for a millennium, corkscrews have been around for only about three hundred years. The first one came on the scene in the late 1600s and was actually a firearm mechanism doing double duty. The story has it that a group of English soldiers couldn't extract a recalcitrant cork from a bottle of cider, so they used the ramrod of a flintlock pistol to dig out the cork.

The correct way to open a bottle of wine is first to take a small knife, cut away the capsule (the sheet lead or foil covering) below the collar (the ridge below the bottle's mouth), and remove it (while it is not necessary to remove the whole capsule, only the part that may come into contact with the wine, it is usually proves easier and more expedient to tear it off in its entirety). If the bottle seems mucky, give it a wipe. Insert the corkscrew into the center of the cork, and gently push and turn. Too much pressure will force the cork down; too little, and you're stripping the cork. Keep turning until you reach the bottom of the cork; then give it a slow, steady pull, taking care not to shake the bottle around, which distributes any sediment that's developed. If you're using a Screwpull or a butterfly lever, a simple push of the "wings" should extract the cork.

WHAT CAN YOU DO WITH A BOTTLE OF WINE THAT WON'T OPEN?

Corks sometimes seem like more trouble than their worth, the most stubborn ones requiring a hundred pounds of pull before coming loose. (The average cork requires about twenty-five pounds.) And some never come out. If you're saddled with such a bottle, wine expert Hugh Johnson suggests the following tactic: "Take the heaviest kitchen knife you can find. Hold the bottle in one hand, with the neck pointing away from you, and the knife in the other, with the blunt edge toward the bottle. Now run the blade up the neck as hard as you can, hitting the 'collar' of the bottle a terrific whack, and the neck should break off cleanly. It's a trick that can look impressive at a dinner party, but you should practice it first."

Yes. Or you could blowtorch the thing open.

But seriously, know you will rarely encounter an indomitable cork with wine that has been properly stored (i.e., on its side). If it hasn't and the cork will not budge, reinsert the corkscrew precisely and try to shimmy it out slowly. If this fails to open the bottle, see above. If the cork becomes gouged beyond extraction or falls into the bottle, see below.

WHAT DO YOU DO IF THE CORK BREAKS?

Moldy or spoiled corks, estimated at about one in thirty, can crumble or split apart, no matter how delicately you apply the corkscrew. One trick to extracting a broken cork is to reinsert the screw at a different angle, hopefully getting a bite that will extract enough cork to make the wine pourable. You might also try a two-pronged cork-pull device called, in America, an Ah-So; in England, it's "the butler's friend." The Ah-So's thin blades surround the cork instead of puncturing it, allowing for what some wine enthusiasts feel is a more assured pull. If all else fails and you succeed in merely pushing a cork in deeper, push it in all the way, but gently, as a sudden push can result in a big splash. If your bottle has a good shoulder, the cork should bob beneath it, making the wine pourable. If not, insert a slender object (like a skewer) into the neck of the bottle, push the cork to one side, creating a vacuum, and pour. Any bits of cork that wind up in your glass can be fished out; they're a nuisance but won't affect the taste.

WHY DO PEOPLE SMELL THE CORK?
Usually to determine if the cork has molded. If it has, this means the wine has probably spoiled.

WHAT'S THE PROPER WAY TO ORDER AND TASTE WINE IN A RESTAURANT?
The protocol depends on the restaurant. If you're going low-budget, simply tip the bottle or carafe and hope for the best. Better restaurants, and especially those that pride themselves on their wine lists, will be enthusiastic about helping you pick the wine. Indicate to the wine steward or sommelier what wines you've enjoyed in the past and the preferences of table. While it is not necessary to "match" the wine to the food (the old "red wine with meat, white wine with fish" saw), you do want the wine to complement what you're dining on.

When the bottle comes to the table, it is not necessary to sniff the cork, as a moldy cork should be detected by the sommelier straightaway. Let him pour an ounce or so of wine into your glass. You may hold it up to the light, to judge the color and clarity. While this may not tell you anything about the way this particular wine tastes, it will familiarize you with this specific wine and help to release the bouquet. Swirl the wine around a bit in the glass, and sniff. Does it smell all right, or is it off? If you're not sure, ask someone else at the table, or the sommelier, to smell it. Then taste, swishing it around your mouth a bit to get the full flavor. Is it pleasing, tannin-rich, acidic? If it's to your liking, tell the sommelier to serve it forth; if not, you are well within your rights to send it back. After all, you're paying for it.

HOW CAN WINE HAVE LEGS?

Place a small amount of wine in a glass and swirl the liquid around. The tendrils of wine that cling to the glass and slowly slide down are called "legs," or "tears." Their significance, however, is all but negligible when it comes to judging wine. In fact, true oenophiles regard with humor the tyro's tendency to consider a wine with good legs a good wine.

Scientifically, legs are caused by the high sugar content and/or natural viscosity of a wine. Wines that are high in sugar (like Chardonnay) or alcohol (like brandy) tend to be more viscous and will give a good leg. But this is simply a function of the differential in surface tension between water and alcohol, not an indication of quality. As viscosity tends to break down with age, there are extremely fine twenty-five-year-old bottles of wine that give no legs at all but taste sublime.

While there is no harm in checking for legs (hey, it's fun), there are only three things that really matter when judging wine: color, nose, and taste.

WHAT ARE SULFITES, AND WHY ARE THEY SOMETIMES ADDED TO WINE?

Sulfites, or the salts of sulfuric acids, are used as a preservative. In 1986, after determining that sulfites can, in rare cases, cause allergic reactions (from hives to anaphylactic shock), the U.S. Food and Drug Administration banned their use on fresh fruits and vegetables, and required other foods containing sulfites to be clearly labeled; hence wineries were now required to include the tiny "Contains sulfites" on their bottles.

It was a lose-lose situation. Consumers were suddenly suspicious of their favorite Chianti, and vintners were put on the defensive over something they'd long employed.

Ten years later, sulfites are still found in almost all commonly available, moderately priced wines. They are said to not affect the taste of wine. If you have a known sulfite allergy, seek out wines without them; otherwise, drink with impunity.

WHAT ARE COOKING WINES? CAN RED AND WHITE WINES BE USED INTERCHANGEABLY IN RECIPES?

A century ago, Americans used something called "cooking wine" in their beef Bourguignonne and coq au vin. It was foul stuff, adulterated with salt, which began to be added in the late 1800s, in hopes of keeping the help from hitting the sauce. Thankfully, the market for cooking wine disappeared when America became savvy about drinking wine.

Logic tells us you shouldn't cook with anything you wouldn't drink. Yet the cook should also beware the ludicrous (and potentially bank-breaking) suggestion to cook with the same wine you're serving with the meal.

When cooking with wine, make sure whatever wine you're using is neither too sweet nor too acidic for whatever dish it's being mixed into. Most recipes will suggest a specific wine. If you don't have it (and don't feel like running to the store for it), substitute wine of similar character: dry reds for a dry red, sweet whites for sweet whites. Sparkling white wines (with the exception of sweet ones) may be substituted for white wines, as heat releases carbonation.

Substituting red wine for white is generally not a good idea. While cooking is all about experimentation and judgment, the flavor of red wine, to say nothing of the color (pink beurre blanc?) may prove heavy and incongruous. White wine can occasionally be substituted for red, though the flavor will be less pronounced.

In recipes that call for small amounts of wine, know that the alcohol evaporates (when heated to 172 degrees Fahrenheit) and is therefore safe to serve to teetotalers and children.

Health Food

> "Part of the secret of success in life is to eat what you
> want, and let the food fight it out inside,"
> MARK TWAIN, circa 1890

A walk down the bread aisle of any major supermarket reveals a dizzying array of back-to-the-land alternatives. "Home-style hearth," "country potato," and "wheatberry" loaves are as popular as bleached-to-the-bone white and pallid whole wheats. After a century of robbing food of its inherent nutrients, producers are finally putting back in a little of the stuff that's good for you, like bran and fiber, and consumers are eating it up.

Sometimes.

After nearly a century of stuffing ourselves with convenience foods (and making up for their nutritional paucity with vitamin tablets), there is understandably some suspicion about health foods, especially when they bear little resemblance to anything we've eaten before. There's a reticence about foods our parents didn't serve us, a feeling that these so called "health foods" are for some other segment of the population. And so we fail to investigate; we categorize health food as a little too crunchyfeelie for our tastes, then storm the supermarket for the latest variety of fat-free cookie.

This distrust of complete foods is rather silly. Choosing to eat yogurt with acidophilus doesn't make you a subversive. It simply means you want food to pack as much of a health punch as it can. Fear of tofu (which, granted, looks like astronaut food and doesn't really taste like anything) can be ameliorated by knowing that it is high in protein, low in fat and calories, and about as versatile as any other food in the world.

WHAT IS TOFU?

Tofu is a curd made from soybean milk. The staple of Chinese cuisine for 2,000 years, it is said to have come about by accident, when some sea salt (which contains the coagulant calcium sulfate) tipped into a vat of heated soy milk, causing it to curdle. The resulting product—smooth, somewhat firm, and high in calcium, iron, and protein—found its way to Japan, where it's been prepared thousands of ways for more than a thousand years.

While Americans have become hyperconscious about their fat and cholesterol intake, they have been slow to recognize the benefits of tofu, which has neither of these properties in abundance: a four-ounce slice of tofu has 120 calories, ten grams of protein, six grams of fat and zero milligrams of cholesterol. It's also inexpensive and easy to prepare. Asian and vegetarian cookbooks, especially, make use of tofu, and many other cuisines are slowly warming to its benefits and flexibility.

Tofu can be purchased silken (a Japanese tofu that is extremely delicate), soft (the most commonly found variety), or firm (which is more resilient and flavorful). Fresh tofu is almost always packed in water, which should be changed daily to prevent spoiling. Tofu is highly perishable and should be eaten within a week of purchase.

WHAT IS TEMPEH?

Tempeh is a fermented soybean product made by combining cooked soybeans with a culture called rhizopus, made from the beans themselves. Fermentation gives tempeh a stronger flavor and heartier texture than tofu. Unlike tofu, which can be eaten raw, tempeh is always cooked before it is eaten. (Try it uncooked, and you'll see why.) A bit unusual looking (bumpy and dry, with black specks of rhizopus spores), it is nevertheless an extremely popular source of protein that takes especially well to frying.

WHAT IS SOY MILK?

Cuisines are, of course, built on indigenous foods. In parts of Asia, the soybean is plentiful and cheap, and has spawned hundreds of products, from tofu and tempeh to oil and flour. Soy milk is a nondairy milk made from pressing ground, cooked soybeans. It is high in iron, low in fat, and cholesterol-free. And, while not a very good source of calcium, soy milks are usually fortified with calcium, making them nutritionally comparable with cow's milk.

Soy milk tastes like thin, sweet milk and makes an excellent substitute for people (including infants) who are milk-allergic. Vacuum-packed, soy milk lasts on the shelf six months; once opened, it will last in the refrigerator up to ten days.

WHAT IS RICE MILK, AND WHY IS IT SWEET?

Rice milk is made from brown rice and water. An enzyme process breaks down the starches to sugars, turning the rice milk sweet. (A few brands add brown rice syrup, making it even sweeter.) Rice milk has the consistency of a thin milkshake and a rich, maple-wheaty taste. While it doesn't have the nutrients of cow's milk, it is usually enriched with calcium and vitamins A and D. Vacuum-packed, it lasts up to one year; opened, it will last in the refrigerator two weeks.

What is acidophilus, and why is it in yogurt and milk?

Acidophilus is the bacterium *Lactobacillus acidophilus,* which grows in milk and which, under certain conditions, alters the microflora of the intestinal tract. While yogurt naturally contains acidophilus, adding acidophilus to yogurt, milk, and soy products increases the "friendly flora" in the intestines. For this reason, doctors often prescribe acidophilus for people taking antibiotics, which tend to destroy beneficial intestinal flora. Regular use of acidophilus is also believed to eliminate bad breath and sour stomach, and help control acne.

Is it safe to eat unpasteurized milk and cheese products?

Pasteurization was named for Louis Pasteur, who discovered the process in the 1860s. It involves heating milk and other liquids to destroy microorganisms (such as tuberculosis bacteria), yeasts, and molds. The result is a more disease-free product and one that stays fresher longer. This does not mean that unpasteurized products are unsafe, simply that producers (and consumers) need to take more care in the making and storing of unpasteurized dairy products.

Advocates of unpasteurized dairy products claim pasteurization kills nutrients and alters flavor. They prefer to buy unpasteurized "raw" milk and cheese. As dairies certified to sell raw milk products must, by law, maintain stringent hygiene standards and have their cattle inspected on a regular basis, the likelihood is that their products are safe.

WHAT IS PROTEIN POWDER MADE OF?

Protein powder is made up of various proteins, usually from soy, calcium, or egg. These proteins are dried, mixed with vitamins, sweeteners, and flavorings, and processed into a powder. This powder is mixed with milk or juice, or added to foods, a serving of which supplies fifteen grams of protein, or about 25 percent of the recommended daily allowance (RDA).

People often use protein powders to supplement their diets, erroneously believing they are not getting enough protein from flesh foods and legumes. In fact, many vegetables and grains we don't think of as high in protein are actually loaded with it, like spinach (49 percent protein), broccoli (45 percent protein), and wheat germ (30 percent protein). Even rice, rumored to be an incomplete protein when not combined with flesh foods or beans, is a rich source of protein in and of itself, containing five grams of protein per one-cup serving.

WHAT IS EGG SUBSTITUTE?

Egg substitute is a yolk-free, liquid product made of egg whites, milk powder, corn oil, and various vegetable gums. It pours and measures like eggs, and tastes similar enough to be acceptable to those concerned about ingesting the cholesterol found in egg yolks. It can also be used in baking, with the understanding that whatever you're making will not have the richness and color of a dish made with real yolks.

There is also something called "egg replacer," made of potato starch, tapioca flour, and a leavening agent. Combined with water, it acquires an eggy consistency and is used in batters as eggs would be by people who want to avoid eggs altogether. It cannot, however, be scrambled or fried.

There is also a product on the market called WonderSlim, made of whipped prunes, that purports to take the place of butter and eggs (and some of the sugar) in baked goods.

WHAT DOES *GRANOLA* MEAN?

While the 1970s brought America a spate of so-called health foods, one of the most popular, granola, is based on a cereal developed in the 1890s. Dr. John Kellogg, who would later create Corn Flakes and a panoply of other breakfast cereals in his Battle Creek, Michigan, laboratory, came up with a crunchy cereal called Granola, based on his morning constitutional of seven graham crackers. In 1907, a rival cereal called Grunola, made of graham crackers and bran, hit the market.

Both of these, however, were preceded by muesli, developed by a Swiss nutritionist named Dr. Bircher-Benner in the late 1800s. His recipe called for soaking oat flakes overnight in water, and in the morning adding sweetened condensed milk, a grated apple, lemon juice, and chopped hazelnuts or walnuts, which seems to be closer to today's versions of granola than a bowlful of crumbled graham crackers.

WHAT IS LECITHIN?

Lecithin is a fatty substance derived from egg yolks and beans that is often used to preserve and emulsify foods. It is also used in pan sprays and cosmetics.

More important, however, is lecithin's nutritive value. As one of the body's most integral components (40 percent of the brain is made of lecithin, as are the cell membranes), adequate supplies of lecithin are essential to good health, indeed to life itself. Largely composed of the B vitamin choline, lecithin also contains linoleic acid and inositol, which keep cholesterol down by helping the liver function properly.

Lecithin is available in capsule or granular form, is virtually without taste, and is easily mixed into hot or cold drinks and other foods.

WHAT'S THE DIFFERENCE BETWEEN FAT-FREE AND LOW-FAT?

About three grams of fat per serving (100 grams). That's the limit for low-fat foods, whereas fat-free foods must have less than a half gram per serving. *Reduced fat* means the fat has been reduced by at least 25 percent of a comparable food, and *light* (*or lite*) means the food has 50 percent less fat than a comparable product. *Low calorie* usually means a food has 40 calories or less per serving.

Cholesterol-free means that a product has less than two milligrams of cholesterol per serving (100 grams), whereas *low cholesterol* means it has 20 milligrams or less of cholesterol, and two grams or less of saturated fat.

Sodium-free means a product has less than five milligrams of salt per serving (100 grams), *very low sodium* indicates less than 35 milligrams, and low sodium means less than 140 milligrams.

Good source (of vitamins, minerals, fiber, and/or protein) means a serving of the product supplies at least 10 percent of the FDA-suggested requirement of the nutrient(s). *High in* (or *excellent source*) indicates the product supplies at least 20 percent of the nutrient(s).

ARE ORGANIC FOODS BETTER?

Though often more expensive, and usually not as comely, organic foods (usually fruits and vegetables) probably are more healthful. At the very least, they are less adulterated by the pesticides and chemicals that the big food producers routinely use to guarantee large crops.

Organic food is cultivated and processed without chemicals of any sort. Because there is nothing to kill the bugs, broccoli may become infested with aphids, and unwaxed apples may have less luster. All this puts off American consumers, who've been spoiled by the pulchritude of fruits and vegetables doused daily in beauty-abetting synthetic fertilizer and insecticide.

In terms of sound land policy, organic is better, as the runoff from fertilized fields feeds into rivers and oceans, potentially polluting the water and posing hazards to life in and around it. Environmentalists believe using chemicals to grow foods is tantamount to loading the gun that will eventually kill us. Marilyn Diamond, author of *The American Vegetarian Cookbook from the Fit for Life Kitchen*, writes, "While the rise of pesticides and synthetic fertilizers has increased *tenfold* in the last forty years, crop losses to insects have *doubled*. Organic methods, on the other hand, build up the soil, creating stronger, more disease-free plants." She also quotes a *Los Angeles Times* story as stating, "An overwhelming majority of Americans say they would buy organically grown food if it cost the same as fruits and vegetables treated with pesticides."

Though more farmers have been taking part in urban "farmer's markets" (selling directly to the consumer, and thereby eliminating the middleman and keeping costs down), the vast majority of Americans still get their perfect produce, for less, in the supermarket and will continue to do so until escalating costs or declining quality motivates them to make sounder nutritional and ecological choices. Of course, depending on marketing strategies, they may just as easily turn to hydroponics or irradiated produce.

What are hydroponics?

Hydroponics are a way to grow plants without soil. The plants are cultivated by placing their roots in liquid nutrient solutions. While American farmers have been flirting with hydroponics, it has yet to yield wholescale crops. Some of the more popular produce grown through hydroponics include herbs and lettuces.

What's irradiated food?

Whereas pasteurization destroys microorganisms through the use of heat, irradiated food is subjected to large doses of gamma rays in order to prolong shelf life. While the intent is to inhibit maturation so food stays fresher longer, one has to wonder: why? Isn't food supposed to go bad after a certain period of time? What benefit am I deriving from a tomato that was picked five weeks ago but still looks perfect?

There are also health risks involved. Eating food that has been exposed to radiation has, understandably, gotten a lot of people rather worried. One study shows food being irradiated in doses up to 100,000 rads, which is about 100,000 times more than what the dentist shoots into you for a X ray.

While fruits, vegetables, herbs, pork, potatoes, and tea have all been approved by the Food and Drug Administration for irradiation, the market has been slow on the uptake. Foods that are irradiated (with the exception of herbs) must, by law, carry an international symbol, a plant within a broken circle.

What is the difference between dextrose, fructose, lactose, maltose, and sucrose?

All are sugars; all have different origins.

Dextrose, made from grapes or corn, is a form of dextroglucose, more commonly called *glucose.* Glucose has about half the sweetening power of sugar and tends not to crystallize. The most popular kinds of dextrose are honey and corn syrup.

Fructose is a natural byproduct of fruit. It is extremely sweet (twice as sweet as white sugar, though it has half the calories) and comes in either liquid or granulated form. *Lactose* is a sugar that occurs naturally in milk. It is the least sweet of all sugars and is used in the production of baby food and some candies. *Maltose* is malt sugar, derived from a grain (usually barley). It is used as a sweetener and nutrient, and is the basis of many malt products.

But by far the big daddy of sweeteners is *sucrose,* derived primarily from sugar cane and sugar beets. Sucrose's many forms include white sugar, brown sugar, molasses, maple syrup, and sorghum.

WHAT'S A WHEATBERRY?

Not a berry at all but a whole, unprocessed kernel of wheat, including the endosperm. The wheatberry is full of protein and is rich in iron and niacin. The tiny brown berries can be sprouted and added to salads and soups. Parboiled, dried, and cracked, wheatberries become bulgur (the Turkish word for "cracked wheat"), the base of *tabbouleh,* and can be cooked and eaten like rice, baked into bread, and often become the base for what are called "garden burgers" or "veggie burgers."

WHAT'S SO POWERFUL ABOUT POWER BARS?

Power Bars and other sports bars are made primarily from fructose and fruit juice concentrates, complex carbohydrates that the body can digest immediately, a boon to the marathon runner or those experiencing a plummet in blood sugar. A piece of fruit will, of course, do the same thing, though it doesn't pack as easily or taste nearly as much like candy.

As far as quick snacks go, sports bars aren't a bad choice. They are fortified with about a day's worth of vitamins, contain ten grams of protein (derived from milk powder), are low in fat (about three grams per bar, depending on flavor), and calorically sensible (around 250 per bar). While they may not make you mightier, they are a reliable convenience food that can survive months in your glove compartment and still taste good.

Is MSG DANGEROUS?

Some people who ingest monosodium glutamate experience a number of distressing health problems—headache, nausea, shortness of breath—and erroneously attribute them to some chemical found in MSG. In fact, MSG is derived from glutamic acid, a naturally occurring amino acid found in the body as well as in seaweed, sugar beets, and other vegetative products, from which MSG is derived. Also masquerading under the name "natural flavoring," MSG is hard to avoid.

MSG's prevalence calls into question the validity of Chinese restaurant syndrome, the debilitating side effects also known as Kwok's disease, named after Dr. Robert Ho Man Kwok, who in the 1960s researched the effects of MSG on the body. Though the findings were inconclusive, it was assumed that an excess of glutamic acid overstimulates the nervous system, causing malaise in some individuals.

There are also those who argue most MSG "allergic reactions" are a result of mild phobia; that the corner coffee shop uses just as much MSG (sold in the United States under the brand name Accent) as the local Chinese takeout.

Sauces and Spices

There is no sauce in the world like hunger.
—MIGUEL DE CERVANTES, Don Quixote, 1615.

Many older cookbooks (and many current European ones) assume the cook has a working knowledge of the basics. A recipe for rabbit stew might, for instance, begin by instructing the chef, "Make a mirepoix," without giving any instruction toward ingredient, amount, or procedure.

The fact is, most Americans don't spend enough time cooking from scratch to be proficient in fundamental sauces and seasonings. Tighter schedules, lighter eating, and prepackaged foods have stalled our ability to master the requisite foundations, feel confident improvising with herbs, or spontaneously whisking together a beurre blanc.

As handy as garlic salt and ketchup ("the American béarnaise," a French waiter recently sniffed when asked to fetch a bottle of Heinz) may be, they are constricting and monochromatic, like wearing the same jacket with every outfit.

Often, taste's not to blame, but naïveté. If you're unaware of aioli, you may forever dip cocktail shrimp in jarred tartar sauce and never experience the pleasure of the luxurious garlicky mayonnaise of Provence.

Becoming versed in sauces and spices is very, very easy. The key is exposure and a curious mind and palate. So the next time a recipe begins, "Make a white sauce," don't turn the page. Give it a go. In doing so, you open a window on an infinite vista of tastes from the world over.

WHAT'S A ROUX?

A roux is a thick paste made of flour cooked in butter (to rid the flour of any chalky taste) or other fat, such as oil, lard, or beef drippings. Roux is used as a base for gravies and sauces, and as a thickening agent in dishes such as étoufée and gumbo.

While Northerners simply stir a little flour into butter to thicken their gravies, roux is taken very seriously down South, particularly in Cajun and Creole cookery, with some lard-based rouxs being cooked for an hour or more, until the mixture turns mahogany and the flavor becomes deeply roasted. This is called *brown roux;* mixed with beef stock, it becomes the base for brown sauce, which occasionally goes under the name *Espagnole*. There is also *white roux,* barely cooked and suitable for light white sauces, and the longer-cooked *blond roux,* pale gold and slightly nutty, the choice for gumbo and other dishes that require a stronger flavor.

HOW DO I MAKE A WHITE SAUCE?

A white sauce is a milk sauce thickened with a roux, a mixture of flour cooked in butter or other fat. White sauce is relatively plain yet rich and velvety, the kind of simple sauce our grandmothers spooned over croquettes. Also called *béchamel* sauce, after its purported inventor, Louis de Béchameil, steward to Louis XIV (some say Béchameil merely took credit for a centuries-old sauce), white sauce is the base for dozens of other sauces. For this reason, is known as one of the three Mother

Sauces, the other two being brown sauce (brown stock thickened with roux) and velouté (light stock thickened with roux). The Mother Sauces and their many offspring were all but excised from the kitchen when calorie- and cholesterol-conscious avengers slashed their way into the fatty heart of our cuisine, which is a shame, as many dishes depend on a good white sauce or one of its many variations: Add stock and cheese to white sauce, and you have Mornay; sautéed onions gives you Soubise; cream and shellfish butter yields Nantua.

Any comprehensive cookbook includes a recipe for white or Béchamel sauce. Here is a simple one:

White Sauce
4 tablespoons butter
4 tablespoons flour
2 cups milk
Salt and pepper, to taste

Melt butter in a heavy saucepan over medium heat. Add flour and stir with a wooden spoon or whisk for three to five minutes. Add hot milk, whisking as you do, and continue cooking for two to three minutes. Add seasoning to taste.

HOW CAN I SAVE A SAUCE THAT'S CURDLED?
Curdling, also called "breaking," most often occurs when liquid is added too quickly to a hot fat mixture. To avoid curdling, always add the liquid slowly, stirring (or whisking) as you do so. Also, try adding any wine *before* the other liquids, as wine tends to thin a sauce quickly.

Another culprit is temperature. Cold water/stock/milk added to a hot roux can cause the roux to break down. Try to have liquid ingredients at room temperature before adding them to hot fat. Cold sour cream added to any hot sauce will also curdle, so add it last, and slowly, after you've taken the sauce off the heat. If you use raw milk, remember to scald it first. (Pasteurized milk need not be scalded, as the enzymes that keep milk from doing its thickening job are killed in the pasteurization process.)

If your sauce is still full of lumps or runny, here are a few remedial hints:

Whisk the sauce very well, which helps the emulsification process. Whisking a bit of cornstarch thinned with cold water into the simmering sauce will help thicken it. Alternately, make a bit of roux and slowly whisk the sauce into it, stirring constantly over low heat. If your sauce is too thick, a little cream, stock, or water (depending on the sauce) added should do the trick.

How do you make gravy without lumps?

Whisking together flour and water, and adding it to hot pan juices tends to produce lumps. Instead, make a roux, and add your hot water (or stock) to this, whisking consistently over a low flame. This should produce a lump-free gravy. If not, you may strain the gravy, and reheat it gently. If all else fails, and your gravy makes up in taste what it lacks in looks, keep the lights dim during dinner.

What is demi-glacé?

Demi-glacé (French for "half-glaze") is a meat stock (usually made from veal or beef bones) or poaching liquid that has been reduced by to a light, syrupy consistency. It is used as a base for sauces (such as Madeira, the piquant sherry-and-butter-enriched sauce served over filet mignon) and to enrich and color sauces and stews.

Glacé ("glaze") is stock or poaching liquid that has been reduced further, until it is extremely thick and syrupy. It is extremely strong and concentrated, and a little goes a long way in terms of flavoring. Chilled, glacé becomes hard and rubbery but is easily remelted.

WHAT'S THE DIFFERENCE BETWEEN HOLLANDAISE AND BÉARNAISE?

Hollandaise (meaning "from the Dutch") is made from egg yolks and clarified butter, and flavored with lemon juice. A thin yet extremely rich sauce, it is always served with eggs Benedict, and often with fish.

Béarnaise is a creamy sauce made from egg yolks, shallots, and reduced vinegar mixed with butter. It is heartier than hollandaise and usually served with meats and vegetables.

WHAT IS AIOLI?

Aioli is a garlic mayonnaise from Provence, usually eaten with cold vegetables, meats, and fish. You can try stirring a few cloves of minced garlic into a cup of prepared mayo, but you're better off making it yourself.

Aioli
6 cloves garlic
2 egg yolks
1 tablespoon lemon juice
1 teaspoon Dijon mustard
Salt and pepper
1 1/2 cups olive oil

Purée garlic in food processor or blender. Mix egg yolks and lemon juice, and allow the mixture to stand for ten minutes. Add yolk mixture, mustard, salt, and pepper to garlic purée, and blend. With the motor running, pour olive oil in a slow, steady stream, blending until the combination is shiny and thick. Transfer the aioli to a bowl and refrigerate, covered, until ready to use.

What's a mirepoix?

Mirepoix is a mixture of diced celery, carrots, and onion, sautéed in butter; if the mixture is minced, it is called a *matignon*. Both occasionally include a bit of chopped ham, salt pork, or bacon and are used in the making of hundreds of soups, stews, and sauces.

What is *battuto*?

Battuto is a sort of Italian mirepoix, made by sautéing chopped onion, minced rosemary, and a little prosciutto (or bacon) in olive oil. It is easily prepared and makes a lovely base in which to sauté winter vegetables, such as potatoes or cabbage.

What is caponata?

Caponata is the Italian version of France's ratatouille, but even more luxurious, as the vegetables—eggplant, onion, tomato, peppers—are cooked separately in hot olive oil, until each ingredient reaches its peak of perfection. Only then are they mixed with olives, capers, and various herbs and served at room temperature as a salad or relish.

What is a *coulis*?

Originally, a coulis was a concentrated stock, made by bathing and rebathing meats in stock until the juices were rich and strong, almost a demi-glacé. Over the years, coulis has come to mean a stock-based sauce that is neither thickened nor enriched. The term also applies to fruit- or tomato-based sauces that have been puréed and strained.

WHAT IS GERMOLATA?

Germolata is a mixed of minced garlic, lemon zest, parsley, and other herbs, such as rosemary or sage. It is patted onto *osso buco* (braised veal shanks) and other meats before cooking and is also sprinkled into soups, stews, and vegetable dishes. Mixed with olive oil, it is used as a dip for bread and *crostini* (bread sticks).

IS KETCHUP AN AMERICAN FOOD?

The tomato-based sauce we know as ketchup is a descendent of a Chinese sauce called *ke-tsiap,* made of pickled fish and spices. Crossing over to Malaysia, this sauce was sweetened up a bit and became *kĕchap* (meaning "taste") and exported by British seaman to England. There, it became quite a sensation, was doctored with English spices instead of Eastern, and renamed *ketchup*. Sometime in the late 1700s, this condiment reached America, the fish were forgotten, and the tomatoes were added.

In 1876, a German-American businessman named Henry Heinz doctored the sauce with sugar and spices, and sold it as Heinz Tomato Catsup, touted as "Blessed Relief for Mother and the other women in the household!" By 1895, Heinz actually offered three types of relief, in the form of three grades of ketchup: Heinz Catsup, Duquesne Catsup, and Heinz Ketchup, the last being the highest quality. When consumers showed a clear preference for ketchup, both catsups were discontinued, leaving consumers with a product virtually identical to the Heinz ketchup we buy today.

IS THERE A SIMPLE RECIPE FOR PESTO?

Pesto is a Genoese invention that America took to heart in the seventies. Translated, the word means "paste," and a true Genoese pesto is a paste of basil, pine nuts, and garlic, crushed together in a mortar and pestle, thinned with olive oil, and spiked with a bit of Parmesan cheese. Tossed over hot pasta, stirred into soup, or spread on bread, it is smooth, verdant, and extremely good.

Over the years, Americans have appropriated this simple sauce, substituting walnuts for pine, broccoli for basil, adding hot peppers and cream and much too much cheese, and creating newfangled pestos that mar the silken simplicity of the original.

This is all you need:
2 cups basil leaves, washed
1–2 cloves garlic, minced
2 tb pine nuts (or walnuts)
2 tb freshly grated Parmesan cheese
⅔ c. olive oil

Blend all the ingredients except the olive oil in a food processor. Add the olive oil and process until smooth. Makes about one cup.

What is *NUOC MAM*?

Nuoc mam, Vietnamese for "fish sauce," is the liquid that results from fermenting anchovies or other tiny fish in salt. (In Thailand, the same product is called *nam pla;* in Japan, *shott-suru.*) Nuoc mam is extremely pungent, with a strong odor that some people compare to dirty socks. However, it is almost as essential an ingredient to Asian food as soy sauce.

Nuoc mam is sold in large glass bottles. After opening, it should be stored in the refrigerator, where it will last up to one year.

WHAT IS OYSTER SAUCE?

Made of oysters, brine, soy sauce, and seasonings simmered until it is thick and concentrated, oyster sauce (which does not in fact taste like oysters—they are strained out) is used in preparing numerous Asian dishes, such as stir-fries. It is also used as a table condiment, second only to soy sauce.

WHAT EXACTLY IS SOY SAUCE?

Soy sauce, the world's most popular condiment, is made of roasted soybeans and barley (or wheat) that have been allowed to ferment.

While Americans generally enjoy one kind of soy sauce, there are actually four. The first is light soy, the kind we buy in a bottle; the second is dark soy, thicker, darker, not as salty, but very strong. The third is Chinese black soy, quite thick and as dark as molasses. The fourth, Japanese *tamari*, is dark, thick, and less salty than Chinese soy sauces.

While we think of soy as that stuff that comes gratis in a tiny plastic packet, soy sauce has an auspicious three-thousand-year-old tradition. It began in China, with a long-fermented porridgelike mixture called *chiang*, made of seafood or meat, brine, and rice wine. Over time, new ingredients were fermented; by A.D. 600, the spread of Buddhism, with its regime of vegetarianism, in China encouraged the use of protein-rich soybeans. A century later, Japan began its own cuisine based on soy, creating *miso* (fermented soybean paste) and tamari. When soy moved into Indonesia, it was sweetened with palm sugar and called *kĕchap*, the origin of America's favorite condiment, ketchup.

WHAT IS TABASCO SAUCE MADE OF?

Tabasco is the world's favorite hot sauce despite only three ingredients: tabasco peppers (tiny, hot, and fiery), vinegar, and salt. Why it remains the world's best-selling hot sauce (75 million bottles annually) may have something to do with continuity. The peppers are grown from the same strain of seeds that were originally planted on Avery Island, Louisiana, just after the Civil War, and the salt comes from the island itself. The peppers and salt are fermented for three years before the vinegar is added, just as it was when Tabasco was first marketed, in 1868.

Other hot sauces may be made in much the same way, but they rarely have the smooth bite of Tabasco. Either they are underfermented and wind up tasting raw, or a lot of other ingredients are added (like sugar, liquid smoke, various vegetable gums), which mars the pure sting people seem to like in a hot sauce.

WHAT IS TAHINI?
Tahini is a paste made of crushed sesame seeds. It is has the consistency of smooth, thin peanut butter and is used widely in Middle Eastern dishes such as baba ganoush (eggplant purée seasoned with tahini, olive oil, lemon juice, and garlic) and hummus (chickpea purée).

Tahini can vary in color, from off-white to brown, depending on how long the sesame seeds have been roasted. The darker the roast, the stronger the flavor. Like other nut-and-seed butters, tahini tends to separate; any top layer of oil should be remixed into the tahini before use.

In a pinch, peanut butter may be substituted for tahini, though the flavor will be sweeter and less subtle.

WHAT IS *TAPENADE*?
Tapenade is a Provençal dip with a base of chopped olives, capers, anchovies, and sometimes a bit of tuna. It is lusty and

vibrant, and is usually served with crudités, stuffed into hard-cooked eggs, or tossed over hot pasta.

WHAT IS WORCESTERSHIRE SAUCE MADE FROM?

Worcestershire sauce, "from the recipe of a nobleman of the country," as the Lea & Perrins bottle tells us, is based on a sauce that Sir Marcus Sandys, governor general of Bengal, brought back to his native England in the early 1800s. Not having the exact proportions, he commissioned two chemists, John Lea and William Perrins, to duplicate it. They did, but the result was deemed unacceptable. After two years in a cellar, however, the aged sauce was proclaimed a success and was soon a worldwide sensation.

The sauce, made of shallots, tamarinds, anchovies, molasses, and soy, among other ingredients, is still based on the same recipe and aged more than two years. It is used the world over, as a piquant addition to sauces, gravies, meats, and seafood.

WHAT'S THE DIFFERENCE BETWEEN AN HERB AND A SPICE? IS ONE PREFERABLE TO THE OTHER?

Herbs are the fragrant leaves of plants that do not have woody stems. Spices are the barks, berries, roots, fruits, and stems of various plants, trees, and vines.

In general, the more vibrant an herb or spice's color, the more of its flavor has been retained. Fresh herbs are usually preferable to dry; freshly grated or ground spices are more potent than preground.

WHAT'S THE BEST WAY TO KEEP HERBS FRESH?

Keep fresh, leafy herbs such as basil and mint with their stems immersed in a small jar of water in the refrigerator. The herbs should stay fresh and green for up to ten days. Alternately, they may be wrapped in a damp paper towel, placed in a sealed plastic bag, and kept in the refrigerator.

Although refrigerating sturdy, smaller-leafed herbs, like rosemary and oregano, will do no harm, they retain their flavor and body without it. Simply tie and hang at room temperature.

Herbs may also be frozen. Take large-leafed herbs off the stem, pack them into plastic bags, seal, and freeze; smaller-leafed herbs may be frozen and sealed in plastic, still on the stem.

Another fine way to freeze herbs, especially basil and parsley, is to purée them with olive oil, pour them into ice cube trays, and freeze. Transfer frozen herb cubes to a plastic bag, and use as needed. (Herbs may also be puréed with butter, rolled into logs, wrapped in plastic, and frozen until ready to use.)

WHAT'S THE BEST WAY TO DRY FRESH HERBS?

While herbs can be dried in a very slow oven (150 degrees Fahrenheit), their aromatic oils are usually far too fragile to withstand heat higher than 86 degrees. Air-drying is a more delicate, if slower, process.

Brush fresh herbs free of dirt; if they are very gritty, rinse and pat them dry. Hang them in a dry, airy room free of drafts for up to one week. Check daily; some leaves, like mint, dry quickly, while basil can take up to a week. Properly dried herbs should have leaves that are crisp but not ashen.

When free of all moisture (any dampness will cause the herbs to mold), strip them from their stems and pack into airtight jars or tins. Jars have the advantage of allowing you to see the herb, but they must be kept in a cool, dark place, as sunlight quickly leeches herbs of their flavor. If you want to display the herbs, you can pack them in colored glass jars, which protect the herbs from light. Whatever you pack the herbs in, all containers should be quickly resealed after use, as air robs herbs of their potency.

CAN YOU SUBSTITUTE DRIED HERBS FOR FRESH?

Sometimes. It all depends on the consistency of the dish and whether the herb is playing the predominate role. You certainly cannot make pesto with dried basil, but you can substitute dried oregano for fresh in a ragù sauce.

The rule of thumb when substituting is 1:3, dried to fresh. This varies widely, however, by herb and taste. Let your taste be the judge, starting out with a smaller amount and adding more as you see fit.

HOW LONG DO DRIED HERBS AND SPICES RETAIN THEIR FLAVOR?

A friend who prepares an Indian brunch every Sunday recently ran out of spices for her homemade curry, and needed to purchase fresh cumin, fenugreek, and mustard seed. Brunch the following week had her guests in tears, the curry was so powerful. The hostess was delighted. "I should have replaced those spices *years* ago," she trilled, fetching more fire-dousing *lassi*.

As a rule, spices and dried herbs lose at least 50 percent of their flavor after one year. Beyond that, they can begin to taste soapy (cardamom), dusty (allspice), or timid (oregano). There are exceptions, notably hot red pepper flakes (a jar of which can pack a punch a decade down the line), as well as those herbs that never really taste very good in dried form (basil). When in doubt, smell and taste any herb or spice before tossing into a recipe.

If dumping and replacing the entire spice cabinet seems an exhausting (and exorbitant) task, buy spices in small quantities, thus assuring they'll run out before spoiling.

WHAT IS BOUQUET GARNI?

Bouquet garni is a bundle of herbs, usually tied in cheesecloth, that is used to flavor stocks, soups, and stews, then fished out and discarded at the end of cooking. The classic bouquet garni consists of thyme sprigs, parsley, and a bay leaf; however, in recent years, cooks have taken liberty with the phrase, expanding their bouquet garnis to include such items such as peppercorns and fennel.

CAN FLAT-LEAFED AND CURLY-LEAF PARSLEY BE USED INTERCHANGEABLY?

Yes, but know that flat-leafed, or Italian, parsley has more flavor and a smoother texture than curly-leafed.

Though we tend to think of parsley as the ubiquitous garnish, parsley is prized as an herb the world over. One very popular parsley-based recipe is the French persillade (the French word for parsley is *persil*), a mixture of parsley, bread crumbs, and chopped shallots and that is sprinkled on meats (especially rack of lamb) before grilling, creating a crunchy topping.

ARE CORIANDER, CILANTRO, AND CHINESE PARSLEY THE SAME THING?

Chinese parsley, better known as the herb coriander, looks a lot like Italian parsley but has a distinct, powerful taste. While slow to gain popularity in Europe and America, coriander is a mainstay in many cuisines, particularly Chinese and Thai, where it is liberally mixed into salads, noodle and meat dishes, and Mexican fare, where it gives a bright, zippy taste to salsas and soups.

Coriander is also a food that inspires fierce division. Some find it minty and fresh; others think it tastes like soap or perfume. Many chomp whole stalks to freshen their breath, while others feel even the tiniest leaf ruinous to a meal. The latter group may look to etymology to support their abhorrence: the word *coriander* comes from the Greek *koriandron,* meaning "bedbug;" the former may rejoice in knowing coriander is the world's most popular herb.

Coriander seeds, while from the same plant, have a faintly anise flavor and cannot be substituted for fresh coriander.

WHAT'S THE DIFFERENCE BETWEEN QUATRE EPICES, FINES HERBES, AND HERBES DE PROVENÇE?

All are classic French herb mixtures, used in flavoring savory dishes.

Quatre epices ("four spices"): Includes cloves, dried ginger, nutmeg, peppercorns, and occasionally cinnamon. It is used to flavor charcuterie (pork specialties such as pâtes and sausage) and dishes that require long, slow cooking, like stews.

Fines herbes: An herb mixture of fresh or dried chervil, chives, parsley, and tarragon, used to enhance the flavor of fish, chicken, and sauces. These herbs are usually added at the last moment, to retain their full flavor.

Herbes de Provençe: An herb mixture of either fresh or dried basil, bay leaf, rosemary, summer savory, thyme, and often lavender. It is used on grilled meats, poultry, and vegetables.

All three herb mixtures are available premixed, usually in small, overpriced earthenware crocks. If you enjoy the taste of any of the above herb mixtures, you can save yourself a pretty penny by mixing them yourself.

WHAT'S ALLSPICE?

Contrary to the notion that allspice is a combination of cinnamon, nutmeg, and cloves, allspice is a single spice that happens to taste like all three.

A berry of the evergreen pimiento tree, allspice is grown primarily in Jamaica (hence its other name, Jamaica pepper), where its peppery-sweet goodness is a staple in jerked foods. Allspice is also used in baking, marinades, and pickling brines.

IF THERE'S NO SUCH THING AS CURRY POWDER, WHAT AM I BUYING WHEN I PURCHASE DRIED CURRY?

Curry powder is not a spice in itself but a mixture of spices, sometimes twenty or more. In India, where curry took its name *(kari* is a southern Indian word, meaning "sauce"), curries are mixed fresh and can include cardamom, cinnamon, cloves, coriander, cumin, fenugreek, mace, nutmeg, red and black pepper, tamarind, and turmeric (which gives curry its characteristic yellow color).

The curry powder we buy in the store is predominately turmeric and cumin, and the taste is rather dusty and blah; curry powders marked "Madras" are slightly hotter. As these spices lose their flavor very rapidly, we are usually purchasing little more than a box of dust that turns food yellow, hence—curry!

This is not what good curry is about. In fact, the use of the term *curry* strikes many as an ignorant misnomer. Madhur Jaffrey, the world's foremost author on Indian food, has a special dislike for the word. In her book *An Invitation to Indian Cooking*, Jaffrey writes: "Curry is just a vague, inaccurate word which the world has picked up from the British, who, in turn, got it mistakenly from us. It seems to mean different things to different people. Sometimes it is used synonymously with all Indian food. In America, it can mean either Indian food or curry powder. . . . Of course, when Indians speak their own languages, they never use the word at all, instead identifying each dish by its own name."

While the word cannot be eradicated from the language, bad

curry can. When making a curry, mix the spices yourself or buy them freshly blended from a spice shop.

Having stated all this, know there is such a thing as curry leaves, which look like and are used like bay leaves.

WHAT IS EPAZOTE?

Also known as *wormseed* and *stinkweed*, epazote is a wild herb used primarily in the cooking of southern Mexico. Though it smells, in its raw form, somewhat like kerosene, the flavor is lively and piquant, not unlike coriander. It is also purported to be carminative, meaning it reduces gaseousness.

WHAT IS FILÉ POWDER?

Filé powder (from the French *filer*, to spin) are the dried, ground leaves of the sassafras tree. The Choctaw Indians of Louisiana are credited with first using filé as a thickener and a spice. It has since been appropriated by Creole cuisine, which uses its woody flavor and thickening power in gumbos and other dishes.

WHAT IS FIVE-SPICE POWDER?

Five-spice powder, used primarily in Chinese meat and poultry dishes, is a pungent combination of cinnamon, cloves, fennel seed, star anise, and Szechwan peppercorns, though may also include powdered ginger and nutmeg. It is available prepackaged and should be purchased in very small quantities, as the flavor tends to dissipate rapidly.

WHAT IS GARAM MASALA?

From an Indian word for "warm" or "hot," garam masala is a blend of spices that can include black pepper, cardamom, chilies, cinnamon, cloves, cumin, fennel, nutmeg, and mace, among others. It is a form of curry powder and is best purchased fresh, so that the spices retain as much "warmth" as possible.

WHAT IS LOVAGE?

Lovage, also called "love parsley" and *céleri bâtard* ("false celery"), is an herb with a bitter-sour celery flavor. Used as a food and a medicinal by the ancient Greeks (who believed it cured everything from indigestion to freckles), its leaves are currently used in salads and soups, and its seeds in baked goods and pickling brines. The stalks (lovage can grow up to six feet high) are steamed and eaten like celery, or candied into the confection *angelica*.

WHAT IS SAFFRON, AND WHY IS IT SO EXPENSIVE?

Saffron are the yellow-orange stigmata (the stamen of the female flower) from the purple *Crocus sativus,* grown primarily in Spain. Harvesting even the tiniest amount of saffron is extremely labor-intensive, as each crocus has only three stigmata. With over 12,000 needed to produce a single ounce, the price of saffron is understandably outrageous, about twenty dollars for a thimble-size packet containing a dozen or so burnt-orange threads. Luckily, it takes only a few threads to perfume and deeply color the broth that flavors paella, risotto, and bouillabaisse.

If you don't see saffron with the other spices at your local market, ask the manager; it's usually kept under lock and key.

And, if you ever run into powdered saffron at a ridiculously low price, it's probably turmeric, which is occasionally marketed as saffron, particularly in the Caribbean. While turmeric will give foods a deep amber glow, it cannot impart saffron's subtle, rich, smoky flavor.

WHAT IS THE DIFFERENCE BETWEEN SALT, KOSHER SALT, AND SEA SALT?

Regular salt and kosher salt are both harvested from salt mines, whereas sea salt comes from the sea.

Regular salt, also called table salt, is fine-grained and may or may not have iodine (sodium iodide) added, for nutritional purposes, as well as free-flowing agents to keep it from clumping.

Kosher salt is manufactured under the supervision of a rabbi, making it suitable for kosher diets. It is coarser and may or may not have had iodine added. Many chefs prefer to use kosher salt when cooking, because it is easier to grab with the fingers. It is used at a 1:1 ratio with table salt.

Sea salt is harvested from seawater, which is allowed to evaporate naturally, leaving semi-opaque, irregularly shaped salt crystals. It can be used in place of kosher salt.

Other types of salts include:

Pickling salt is like table salt, except that it has no additives, which might cloud the resulting pickle.

Rock salt, also harvested from salt mines, is a grayish-white, unrefined salt not approved by the FDA for human consumption. Its large crystals are primarily used in old-fashioned ice-cream cranks, or as a stable bed on which to rest baked oysters, in the shell. It's most popular use, however, is for melting snow.

Epsom salts is made from magnesium sulfate. While it is nontoxic in small amounts (it is occasionally used for laxative purposes), it is never, ever used in cooking.

Sour salt is not a salt at all but rather citric acid extracted from citrus fruits. The very sour white powder is used to add tartness to foods such as borscht.

How can you keep salt from getting clumpy?

Though many salts have anticlumping agents added to them, humid weather can cause salt to absorb moisture. The only real solution is keeping salt very dry, by placing a piece of tape over the pouring spout or keeping the salt in an airtight container. Otherwise, toss a few grains of rice into the shaker; they will absorb excess moisture and keep the salt flowing. Replace the rice when you replenish the salt.

Why add salt at the end of cooking?

Recipes that require long cooking, like soups and stews, are always salted at the end because, as the liquid reduces, the flavor intensifies. If you salt-to-taste two quarts of chicken stock, your eventual one quart of long-simmered stock will be very salty, indeed. Remember: You can always add more salt later, but it is nearly impossible to take salt out.

What is arrowroot, and can it be used interchangeably with cornstarch?

Arrowroot is the dried powder of the tropical tuber of the same name. Like cornstarch (which is derived from the endosperm of the corn kernel), it is used as a thickening agent for puddings and sauces. It is colorless when mixed with water, but, unlike cornstarch, will not impart a chalky taste or texture.

Arrowroot and cornstarch are used slightly differently:

- Arrowroot is dissolved in warm water before being stirred into the liquid it is to thicken, whereas cornstarch is stirred into cold.

- Arrowroot thickens at a much lower temperature than cornstarch (158 degrees Fahrenheit versus 198 degrees).

- Arrowroot does not have the holding power of cornstarch, and any recipe thickened with arrowroot will begin to thin if left longer than fifteen minutes, or if reheated.

Arrowroot's powers, while fragile, are the perfect thickener for delicate sauces (particularly fruit-based sauces) and desserts, whereas cornstarch does a yeoman's duty on heavier gravies, sauces and puddings.

WHAT ARE CAPERS?

A caper is the bud of the caper bush *(Capparis spinosa)*, a small, spiny shrub that grows in the Mediterranean. Picked before they bloom into pink and white flowers, the caper buds are pickled in a vinegar brine or packed in salt (rinse before using.) Their sharp, distinct flavor, like a salty-sour pickle, is used to brighten salads, sauces, and condiments.

WHAT ARE *CORNICHONS*?

The small gherkins called cornichons (derived from word *corne*, meaning the horn of an animal) are made from a special variety of cucumber, picked when very young, and pickled in a vinegar brine. They are ubiquitous in France, where they are quite tiny (between one and two inches long), and are almost always served alongside pâtés and smoked meats.

THIRTEEN

Technique and Terminology

*One cup sugar, two cups salt, lots of chocolate on the side,
three cups potatoes, four cups cinnamon. Get a huge bowl
and put all the stuff in it except for the
chocolate and cook it for 20 hundred minutes at
5 temperature.*

—FOUR-YEAR-OLD'S RECIPE FOR APPLE PIE,
FROM A NURSERY SCHOOL COOKBOOK

I baked my first cake when I was eight. The recipe I used called for "creaming the butter with the sugar." Having no idea what that meant, I added a small dash of heavy cream to the batter. The next quandary was "1 teaspoon soda." We didn't have any soda; I substituted Kool-Aid. I enjoyed "sticking a toothpick in the center," even if I didn't know what "comes out clean" meant or how to "cool the cake on a rack." My mother found the cake an hour later, perched precariously where the bathroom towel usually hung.

Cooking is, or can be, an art. But becoming fluid and confident requires a certain mastery of technique, the fine points of which are often overlooked in cookbooks. While just about every cook knows the difference between a *t.* and a *T.,* how about understanding why certain dishes won't set in wet weather or rise on top of a mountain? Or recognizing a salamander from a China cap from a mandolin? Or how much, exactly, is "butter the size of a walnut"?

WHY DO SO MANY OLD COOKBOOKS USE THE MEASUREMENT "BUTTER THE SIZE OF A WALNUT"?

Though cookbooks have been around for thousands of years (the oldest being that of Archestratus, printed in the fourth century B.C.), they were not popular until the nineteenth century, when literacy boomed. Before then, cooks had their own ways of gauging quantity, based on existing foods. Measurements like "butter the size of a walnut" were easily understood and translated, as almost everyone knew how big a walnut was.

Everyone, that is, but twentieth-century cooks, who rely on weight or measure. For conversion purposes, butter the size of a walnut is about one and a half tablespoons.

WHY DO SO MANY RECIPES SPECIFY UNSALTED BUTTER?

Because it allows the cook to regulate better the amount of salt in a recipe. Salted butter can contain up to 3 percent salt (by weight), or less than one third that amount. To the serious cook, the chance is not worth taking. Unsalted butter also tends to be fresher (salt acts as a preservative).

Eating butter is another story. While purists insist unsalted butter has a more delicate flavor than salted, many people find butter without salt decidedly blah. And then there are those who cut it both ways, like the writer Laurie Colwin, who liked to spread her bread "with sweet butter and sprinkle salt on top. When people asked why I didn't simply buy salted butter, I pointed out that sweet butter—even with a little salt on top—has a totally different flavor."

How do you clarify butter, and why would you want to?

Clarified butter, also called drawn butter, is melted butter with its milky deposits removed. It has a higher smoke point than unclarified butter, meaning it will not burn as quickly, and is clear instead of cloudy. This latter quality is particularly desirable when the melted butter is to be used for dipping.

To clarify butter, melt it slowly over a low flame, skimming off any foam. Remove it from the heat and carefully pour off the clear, golden liquid, tossing the milky sediment at the bottom.

Clarified butter can be kept, refrigerated, for as long as you would keep regular butter. To liquefy, simply reheat.

What is ghee?

Ghee comes from the Hindi word for clarified butter, *ghī*. In India, they use two forms of ghee. The first is usli ghee, or true clarified butter, simmered until some of the water evaporates and the liquid turns a deep gold. The second ghee is not butter at all but rather melted vegetable shortening. In India, where butter is a luxury for most of the inhabitants, ghee is used every day; usli ghee is reserved for special occasions.

Can butter and margarine be used interchangeably?

Yes and no. While they look alike and are often substituted measure for measure, margarine usually makes a poor substitute for butter.

The first and foremost reason is taste. Margarine, a solidified, hydrated oil, has a neutral, greasy taste and a tongue-coating texture. Flavorings and a bit of cream or milk are sometimes added to margarine to make it taste more "buttery," yet no one ever makes butter taste like margarine.

The most common reasons people use margarine instead of butter seem to be economics and health, though the latter is a misconception. Margarine may cost about half as much as butter, but margarine's purported cholesterol-reducing properties have recently been proved erroneous. In his book *Kitchen Science*, Howard Hillman explains that, while most margarine is made with unsaturated fats (which, according to studies, can help lower serum cholesterol), hydrating "adds hydrogen atoms to the molecular chain, which converts the unsaturated oil molecules into saturated ones."

One advantage margarine does have over butter is its ability to be heated to higher temperatures. Butter burns at a 250 degrees Fahrenheit. Clarifying it removes the protein in butter that burns, raising its smoke point to about 350 degrees, less than the smoke point of margarine, whose smoke point depends on the oil it is made from. However, know that low-fat margarines have quite a lot of water and air "whipped" into them, lowering the fat ratio, which results in poor stability, and hence not a lot of frying power.

How can you tell if oil is hot enough to deep-fry in?

Oil must be at least 365 degrees Fahrenheit but not more than 375 degrees to fry food properly. That's a pretty small window, and the old adage "Heat until hot but not smoking" is a little vague for anyone without frying experience. Oil heated to a temperature higher than its smoke point breaks down the oil irreversibly, preventing reuse and posing the possibility of fire. (Smoke points for some popular oils are: olive, 375 degrees, vegetable shortening, 375 degrees, corn, 440 degrees, soybean, 495 degrees, and safflower, 510 degrees.)

The best way to ensure good results is to use a candy or deep-fry thermometer, which can read temperatures up to 400 degrees. Lacking such a thermometer, a bread cube will do: Take a one-inch cube of bread and submerse it in the hot oil; if it browns evenly within one minute, the fat is hot enough to fry.

Try to keep the temperature of hot oil steady; don't be tempted to turn up the heat when submersing cold food, which brings the temperature down slightly, as foods fried at too high a temperature invariably burn on the outside, while leaving the inside raw. Foods fried at temperatures that are too low absorb too much oil, and wind up bloated by the time they are done.

CAN YOU SUBSTITUTE CORN OIL FOR SAFFLOWER OIL? OLIVE OIL FOR WALNUT OIL?

Flavorless oils, such as corn and safflower, may be substituted for one another, taking into consideration that some oils are able to withstand higher temperatures than others. Solid vegetable shortening, however, should not be melted and substituted for flavorless oil, as it will reset when it comes to room temperature, leaving whatever recipe it's been used in flecked with white fat.

Flavored oils, such as olive and sesame, should not be substituted for flavorless oil, as they will impart an uncomplementary flavor. Substituting one flavored oil for another is a matter of taste. Using walnut oil in place of olive in a salad dressing, for instance, will alter the flavor but not ruin it; doing the same in a tomato sauce might bring unappetizing results.

HOW LONG CAN OILS BE KEPT BEFORE THEY BECOME RANCID?

Oil can be kept, in a cool, dark place, for about a year, provided it is relatively fresh when you purchase it. Chilled, it will keep longer, though it will solidify somewhat. To liquefy thickened oil, leave at room temperature for a few minutes or run the container under warm water.

If you're not sure whether oil is good or not, smell it. Oil that's gone rancid gives off an offensive petroleum odor. Throw it away.

WHAT'S THE BEST WAY TO REMOVE FAT FROM THE TOPS OF SOUPS, STOCKS, AND GRAVIES?

You can skim the top of hot soup by hand, but it's not very efficient. The best and easiest way it to chill the soup, allowing a disk of fat to form at the top. Once cold, the disk is simply removed and discarded. Or you can invest in a small, inexpensive kitchen device called a degreasing cup, which looks like a measuring cup with a long spout that begins at the cup's base. The design allows the liquid to be poured out, while the fat stays in the cup.

WHEN COOKING, CAN YOU SUBSTITUTE WHOLE MILK FOR NONFAT, AND VICE VERSA?

Fat adds flavor and richness, so while milks may be substituted, the results are not always satisfying. Think of New England clam chowder made with nonfat milk, and you get the idea. However, nonfat, low-fat, and whole milk all heat and blend the same way and may be used interchangeably.

The exception is buttermilk, which is quite sour, and separates into curds and whey if heated. Buttermilk may, however, often be substituted for yogurt, so long as the consistency of the final product is not reliant on yogurt's thickness or buttermilk's liquidity.

WHAT DOES IT MEAN TO SEASON A CAST-IRON PAN?

Cast-iron pans should be seasoned (or prepared) before use, to smooth out any roughness and prevent foods from sticking. To season a pan, wash it with warm water and soap, and dry it well. Next, rub a thin coat of unflavored oil onto the pan and place it in a 300-degree Fahrenheit oven for one hour. Turn off the oven and leave the pan in overnight. In the morning, rub the pan clean. It should retain a smooth, shiny glaze.

You should not use soap on an already seasoned cast-iron pan. To clean, rinse with hot water, scrubbing, if necessary, with a wire brush. Cast iron should be dried immediately, or it will rust. If this happens, scour the pan with salt, wipe it out, and reseason the pan.

A properly cared-for cast-iron pan should last indefinitely. Not only does it conduct heat beautifully and evenly, but it imparts iron to the foods cooked in it as well.

WHAT IS A REACTIVE PAN?

Reactive pans are made of metals that react with certain acidic foods, like wine and tomatoes, causing both pans and food to discolor and impart an off, metallic flavor. These pans include unlined copper, aluminum, and cast iron, all of which are fabulous heat conductors. Lined with either stainless steel or a porcelain-enamel coating, these pans will not discolor but tend not to brown as well, either.

WHAT DOES DEGLAZING MEAN?

Deglazing is a method for loosening browned bits of food that have stuck to a pan during roasting or sautéing. The food, usually meat, is removed and a small amount of liquid (wine, water, or stock) added to the hot pan. The mixture is then boiled until any caramelized food scrapes up easily.

The resulting sauce is served as is, or used as an addition to whatever sauce is served with the meat. Besides adding a wonderfully rich taste to the sauce, deglazing makes cleaning the pan a snap.

HOW DO YOU CONVERT FAHRENHEIT TO CENTIGRADE?

On the scale of centigrade (also called Celsius, after its devisor, Swedish astronomer Anders Celsius), 0 degrees equals freezing, and 100 degrees boiling. To convert centigrade to Fahrenheit, divide the Celsius figure by 5, multiply by 9, and add 32. To convert Fahrenheit to centigrade, subtract 32, divide by 9, and multiply by 5.

A few standard conversions are: 350°F = 177°C; 400°F = 205°C; 450°F = 232°C.

HOW DOES A CONVECTION OVEN WORK?

Gas or electric convection ovens contain a fan that continually circulates hot air, cooking food faster and more evenly. The oven heats up almost immediately, thereby eliminating the need to preheat, and contains no cold or hot spots. Because these ovens are so efficient, temperatures are usually lowered by 25 degrees. While convection ovens work wonderfully with sturdy foods, like roasts and casseroles, delicate batters have a tendency to become wind-blown and can bake up crooked.

Convection ovens require no special cookware, except if you use a combination convection-microwave oven, in which case the rules of microwave apply, that is, no metal.

How long does it take to preheat an oven?

Most gas and electric ovens preheat in fifteen to twenty minutes, though a little longer never hurts. Not preheating can do damage, especially to baked goods, whose leavening agents often work in conjunction with heat. Double-acting baking powder, for instance, works twice: once, when it comes into contact with a liquid, and again, when it is exposed to oven heat. Inadequate initial heat will inhibit its progress and result in a lopsided product.

How do you use a meat thermometer?

A meat thermometer should be inserted into the meat toward the end of the cooking time. The best meat thermometers have small, round faces atop a slender stem. Insert far enough to read the heat at center of the meat, which cooks last, but not so far that it touches any bone, as this will measure the temperature of the bone, not the meat. Don't overdo it. Each hole inserted into meat is a channel for the juices to run out, and overpoking can result in a juiceless roast.

To test the accuracy of a meat thermometer, submerge the stem in boiling water; it should read 212°F.

How can you tell if a cake is done?

Each baker develops his or her own sense of when a cake is finished, usually using a hybrid of the following three methods:

First: The most popular and most reliable is the toothpick method. Insert a toothpick or metal cake tester into the center of the cake. If it comes out clean (i.e., with no gooeyness), the cake is done. However, the cake also may be overdone, and this method does not work on those that intentionally stay "wet," like mousse cakes.

Second: See if the cake is pulling away from the sides of the pan *slightly*. This indicates that an appropriate amount of moisture has evaporated, and that the cake is sufficiently done. Again, however, it may be overdone.

Third: Touch the top of the cake with your finger. If it leaves an indentation, the cake is done.

Most cakes call for the pans to be rotated midway through the baking process. This is the time to eyeball the cake and see if it looks to be on schedule. Make a mental note of its progress, and check accordingly. And *always* check a cake five to ten minutes before the allotted baking time, as dozens of variations (in flour, oven temperatures, pan sizes, the weather), and not just ingredients and technique, determine the outcome of a cake.

Cakes with a very wet filling, like cheesecake and pumpkin pie, do not follow any of these rules. In such cases, the cake is done when a small crack forms in the center.

WHY DO YOU SIFT FLOUR? DO YOU MEASURE FLOUR BEFORE OR AFTER SIFTING?

Years ago, when flour was less well milled, sifting removed bits of chafe and other impurities. With the exception of whole-grain flours, today's flours are milled to within an inch of their lives and carry no such grainy particles.

The reason we sift flour (and powdered sugar) today is to remove lumps and add air, making it lighter. Sifting flour with leavening agents, such as baking powder, also assures that all ingredients are well distributed.

As sifting changes the volume of flour by about 12 percent,

flour should be sifted before or after measuring, according to the recipe. If a recipe calls for: "1 cup flour, sifted," measure and then sift. If it calls for: "1 cup sifted flour," sift one cup of flour onto a piece of wax paper, measure, and use any remaining flour for another purpose.

How does altitude effect cooking?

Less atmospheric pressure at high altitudes means leavening agents encounter less resistance. Hence, that teaspoon of baking powder that leavens perfectly at sea level may blow up your bread at 7,000 feet. The rule at above 3,000 feet is to decrease double-acting baking powder one quarter to one half a teaspoon for every teaspoon called for. Some bakers also find decreasing the sugar (one tablespoon at 3,000 feet, two tablespoons at 5,000 feet, and three tablespoons at 7,000 feet) and increasing the liquid (one tablespoon at 3,000 feet, two tablespoons at 5,000 feet and three tablespoons at 7,000 feet) gives better results. The only way to tell what really works in your area or during that camping trip is trial and error.

Boiling is also affected. At sea level, water boils at 212 degrees Fahrenheit, whereas at 3,000 feet it boils at 205 degrees; 5,000 feet, at 203 degrees; and 7,500 feet, at 198 degrees. Because foods (like soup, pasta, vegetables) are cooking at a lower temperature, they will take longer to cook.

How does wet weather affect cooking?

Anyone who eats a doughnut or croissant every day will notice fluctuations in texture due to the weather. High pressure and humidity prevent certain foods, notably those with a high air content, from setting and/or rising. Puff pastry, for instance, becomes too soggy to properly "puff," and meringues, which depend on the airiness of beaten egg whites for their shape, become sticky and flat. Yeast, always a temperamental spirit, reacts differently to damp weather than to dry. (Sometimes to good effect: The distinct tanginess of San Francisco sourdough is attributable to the weather conditions in the Bay area.) And many confections, such as divinities and pralines, will not set properly during a rainstorm. Honey also attracts moisture, so avoid any honey-based sweets on a stormy day.

If you do elect to make fudge some rainy day, know that you will need to cook it longer, at a heat at least two degrees higher than normal.

WHICH IS BETTER—KNIVES SHARPENED WITH A WHETSTONE OR A MACHINE?

Cooks are sharply divided over this question. The stone scribes insist a machine is not only unnecessary but is even harmful to the knife, as you have less control over the honing. Machine enthusiasts say phooey; their knives are as sharp, for as long, with less work.

I tend to side with the manual sharpeners, using a little tool called the Sharpery, imported from England. Instead of a blunt, flat stone, the Sharpery has two carbon rods, crossed into the shape of an x. The knife is drawn through the base of the x, causing both sides of the knife to become sharp at once. It's easy and quick, and it doesn't require electricity.

There are two other ways to sharpen knifes. The first is to let your butcher do it; most will sharpen a whole batch for a very low price. The other is to run the knife across the rough bottom rim of a ceramic coffee mug. While this does not give razor-sharp results, it certainly works in a pinch.

WHAT IS THE BEST WAY TO STORE KNIVES?

The two best ways to store knives are in a knife block or on a heavy, magnetized strip. The worst way is to throw them chock-ablock into a kitchen drawer. Not only is this habit dangerous, but the constant opening and closing of the drawer jostles the knife blades together, causing them to lose their edge.

HOW DO YOU KEEP CUTTING BOARDS FROM MOVING AROUND WHEN IN USE?

The easiest way is to place a damp kitchen towel beneath the cutting board. You can also purchase rubberized skid pads, or invest in a chopping board heavy enough to stay in place on its own, such as one made of wood or marble.

To keep a mixing bowl in place, wet a kitchen towel, wring it out, and twist it. Place the mixing bowl on the counter, and wrap the twisted towel around the base. This will keep the bowl from moving around during use.

WHAT IS MEANT BY "THREAD STAGE"?

Thread stage is a term used in determining the temperature of sugar syrup. The hotter the syrup, the harder the thread.

For candy to set, sugar needs to crystallize—by creating a syrup of sugar and sometimes other ingredients. The syrup is cooked in a heavy saucepan over a medium flame until it reaches a specific temperature, most easily and safely read on a candy thermometer.

Should there be no thermometer available, however, you can test the syrup's temperature by dropping a strand of syrup into a glass of ice water and "reading" the reaction:

Thread (230°F to 234°F): Syrup forms a soft thread.

Soft ball (234°F to 240°F): Syrup forms a ball that flattens of its own accord when removed.

Firm ball (244°F to 248°F): Syrup forms a firm ball that flattens when pressed between the fingers.

Hard ball (250°F to 265°F): Syrup forms a hard ball that is hard yet pliant when pressed.

Soft crack (270°F to 290°F): Syrup separates into hard, bendable threads

Hard crack (300°F to 310°F): Syrup separates into hard, brittle threads

Caramelized sugar (310°F to 338°F): Syrup turns golden.

Heated above 350 degrees, sugar syrup burns and turns black.

HOW MUCH IS A DOLLOP?

A dollop is a small glob, or a little plop, equal perhaps to a tablespoon or two. However, the amorphousness of the term indicates that the amount is subjective. My idea of a dollop of sour cream may be twice as big as yours, yet both amounts are valid.

WHAT IS ZEST?

Zest is made from the outer, colored skin of citrus fruits, which are full of flavor and oils and color. It does not mean the pith, or the white, bitter underside of the zest.

Making zest is easiest with a small tool called a zester, which scrapes away and shreds only the very top layer. Using a vegetable peeler is another option, but do so gingerly, removing only the colored portion of the peel.

How do you handle a pastry bag?

It takes a while to get the feel of maneuvering a pastry bag, which is used to pipe frosting (or whipped cream, or mashed potatoes) into decorative designs. The cone-shaped, plastic-lined canvas bags tend to be overlong and unwieldy, resulting not in the professional-looking garland you were hoping for, but an indistinct floral collage.

The easiest way to use a pastry bag is to insert the tip you want to use, stand the bag in a pitcher, and fill the bag two thirds of the way with whatever it is you plan to pipe. Gently gather the empty part and give a gentle twist, so that there's no air pocket left on top of the bag, which can cause big expulsions at the other end. Lift the bag from the pitcher and, holding the base of the bag (near the piping tip) in your dominant hand, start decorating.

If you know you will changing tips often, invest in something called a cup-link, which attaches tips to the pastry bag from the outside.

Is there an easy way to measure honey?

The best way to measure honey, or any sticky liquid, is to lightly oil the inside of the measuring cup before filling. The poured honey will then slip right out, giving you an accurate measurement without waste.

To loosen the dregs from a jar of honey, heat it in the microwave for about fifteen seconds. The result will be loose but quite edible.

Is honey that's become cloudy still edible?

Nectar of the "white man's fly" (or so the Native Americans called the honeybee, which was brought to America by English colonists) turns cloudy, white, or solid when it is exposed to cold. It is fine to eat and simply needs to be reliquified. To do so, set the jar of honey in a pot of warm water, and allow the liquid to return to its original color and consistency. Do not, however, heat honey hotter than 140 degrees, as overheating causes honey to lose flavor and color.

HOW DO YOU KNOW WHEN TO FLIP A PANCAKE?

A little of this depends on what kind of pancake you're flipping. Ultra-thin Swedish pancakes cook almost as soon as they hit the hot pan, while big, fluffy buttermilk pancakes require a few minutes to puff and brown.

First, you need to have the pan or griddle good and hot, at least 325 degrees but not more than 425 degrees. While some old electric griddles allow you to set the temperature, most of us have to rely on the dancing-drop-of-water test: Flick a few drops of water on the hot surface. If they jump up and evaporate, the pan is ready.

Next, pour the batter onto a greased (or Teflon-coated) pan. If the pan is hot enough, the batter will begin to set immediately instead of running all over the pan. Wait for bubbles to appear on the surface of the pancake. When it is fairly bubbling all over, lift one edge. If the underside appears lightly browned, flip with confidence.

WHAT'S THE BEST WAY TO COOK AND PEEL A HARD-BOILED EGG?

There are at least a dozen tricks to hard-boiling eggs. These include poking a hole in the small end of the egg with a straight pin (to encourage an air pocket, which helps the shell slip off more easily), and adding white vinegar to the water, to keep the egg white. Both of these steps are mostly unnecessary. The one thing you need to know about hard-boiling eggs is that you shouldn't really boil them.

For tender hard-boiled eggs, without rubbery whites and green-tinged yolks (both caused by overexposure to heat), cover the eggs with cold water in a saucepan and set on the stove. If you want the yolks centered (as for eggs that will be stuffed), stir gently while the water comes to a simmer. Simmer the eggs for ten minutes, remove the pot from the heat and pour off the hot water, cover the eggs with cold water again, and peel them when they are cool enough to handle.

If the eggs have not been overcooked, the shells should slip off easily. Crack each egg lengthwise with the edge of a knife, and slip off the shell in two (or so) pieces.

Also know that an older egg will give up its shell more easily, owing to a natural air pocket that forms as the egg ages.

How can you tell if eggs are fresh?

Assuming eggs have been bought very fresh, they will last between thirty and forty days, if kept in the refrigerator. If you are uncertain about the freshness of an egg, crack it. Very fresh eggs tend to have a loose, light yolk and a clear white. The thick, whitish strings that attach the yolk to the white, called the chalazae, will be very prominent in a fresh egg. As the egg ages, the chalazae slacken, the yolk gets dark and tougher, and the white becomes dingy. These are still safe to use. A rotten egg is immediately recognizable, as the smell is powerfully offensive. (For this reason, it's a good idea to break eggs into a separate bowl, instead of directly into a recipe.)

To test an egg without cracking it, place it in a glass of water. The natural air pocket at the end of the an expands as the egg ages. Therefore, a fresh egg will sink; an older one will float.

WHAT'S THE BEST WAY TO STORE LEFTOVER EGG WHITES AND EGG YOLKS?

Leftover egg whites and egg yolks will stay fresh in the refrigerator, covered, for about a week, and in the freezer much longer.

Egg whites may be frozen in an airtight container, preferably in small amounts. Single egg whites can be frozen in ice cube trays, then popped into sealed plastic bags or other airtight container.

Single yolks may be frozen in ice cube trays and stored like frozen whites. Yolks in quantity should be frozen, in small amounts, in airtight containers. For added stability, add one teaspoon of salt for every cup of yolks, if they are to be used for savory foods; or one tablespoon of sugar, if they're earmarked for sweet foods. (You will be wise to label which is which.) Stored thus, they will keep for up to six months without becoming gummy and hard to mix.

Both yolks and whites may be thawed in the refrigerator or at room temperature. Do not attempt to refreeze thawed eggs, as they will lose both flavor and texture. Nor should eggs be frozen in the shell, as an egg expands when it is frozen, causing the shell to crack.

WHAT'S THE BEST WAY TO WHIP EGG WHITES?

As egg whites can expand eightfold during the whipping process, the important thing is to give yourself enough room. A large bowl and a big whisk are a must, as are egg whites at room temperature. The bowl and whisk must be completely free of grease, or the whites will not whip. For this reason, eggs should not be separated over the bowl you plan to whip in, as even the tiniest bit of yolk (which is 32 percent fat) will prevent the whites from puffing up.

Place whites in a bowl—copper, if you have it, which seems

to aid in whipping and adds volume. (Do not use an aluminum bowl, which can discolor the eggs). Begin incorporating as much air into the whites as possible, using a brisk, wide stroke. When the whites are frothy, add a pinch of salt, which breaks down the whites and helps them to incorporate air. Continue whipping until soft or stiff peaks form, depending on what's called for in the recipe. Follow the same procedure when whipping in an electric mixer, though be careful not to overwhip, at which point the egg whites will separate into a hard, cottony puffs and a watery liquid.

WHAT'S THE PROPER WAY TO FOLD IN EGG WHITES?

Folding is not as delicate a process as it is made out to be. In recent years, most chefs agree it's advisable to stir one third of the whipped whites into the mixture, thus lightening the mixture before folding in the remaining two thirds. Don't be scared; just remember that the whites are there to lighten the load, and overmixing will deflate them.

Let's say you're making a chocolate cake. Stir one third of your beaten whites into the batter with a sure hand, until they are fairly well incorporated. Pile the remaining two thirds on top of the batter, and with a sweeping motion draw your rubber spatula (or spoon) from beneath the batter up over the whites. Rotate the bowl, continuing to incorporate the whites, until the batter is fairly uniform. While you don't want huge clumps of white, a few streaks and stripes are fine, even preferable. Gently transfer the batter into the prepared baking pan, and try not to jostle it too much on its way to the oven.

HOW DO YOU FISH OUT A SPECK OF YOLK?

Two ways. First, take a piece of the broken shell and retrieve the bit of yolk from underneath. If you think you've caught it all, the whites should whip properly. If this fails, or for some reason you no longer have the shell, take a small piece of soft bread and try to trap the yolk against the side of the bowl. Holding it firmly, transfer the whites to another bowl.

You can also use this technique when fishing out eggshells, in which case it is not necessary to transfer the eggs to a clean, grease-free bowl.

WHAT IS A *BAIN-MARIE*?

Bain-marie is the French term for a water bath. Originally a term used in alchemy, *bain de Marie* (Mary's bath) was named after Moses' sister, a known alchemist. And *Larousse Gastronomique* recounts, "It was also considered to refer to the Virgin Mary, the symbol of gentleness, since the term implies the gentleness of this method of cooking."

Bain-marie involves placing a container of food in a shallow pan of warm water and cooking it in the oven, where the food is continually "bathed" by moist heat, allowing delicate dishes like mousses and custards to set without breaking or curdling.

Bain-maries can also be used on top of the stove, a double-boiler being a form of a bain-marie.

WHAT IS A SALAMANDER?

A salamander is essentially a tiny, hand-held broiler. A long-handled instrument with a small metal disk at one end, it is heated on top of the stove until red hot and is used to brown the tops of foods, primarily custards with a layer of sugar on the top, like crème brûlée. In this way, the sugar is quickly caramelized, while the custard stays at room temperature.

WHAT'S A CHINA CAP?

Also called a *chinois,* a China cap is a large, conical sieve with a very fine mesh. It is used for straining foods that need to be extremely smooth; the mesh is so fine, in fact, that foods must often be pressed through. It is used primarily for sauces, soups, and purées.

WHAT'S A MANDOLIN?

A mandolin is a very sharp slicing tool that looks like an isosceles triangle standing on its short end. On one side, it has a sharp guillotinelike blade that is used for cutting hard vegetables and fruits. The food is slid down over the blade, and falls underneath.

Good mandolins are made of steel and fold flat when not in use.

WHAT DOES *MIS EN PLACE* MEAN?

Mis en place is French for "put in place," meaning ingredients and tools are at the ready when making a dish. There's nothing more distracting (or messier) than having to fish around in the back of the utensil drawer for the potato masher with your hands covered in potato gook, and in your haste manage to knock the butter to the floor.

While the term is especially relevent in professional kitchens, the home cook will find making a practice of putting things in place makes for an easier and more satisfying sojourn in the kitchen.

Dining Out

*A true gastronome should always be ready to eat, just as a
soldier should always be ready to fight.*
—CHARLES MONSELET,
Gastronomie: recits de table, 1874

So you're walking through Chinatown, intrigued by all manner
of Asian exotica: crisp-skinned ducks with the heads attached,
skinny green beans as long as batons, bins of ginger and ginseng
and a thousand fragrant teas. Your interest is piqued, your appetite jumps—quick, what do you do?

If you're like most people, you keep walking until you come
to the restaurant you've been patronizing for a decade, and order the same thing you always order.

While it would be useful to have a worldly chum to hand-
lead us through the maze of the earth's cuisines, the likelihood
is we muddle through on our own, stumbling blind until we run
into something we like. And clinging to it, rather than confront-
ing an intimidating, indecipherable menu yet again.

But let's talk turkey. Limiting one's experience of Chinese
food to *moo goo gai pan* is like someone from Beijing deciding
American food means breakfast cereal. Though we needn't

abandon our ethnic comfort foods, we should court the panoptic view, by asking questions, keeping an eye on what the locals are eating, and being brave enough to try something new.

How much is considered a proper tip? Why is it called a tip?

In the United States, a proper tip is generally considered 15 percent of the final bill. However, 20 percent is not excessive if the service has been very good. A wine steward may be tipped separately, depending on the largesse of the diner and how much wine has been served. Similarly, tipping the captain is an elegant gesture but is by no means necessary.

If you have received bad service, it is better to leave a small tip, thus indicating your displeasure, than to stiff the server entirely, in which case they might surmise you simply forgot.

While the word *tip* comes from the verb *to tip,* meaning to hand over or impart information, TIP is informally considered an acronym for "To Insure Promptness."

American

What is nouvelle cuisine, and why doesn't anyone mention it anymore?

In the mid-1970s, the food world began to throw off the mantle of traditional French cooking and the methods of chef Georges Auguste Escoffier (1846–1935), who for a century had been considered a culinary monarch. (Indeed, he'd had a royal title conferred on him by Kaiser William II, who told him, "I am the emperor of Germany, but you are the emperor of chefs.") And Escoffier *could* be dictatorial: His techniques included copious amounts of butter and cream, long-cooking (some say overcooking) of meats and vegetables, and an exactitude, from garnishes to sauces (hollandaise, hollandaise, hollandaise) that was not to be deviated from, under any circumstances. No wonder the chefs of the world began to feel a little stifled.

What started as a subtle rejection soon turned into a full-scale riot, and nouvelle cuisine was born. Instead of heavy sauces, chefs used reductions, or flavored oils. Vegetables were left snappish, and fresh herbs began appearing in everything from salads to sorbets. Food became explosively visual, sprightly, and tonic, as opposed to heavy and rich. The revolution fed into our desire to eat lighter and fresher, but still to eat well.

The problem was, some people took it too far. Portions began to shrink (the theory being, if light is good, lighter is better), chefs went overboard with eye-catching ingredients like kiwi and papaya, and the whole movement started to reach a ridiculous, even parodic, proportion.

In the early nineties, a knee-jerk reaction against nouvelle cuisine began. People had had enough; they wanted veal chops and mashed potatoes and vegetables that didn't bite back. But instead of going back to the heavy days of old, a hybrid cuisine was born, one that judiciously marries the heaviness of the past with the lighter, fresher foods, and serves it in reasonably generous portions. When this kind of food includes homey favorites (like mashed potatoes), it is occasionally called Nouveau Bar & Grill; when the food shows the influence of the Pacific Rim, it is known as California Cuisine.

WHAT IS SPA CUISINE?

Spa cuisine was born at places like California's Golden Door, where very light, low-calorie meals are served to patrons pampering away excess pounds and stress. Spa cuisine is big on broths, salads and vegetables, and fresh fruits. White-meat chicken and fish often find their way onto the menu, as do small portions of grains. Occasionally, a restaurant will seek to bask in a little of that healthy glow, and offer the ladies who lunch (and their calorie-conscious companions) light meals under the heading "spa cuisine."

WHAT'S A BLUE PLATE SPECIAL?

The blue plate special, which one still occasionally encounters on diner menus, is a phrase made popular during World War II, when inexpensive meals were served on large, originally blue plates, often compartmentalized, so that the sauces from the various dishes wouldn't run into one another. The "special" was up to the chef but often consisted of meat with gravy, potatoes, and several vegetables.

Diners and luncheonettes developed their own food language, sometimes called "hash-house Greek." (This term, because so many diners seemed to be operated by Hellenics.) If the waitress called for "Adam and Eve on a raft," for instance, she wanted two poached eggs sitting on a piece of toast. "Moo juice" was milk, and "Eve with a lid," apple pie. The codes apparently evolved spontaneously, as a way for workers to have a bit of fun.

WHAT'S THE DIFFERENCE BETWEEN A SANDWICH AND A HERO?

The sandwich is the eponym of an eighteenth-century gambler named John Montagu, the fourth Earl of Sandwich, and British First Lord of the Admiralty during the American Revolution. Montagu, it seems, was so committed to the gaming tables, he refused to leave even for meals, sustaining himself with an order of sliced meats and cheeses stuffed between two slices of bread.

The etymology of the hero is vague. In *The New York Times Food Encyclopedia*, Craig Claiborne quotes a 1957 article that claims the hero was the invention of an Italian named James Manganaro, who made "whale-sized sandwiches of prosciutto and French bread to nourish himself on all-day fishing trips," and later moved to New York and opened a sandwich shop, where he sold big sandwiches called "heroboys."

While they may call them heroes in New York, in other parts of the country, sandwiches made on long loaves of Italian or French bread are called submarines, grinders, or hoagies.

French

WHAT IS BISTRO CUISINE?

Bistro cuisine is the kind of food one gets in the bistros, brasseries, and cafés throughout France. It is French home cooking taken into the marketplace without a soupçon of pretension or artifice. Relying on fresh ingredients and counting on big appetites, bistro food revels in long-cooked, full-flavored dishes, like daube (beef stew) and bouillabaisse (fish soup), as well as simple, everyday offerings such as pan-fried steak and *pomme frites* (French fries). It is robust and earthy food (as is the wine that usually accompanies it, a hearty Beaujolais), and as such never goes out of fashion.

WHAT CHARACTERIZES PROVENÇAL COOKING?

The cooking of Provence, in southeastern France, emphasizes the flavors of its Italian neighbor to the south: garlic, tomatoes, and olive oil. This cuisine also uses a lot of lamb, goat, and goat's milk products (like chèvre), and seafood from the Mediterranean (especially a local species called rockfish). Bouillabaisse (fish soup) and *pisto* (the pesto of Provence, used to flavor soups and vegetables) are several examples of the region's strong, sunny cuisine.

WHAT DOES *HORS D'OEUVRE* MEAN?

The literal translation is "outside the work," meaning outside the meal. (In French, *hors d'oeuvre* is never pluralized; no matter how many predinner tidbits you serve, there is only one work [*oeuvre*].) Hors d'oeuvre are served as a first course, may be hot or cold, fancy or quite simple. In fact, the only rule for hors d'oeuvre is that they not be excessively filling. They are meant, after all, to stimulate the appetite, not spoil it.

WHAT'S THE DIFFERENCE BETWEEN PRIX FIXE AND TABLE D'HÔTE?

Prix fixe translates to "fixed price" and refers to a menu of set dishes, all of which are offered at a single price. Table d'hôte means "table of the host" and indicates a choice of different courses, the price of which is set by the chosen entree.

WHY DO THE FRENCH EAT CHEESE AFTER THE MEAL?

Not just the French, but many Europeans enjoy a cheese course between the salad (served *after* the entree) and dessert. There are many reasons the French are recognized for this indulgence, not the least of which are the hundreds of cheeses made in France since the Middle Ages. Cheese is also highly nutritious and its creaminess the perfect complement to the sweet acidity of fruit, which often accompany cheese. A cheese course is also a way to extend the meal, which anyone who has enjoyed a three-hour supper sojourn in France well knows.

WHAT DOES THE TERM *BLEU* MEAN?

The French are notorious for eating their meat very rare. If one orders meat *bleu*, meaning blue, it will arrive just warmed through and still rather purple on the inside. The next stage is *à point,* which is the equivalent of a rare steak in America. Asking for *bien fait,* which translates to well-done, will get you a steak cooked to what we call medium. If you want your steak thoroughly cooked in Paris, however, you may be out of luck, as the French consider well-done meat vastly overcooked.

WHAT IS POT-AU-FEU?
Pot-au-feu ("pot of fire") is a dish of boiled beef and vegetables. It is cooked slowly, often three hours or more, so that the beef is very tender, the marrow inside the bones becoming soft and spreadable. Like stew, the flavor of pot-au-feu improves after a day, whereupon it is eaten as a meal in itself, accompanied, perhaps, by gherkins, horseradish, red currant jelly, and lots of French bread.

WHAT'S A GRATIN?
Gratin comes from the verb *gratter,* meaning "to scrape," and originally referred to bits of crisped food scraped off a cooking receptacle and eaten as a tidbit. These days, gratin (or foods served au gratin) refers to the golden crust that forms when a topping is browned, either in the oven or under the broiler. Cheese is usually used in gratins, but bread crumbs, nuts, and egg-and-herb mixtures are also gratineéd. Food served au gratin reaches its popular apex in *la soupe à l'oignon au gratin* (French onion soup), which often appears on bistro menus simply as *gratinée.*

WHAT'S A MOUSSE?
Mousse is the French term for "foam" or "froth," which is the consistency of a properly made mousse. Lightened with whipped cream and/or beaten egg whites, mousses are very light and soft. While we are most familiar with *mousse au chocolat,* there are

many savory mousses, as well, such as *mousse de homard* (lobster mousse).

Italian

WHAT IS ANTIPASTO?

Antipasto literally means "before the pasta" and can refer to any kind of hot or cold hors d'oeuvre. In America, we tend to think of antipasto as a large plate of sliced cheeses, salami, and marinated tidbits, like olives, artichokes, and peperoncini, but in Italy, an assortment of antipasti can include everything from fish to fritters.

WHAT'S A *PRIMI*? A *SECONDI*?

Primi is the first course of the meal (after the antipasto, that is). Small servings of pasta (three pillows of ravioli, a half-dozen gnocchi) is a popular primi, as is soup. (Though salad may be ordered as a primi, the *salade* course is generally eaten after the secondi.) The secondi, or entree, is the largest portion of the meal and can consist of meat, poultry, fish, or larger portions of pasta.

WHAT IS CALAMARI?

Calamari is squid. While Americans eat relatively little of this ten-tentacled mollusk, Italians eat quite a lot of it, baked, braised, boiled, stewed, and, in its most popular guise, fried. Chopped into ringlets, with tentacles intact, pieces of calamari are dredged in flour, fried in oil until crisp, and served with lemon wedges and sometimes dipping sauces. Well-made calamari is crisp and chewy and only slightly "fishy," and is harder to stop eating than French fries.

WHAT IS *CAPRESE*?

Caprese is a simple dish of sliced ripe tomatoes, fresh mozzarella (often buffalo mozzarella), and fresh basil, drizzled with olive oil and accompanied by Italian bread. It is a ubiquitous primi at Italian restaurants, here and in Italy.

IS BUFFALO MOZZARELLA REALLY MADE FROM BUFFALO MILK?

Real buffalo mozzarella, from the south of Italy, is indeed made with the milk of water buffaloes. However, most of the fresh "buffalo milk" mozzarella we eat, tender white orbs packed in water, is actually made with a *combination* of cow and buffalo milk. Like fresh mozzarella made from cow's milk, this hybrid mozzarella has a very short shelf life (about five days before it turns slimy and sour), whereas 100 percent *mozzarella di bufala* is a soft-ripening cheese that lasts five or six weeks. This cheese becomes soft and spreadable as it ages, and can be eaten as you would eat regular mozzarella. However, it is rarely found in America.

WHAT IS CARPACCIO?

Carpaccio is a first course made of paper-thin slices of raw beef, usually drizzled with very good olive oil. In recent years, however, the term *carpaccio* has been applied to any number of foods, particularly salmon, that are sliced thin and served raw.

The name carpaccio comes from the Italian Renaissance painter, Vittore Carpaccio. The story goes that Giusèppe Cipriani, the founder of Harry's Bar in Venice, prepared the raw beef dish for a customer who could not eat cooked beef, naming the dish in honor of the painter, whose works were being exhibited in Venice that year.

What is focaccia?

Focaccia is a descendent of the ancient Latin bread *panis foca-cius*, or "hearth bread," a flat slab of dough cooked under a bed of ashes on a stone hearth.

The Genoese took focaccia into the oven, dimpling the dough with their fingers, and pouring in olive oil and sea salt. This is the kind of focaccia we usually see. It is a flat yet pliant bread, suitable for eating as is, or slicing on the horizontal and filling.

What is the difference between pancetta and prosciutto?

Pancetta is salt-cured, unsmoked bacon. Fatty and flavorful, it is rolled tightly into a salamilike roll and sliced. Unlike American bacon, it is not usually fried and eaten by itself but is used as a savory addition to sauces and pasta dishes, or in a flavorful *battuto*.

Prosciutto is an unsmoked Italian ham that is seasoned, salted, and hung to dry. It is less fatty than American ham, more deeply colored, and rather dry. In Italy, they sell prosciutto two ways: *còtto* (cooked) and *crudo* (raw).

In America, most of the prosciutto we eat is the regal Parma ham, the king of Italian hams. It hails from the northern Italian province of Parma, where pigs fed on a special diet of chestnuts and whey (left over from the making of parmigiano-reggiano cheese) produce this excellent meat. The very best Parma ham comes from the mountain village of Langhirano, where the cool, clean air is said to contribute to the meat's exceptional quality. It is served in very thin slices, atop melon or, if you are very lucky, with chewy Italian bread, jewel-green extra-virgin olive oil, and a hunk of parmigiano-reggiano.

How can olive oil be extra-virgin?

Extra-virgin olive oil is made from olives that have never been touched before. They are cold-pressed, until they surrender their gold-green liquor. Because the nubile olives have so much more to give, two subsequent pressings are called "virgin" olive oil. After that, the olive is handled rather roughly: Solvents are added to extract more oil, the pressings go from cold to hot, and the oil treated more and more slatternly.

Extra-virgin oil can be intensely fruity and has a very low acidity (less than 1 percent). Subsequent pressings yield oils lighter in color, more acidic, and less flavorful. The kind of oil you use depends on what you'll be using it for. Extra-virgin is lovely drizzled on fresh tomatoes, but the flavor is all but lost in the base for tomato sauce. Price is another consideration. Extra-virgin (and extra-extra virgin, as first pressings are sometimes called) can cost twenty dollars and more a pint, whereas a pint of regular olive oil costs about five dollars.

What is so special about parmigiano-reggiano cheese?

Parmesans made in America may have appropriated the name, but they cannot duplicate the legendary flavor of Italy's parmigiano-reggiano. Whereas American and other parmesans are rather soft, mealy, and taste of dairy, parmigiano-reggiano, made only in Parma, Reggio, Modena, Mantua, and Bologna, is a little oily, a little salty, mellow and rich at once. A real parmigiano-reggiano is the color of straw and slightly grainy, with tiny nuggets of "crunch" in every bite. The wheel always has the words *Parmigiano-Reggiano* etched in small black dots on its surface.

Parmigiano-reggiano's unique flavor is achieved during a long aging process. Whereas most parmesan cheese is aged fourteen months, parmigiano-reggiano is aged two years, three years (in which case it is labeled *stravècchio*) or four years (*stravècchiones*). It can be eaten as is (a truly decadent experience) but is usually grated, at the table.

In Italy, parmesan cheeses that are not parmigiano-reggiano are considered *grana,* a cheese of no particular distinction.

WHY IS AN ITALIAN DESSERT CALLED *ZUPPA INGLESE*?

Zuppa inglese, which translates to "English soup," is neither. It is, however, an Italian copycat of an English trifle, made with rum-soaked sponge cake, layered with whipped cream and/or custard, and studded with candied fruits and nuts. The Italians choose to call it soup because it is meant to be eaten with a spoon.

Mexican

WHAT IS THE DIFFERENCE BETWEEN A TACO AND A TACO AL CARBON?

A taco is a folded tortilla (a pancake made of flour or cornmeal), either crisp-fried or soft, filled with any number of things: beef, chicken, pork, beans, cheese, and toppings such as sour cream, lettuce, onion, and tomato. *Al carbón* indicates foods cooked on an open grill; tacos al carbón are soft tacos filled with charcoal-grilled meats and various toppings.

Other popular tortilla dishes include:

Burrito: A flour tortilla wrapped around meat, cheese, chiles, beans, and/or vegetables. It is not native to any particular region of Mexico and, despite its Spanish name (from burro, meaning "donkey"), is more an American invention.

Chimichanga: A tortilla that is filled, rolled, and deep-fried. This dish from Sonora is usually served with guacamole, sour cream, and salsa.

Enchilada: A corn tortilla rolled around a meat or cheese filling, usually served with a tomato-based sauce.

Flauta: Meaning "flute," this flour tortilla is filled and deep-fried. Some fast-food restaurants have taken to calling them *taquitos.*

Quesadilla: A flour tortilla folded around melting cheese.

Tostada: A crisp tortilla topped with refried beans, meat or chicken, shredded lettuce, cheese, tomatoes, and guacamole.

Some other small Mexican savories are:

Empanada: A rich pastry filled with meats, cheeses, or vegetables, folded into a half-moon shape, and baked until flaky and golden. Sometimes they are filled with fruit and/or sweet cream cheese. Small empanadas are called *empanaditas.*

Gordita: A flat *masa* (cornmeal dough) cake, fried, split, and filled.

Pupusas: Masa formed around a filling and grilled.

Tamale: Masa dough wrapped in a corn husk and steamed. Tamales are often filled with *machaca* (shredded meat), green chili, and cheese, or a sweet fruit, like pineapple.

Torta: A big, messy Mexican sandwich made on a French roll, it can be filled with meats and cheeses, and is often topped with beans and mashed avocado.

WHAT IS *CARNE ASADA*?

Carne asada means "grilled meat" and usually refers to grilled beef. *Carne adobado* is a pork cutlet seasoned with a red and smoky paste made from achiote seeds; *birria* is braised goat; *ropa vieja* ("old clothes") is meat braised until it very tender and shredded; *parillada* is a sizzling plate of grilled meats, including beef, pork, and organ meats like sweetbreads; *albóndigas* are meatballs, usually served in soup.

WHAT IS *MENUDO*?

Menudo is a soup made of tripe, green chile peppers, hominy, and seasonings. Served with lime wedges and hot tortillas, it is especially popular on Sunday mornings, as it is reportedly a cure for hangovers. The combination of liquid, tonic ingredients, and calories rehydrates the brain and calms a queasy stomach. The only hurdle to relief seems to be summoning the strength to face tripe first thing in the morning.

WHAT IS MOLE?

From the Nahuatl word *mōlli* ("concoction"), mole is a thick, spicy sauce made from chiles, onions, nuts, or pumpkin seeds (commonly sold under the Spanish name *pepitas,* for "seeds"), unsweetened chocolate, and many spices. Cooked until it becomes brick-brown, it is served, at its apex, over pork, though it often accompanies poultry dishes as well. The state of Oaxaca is known for its moles, particularly *mole rojo* ("red mole") and *mole verde,* a light-green mole made with *tomatillos* (a green, tomatolike fruit with a lemony taste), chiles, cilantro, and cumin, that complements the lighter taste of seafood and poultry, as well as pork.

WHAT ARE *CHICHARRONES*?

Probably the worst thing the American Heart Association could imagine, but never mind, chicharrones are deep-fried bits of pork skin. Fried once and salted, they sometimes accompany meat dishes; fried twice, they puff up into what looks like tan Styrofoam peanuts but taste like little bits of heaven to aficionados.

WHAT IS *ORCHATA*?

Orchata (also spelled *horchata*) is a beverage made from sweetened rice milk. Served chilled, it is slightly thick and is favored by children. More grown-up nonalcoholic beverages are *agua fresca* ("fresh water"), made of fresh fruit blended with water, and the Peruvian *chicha morada,* made from purple corn and fruit juice.

WHAT IS *ESCABECHE*?

Escabeche (a Spanish word dervied from the Arabic *sakbay,* meaning "a stew of meat and vinegar") simply means to marinate food in a mixture of vinegar with herbs and spices and perhaps onion, garlic, and citrus juices. *Camarones* (shrimp) are often served escabeche, as are *pescado* (fish), *pollo* (chicken), and game, such as *conejo* (rabbit).

WHAT IS *CHIMICHURRI*?

Every country needs a standard condiment. America's is ketchup, and Argentina's is chimichurri, a dipping sauce made of olive oil, garlic, oregano, and other herbs. It always accompanies grilled meats, and can be drizzled on everything from salads to bread.

WHAT ARE *CHIFLES*?

Whereas many American entrees come with a side of fries, Central American and Caribbean dishes are often accompanied by chifles (or *plátanos*), which are fried plantain slices. Made from the plantain, a very large, sweet "cooking banana," plantains turn almost caramel-sweet when fried and, with a sprinkle of salt, are utterly addicting.

Indian

WHAT DOES TANDOORI-STYLE MEAN?

Tandoori is food cooked in a clay oven called a tandoor. A smoky fire burning beneath the oven provides both flavor and an intense heat of over 500 degrees Fahrenheit. This process allows food to cook very quickly, keeping it juicy on the inside and crisp on the outside.

While some Indian breads, like nan, are also cooked in a tandoor, it is primarily used for chicken and meats, most of which have been marinated overnight in yogurt and various spices. Chicken *tikka*, skewered chunks of marinated chicken, is one popular tandoori dish.

WHAT IS VINDALOO?

Vindaloo is a marinade of wine and garlic. Meats, poultry, and fish can all be prepared vindaloo-style, roasted, braised, or cooked in a tandoor. The preparation apparently has its roots in the Portuguese *vinho d'ahlo,* meaning "wine and garlic," and was adopted by the people of the port city of Goa, on the Arabian Sea, during the time of Portuguese colonization.

WHAT IS ROTI?

Roti is the general term for bread. The most popular breads in Indian restaurants are different only in their preparation. All are made of flour, water, and a leavening agent, and rise to different dimensions during the cooking process. Chapati is clapped into discs and fried quickly on a hot griddle, where it puffs up slightly in the center. Nan is similarly formed into a flattened disc and laid directly on the wall of the tandoor oven, where it develops patchy burn marks and takes on a slight smoky flavor. *Paratha* is made of a whole-wheat flour dough that is formed into layers, each layer brushed with ghee. This Indian "puff pastry" swells up beautifully into airy pockets when fried on a griddle. *Poori* is a deep-fried, whole-wheat flat bread. Each of these breads is eaten immediately and used to scoop up sauces, *raita* (a cooling yogurt dip), and dal.

Pappadam is not a bread but a thin, crisp cracker made of *urad* dal (a type of pulse, or lentil) that is placed on the table for nibbling at the beginning of the meal, much as Westerners lay out a basket of bread.

WHAT IS DAL?

In America, we tend to think of dal as the dark condiment that comes to the table at the beginning of an Indian meal, that little bowl of soupy something in which to dredge a bit of naan. Made with lentils, onions, and spices and usually puréed, this is indeed dal, though not at its finest.

Dal is the general term for the more than sixty different types of pulses used in Indian cooking. Dals are cooked into such dishes as *moong* dal (a mixture of the moong dal, ginger, lemon juice, herbs, and spices) and *karhi* (made with chickpeas, buttermilk, and spices), and are eaten with rice or bread, and alongside other foods.

WHAT IS CHUTNEY?

Chutney, from the Hindustani word *chatni,* meaning "strong spices," is a sweet-and-sour relish. The most popular variety is made with mango, ginger, tamarind, onion, and various spices, and cooked with vinegar and sugar until it is quite thick. Chutney can also contain any number of fruits (pineapple, coconut, banana) and vegetables (eggplant, tomato, cucumber). It is almost always offered with Indian meals, as a way to enliven and contrast the meal.

While chutney is commonly thought to be the culinary brainchild of one Major Grey, a British officer during the colonial era, the facts of this man's existence are gray, indeed. It's likely that the British were merely the first to bottle the stuff (Major Grey's chutney is the world's best-seller) and over the years somehow received credit for inventing it.

WHAT IS *LASSI*?

Lassi is a yogurt beverage served with the meal to cool down the spicy burn of some Indian dishes. It is made with plain yogurt, ice, and herbs (like mint) or fresh fruit.

WHAT IS CURRY?

Curry is, in fact, a British term, made popular during colonial times, exported to the far corners of the world, and erroneously considered to be the backbone of Indian cooking. "To me, the word 'curry' is as degrading to India's great cuisine as the term 'chop suey' was to China's," wrote Madhur Jaffrey in her book *An Invitation to Indian Cooking.* "But just as Americans have learned, in the last few years, to distinguish between the different styles of Chinese cooking and the different dishes, I fervently hope that they will soon do the same with Indian food instead of lumping it all under the dubious catchall title of 'curry.'"

Unfortunately, Indian restaurants are still seeking to make it easier on the customer, lumping dishes under umbrella titles like "Red Curries" and "Dry Curries," when in fact there simply is no such thing in India as curry, simply dishes flavored with various Indian spices such as cumin, cardamom, and tamarind, combinations of which are called masala. Made into sauces, different masala season poultry, vegetables, and meats, mostly lamb and goat, but never beef, which is not eaten in India.

WHAT IS *METHAI*?

Methai is the term for Indian confections, which tend to be very, very sweet, owing to an abundance of sweetened condensed milk and sugar syrups. The most popular methai are the regrettably named *barfi,* a chewy candy made with nuts; *gulab juman,* fried cheeselike balls made with sweetened condensed milk and brushed with sweet syrup; *rasgolla,* cheese balls served floating in a sweet, creamy syrup; *jelefi,* deep-fried squiggles of dough doused in a rosewater-flavored syrup; and *kulfi,* a cardamom-flavored ice cream.

Chinese

WHAT'S THE DIFFERENCE BETWEEN CANTONESE AND SZECHWAN FOOD?

Different regions of China obviously have different regional specialties, based on available ingredients and cooking techniques developed over many millennia.

Cantonese food was the first type of Chinese cuisine to be widely available in Chinese-American restaurants. Dishes like chop suey and sweet-and-sour shrimp, however, were not authentic Cantonese but imitations made bland and sugary for Western tastes. These kowtowing dishes gave Cantonese food a bad name and a reputation as passé by the time other Chinese cuisines, like Szechwan, hit the scene.

In truth, Cantonese cooking can be as complex as any other Asian cuisine. Very fresh seafood (especially shellfish), skinny chow mein and lo mein (wheat noodles) and *fen* (thick rice noodles) served with sauces made with everything from pork to peanuts, and dim sum are typical Cantonese dishes.

Szechwan and Hunan food, from western China, tends to be spicier. Both cuisines use a lot of chiles, onions, and ginger, and more pork and beef than their seafaring Cantonese neighbors to the south. Of the two, Hunan food is considered the hotter.

Food from Shanghai is noted for the blending of many vegetables, and the use of rich soy, vinegar, and wine-based sauces. This cuisine also specializes in pressed foods (duck and chicken), dumplings, and something called lion's head meatball, an extra-large braised pork ball wrapped in cabbage and served in a rich brown sauce.

Noodle houses, many from Hong Kong, specialize in different noodles served in broth, topped with meats, poultry, seafood, vegetables, and often spiked with chiles and fresh herbs. The diner has a choice of freshly made noodles, including *fen siu* (translucent noodles made from mung bean starch), *fun* (flat rice noodles), *e-fu* (deep-fried wheat noodles), and mein (skinny egg noodles), among others.

WHAT'S DIM SUM?

Dim sum (Cantonese for "heart's delight") are southern Chinese dumplings and pastries traditionally served for breakfast. Individually plated dim sum are wheeled around on carts or brought on trays, the diner picking from dozens of different offerings. In some dim sum restaurants, the bill is tallied simply by counting the plates.

Popular dim sum include *bao,* a yeast-risen bun filled with barbecued pork (*char su bao*), sweet bean paste (*tou sha bao*), or chicken and duck egg (*gai bao*); *chang fun,* rice flour noodles wrapped around fillings such as pork and shrimp; *har gow,* steamed shrimp dumplings covered with a translucent tapioca-flour covering; *pai gwat,* tiny spareribs in black bean sauce; and *siu mai,* open-faced steamed dumplings filled with minced pork or shrimp.

WHAT ARE FERMENTED BLACK BEANS?

Unlike the black beans familiar to Mexican and Caribbean diners, fermented black beans are small black soybeans cooked until soft, then fermented in brine for about six months. They are quite salty and are not served on their own, but used as a seasoning.

IS SHARK'S FIN SOUP REALLY MADE WITH SHARK'S FINS?

Yes. The dorsal, pectoral, and lower tail fins are all used in shark's fin soup. Long prized in Chinese cuisine for its taste (and purported aphrodisiac qualities), the expensive fins are cartilaginous and make a rich, gelatinous soup made all the grander by the addition of pork and prawns.

HOW OLD ARE HUNDRED-YEAR-OLD EGGS?

The same age as thousand-year-old eggs, which is to say, about one hundred days.

To make a hundred-year-old egg, an egg in its shell is covered with a coating of ashes, lime, and salt, and buried for sixty to one hundred days. Unearthed, a properly aged egg should be black and crusty. The white, however, is a lovely amber and the yolk, dark green and creamy. Some find the taste pungent and enjoy the eggs as an appetizer, with soy sauce and minced ginger; others find the taste (and smell) sulfuric.

Japanese

WHAT IS THE DIFFERENCE BETWEEN SUSHI AND SASHIMI?

Sushi is slices of raw fish, mixed with, laid over, or wrapped in or around small, molded pieces of vinegar–seasoned sushi rice. Sashimi is simply the raw fish, sliced very thin and served decoratively.

Most sushi restaurants have charts (often with pictures) helping the diner to decide between the dozens of types of sushi and sashimi. These choices may include *hosomaki* (thin sushi rolls), *futomaki* (thick sushi rolls), and *maki-zushi* (sushi rolls wrapped in roasted seaweed, called *nori*). Sushi can contain thin sheets of seasoned omelet (*charkin*), or bits of tofu (soybean curd).

Both sushi and sashimi are served with traditional raw fish accompaniments: *wasabi* (a fiery sea-green horseradishlike paste), slender slices of pickled ginger (to cleanse the palate), and shredded daikon radish. Accompanying sauces include soy and *ponzu*, a mixture of lime juice, soy, and rice vinegar.

WHAT IS *UDON*?

Udon is one of many types of Japanese noodles. In order of thickness, they are: udon, a thick, white wheat noodle; *ramen*, medium-thin wheat noodles; *sai fun*, potato starch noodles; *soba*, thin buckwheat noodles; and *somen*, very thin wheat noodles.

All Japanese noodles are served either in broths (such as *nabeyaki udon*, a fish broth with udon noodles, or *tanmen*, pork broth with ramen and vegetables) or alone, hot or cold, and topped with a variety of meats, fish, vegetables, and *zuke* (pickled foods).

Many noodle houses serve *gyoza,* or Japanese dumplings, little crescents of gelatinous dough filled with seafood, meats, and vegetables. These dishes are either steamed or grilled, and are served with a dipping sauce, like soy or hoisin, a thick, sweet, somewhat spicy brown sauce made of soybeans, sugar, chiles, and garlic.

WHAT IS MISO?

Because soybeans are indigenous to Japan, almost every staple ingredient, from tofu to oil, comes from soy. Miso, also called bean paste, is another soy derivative, made from fermented soybeans, salt, and a *koji,* a fermenting agent made from soybeans, barley, or rice.

There are three types of miso, of varying intensity: *Shinshu miso* is a light-yellow, all-purpose miso; *sendai miso* has a deep, reddish color and is fragrant and potent; and *hatcho miso* is dark brown and quite strong. All are very thick and rich, used to flavor soups, dressings, main dishes, and as a table condiment.

Thai

WHAT ARE SATÉ AND *PAD THAI*?

Saté are pieces of meat or chicken skewered, marinated, and broiled. It is a particular favorite in the West because it is recognizable (it looks like a slender shish kebab), and because it is easy to prepare and eat. It is served with a dipping sauce, usually sweet rice wine vinegar doctored with crushed peanuts and chiles.

Another Thai standard, though for less understandable if no

less delicious reasons, is pad thai, a mountain of cellophane noodles topped with shrimp, chicken, crushed peanuts, bean sprouts, and fresh coriander.

WHAT ARE CELLOPHANE NOODLES MADE OF?

Cellophane noodles, also known as bean threads, are translucent noodles made from the starch of mung beans. Bought dried, they look like hard, cloudy strips of plastic and require a brief soaking in hot water before they are cooked. (They may be added to soups as is.) They are distinctly chewy and form the basis for many Thai, as well as Chinese, dishes (where cellophane noodles are called *fun siu*).

WHAT'S JOKE?

Joke (pronounced "jook," and sometimes listed as such) is a dish of rice cooked in broth to a porridgelike consistency. It is served with chicken, pork, or seafood and various condiments, and topped with fresh ginger and coriander. Served alone, joke is reputed to be a restorative, as well as an antidote to too-rich food and drink.

Another dish with a provocative name (at least to Americans) is larb, a warm salad made of slices of beef or chicken, dressed with lime juice and dry chilies. Larb made with duck is called *larb pet;* with fish, *larb paduk.*

WHAT DOES PHED MEAN?

Phed is a Thai term used to denote the degree of hotness in a chile. Because Thai food (especially food from the southern provinces) use a lot of chiles, it can be extremely hot. While many standard items, such as *mee krob,* are mild enough for kids (and, in the case of mee krob, some would say *is* for kids, since the deep-fried noodles are drenched with an unctuously sweet, sticky orange sauce), other dishes, like the tamarind-chile dipping sauce *seua rong hai* (literally translated, "it makes a tiger cry"), can leave the diner scrambling for rice and ice water.

The demon pepper that causes all this delicious discomfort is usually the tiny santaka, also known as Thai chile and bird's eye chile, the third hottest chile in the world. Another culprit is the small, dried *phrik kii noo*, a reddish chile that can nestle, chameleonlike, amongst colorful dishes of Thai food.

WHAT IS LEMONGRASS?

Lemongrass is an herb with a sour, lemony flavor. One of the most important flavorings in Thai cooking, it is sometimes used fresh but more often dried, and appears in many soups as woody tubes that look like tiny pieces of bamboo. Other popular herbs include the gingery root *galangal, kaffir* lime leaves, and Thai basil, which has a sweet, aniselike flavor.

Middle Eastern
(Lebanese / Turkish)

WHAT IS BABA GANOUSH?

Baba ganoush (also called *mutabbal*) is a Lebanese spread made of roasted, puréed eggplant, lemon juice, garlic, and oil. It is quite rich and thick, and is used as a dip. Other Middle Eastern spreads include hummus, made of puréed chickpeas and tahini (sesame seed paste), garlic, and lemon, and tabouleh, made of bulgar, chopped parsley, mint, and onions dressed in olive oil and lemon (this is also eaten as a salad). Greeks dip triangles of pita bread in *taramasalata,* made of fish roe, lemon juice, and olive oil, and in *tzatziki,* thin slices of cucumber mixed with plain yogurt.

WHAT'S THE DIFFERENCE BETWEEN *SHAWARMA* AND *SOUVLAKI*?

Shawarma is an Armenian dish made of marinated meat (usually lamb) sliced very thin, skewered, and grilled. The Greek version, souvlaki, is made the same way, except the meat is cut into chunks. Both versions are often pulled off the skewer and tucked into a pita pocket, where they are doused with a thin yogurt-based sauce and garnished with grilled onions and peppers.

WHAT'S FALAFEL MADE OF?

Falafel is made by puréeing chickpeas (or fava beans) with parsley and spices, and deep-frying them into crisp croquettes the size of Ping-Pong balls. They are served as appetizers or packed into a pita, and drizzled with a tahini- or yogurt-based sauce

IS THERE ANY DIFFERENCE BETWEEN SARMA AND DOLMAS?

Sarma (Armenian) and dolmas (Greek) are both marinated grape leaves stuffed with seasoned rice and, sometimes, ground lamb, pine nuts, and onion. They are rolled, like little cigars, and packed tightly so none of the filling spills out. They can be chilled overnight (to let the flavors mingle and develop), served cold or braised, and eaten hot or at room temperature.

WHAT IS MOUSSAKA?

Moussaka is one of the most popular main courses in Greece. Found in nearly every Greek restaurant, it is made by layering ground lamb and sliced eggplant, and covering the mixture with a rich custard sauce that often includes cheese. Moussaka is baked until it is bubbly and brown, and is sliced and served like lasagna.

WHAT IS BAKLAVA?

Baklava is a Greek pastry made by layering butter-soaked phyllo dough with mixtures of chopped nuts and honey. After it is baked, a warm honey-lemon syrup is poured over the baklava, so that the pastry becomes incredibly rich and sweet. It is usually cut into small diamonds, a two-inch piece being more than filling.

A close relative is the Lebanese *kataif*, which is made the same way but uses a pastry dough that looks (and tastes) like shredded wheat to form the layers. Whereas baklava is always baked in a large, flat pan, kataif is often formed into individual rolls that look like small, cylindrical haystacks.

FIFTEEN

Miscellaneous

♈♉♊

"Taste all, and hand the knowledge down."
—GARY SNYDER, *Turtle Island*, "*Ethnobotony*," 1974

There are many things modern eaters take for granted, not least the origin of their food supply. In the nineteenth century, when 75 percent of Americans were involved in agriculture, people's diets were fairly limited: They ate what they (or their neighbors) grew, bought staples such as sugar and salt from the general store, and waited for the Wells Fargo wagon to deliver exotic and expensive comestibles, like oranges.

As we approach the twenty-first century, less than 3 percent of America's population produces its food supply. We buy what we want in whatever amount we choose at the local market, where a cruise through the aisles is like taking a trip around the world: All manner of esoteria, from hundreds of different countries, is right there on the shelves, ripe for the picking.

Which doesn't mean we know what we're eating, where it comes from, or why it looks the way it does. Which is certainly forgivable; only pedants and nutritionists need to know the source of all food. However, a certain affectionate curiosity for the foods we eat every day is not untoward. For instance, what alchemic process gets oil from corn?

HOW IS CORN OIL MADE?

While it's easy to understand how rich foods, such as olive and walnuts, give up copious amounts of oil, how does corn, which is only .8 grams of fat per cup, yield millions of gallons of oil?

The answer is, the endosperm, the center of the corn kernel rich in lipids, protein, and carbohydrate. The endosperm is processed much as other products are for their refined oils: The oil is extracted by pressure under heat, which results in a clear, bland oil. (Unrefined oils are cold-pressed and tend to be cloudy and stronger tasting.)

What the consumer gains in the availability of corn oil, he often loses in other corn products: The nutrient-rich endosperm is removed from most commercially produced corn foods, such as cornmeal and grits.

WHAT MAKES POPCORN POP?

When a dried corn kernel is heated, the moisture trapped inside turns to steam, causing the kernel to explode.

Not all corn will pop. Fresh corn won't, because it has a lower internal moisture content. Similarly, field corn (used as cattle feed) will not pop. Native Americans were the ones who discovered dried corn's popping qualities over 500 years ago, often tossing whole cobs directly onto the fire and gathering up the popped kernels as they jumped from the flames. Necklaces were sometimes made from the popped kernels, and were sold to Columbus, Cortés, and other early explorers. It seems popcorn derived its name from the Old English word *poppe,* meaning "exploding sound."

Make sure to keep popcorn kernels in an airtight container, as exposure to air will rob them of some of their internal moisture, which will in turn keep them from popping.

WHY DON'T YOU EVER SEE CASHEWS IN THE SHELL?

Cashew nuts (*Anacardium occidentale*) grow on the outside of the yellow, red, or white cashew apple, a fruit indigenous to South America and grown in many tropical climates. The apple itself is soft and sweet, but the buttery, kidney-shaped cashew is enclosed in a hard shell so toxic, it can blister the skin and, if ingested, cause death. That's why all shelling and cleaning is done long before cashews reach the market.

ARE PEANUTS REALLY BEANS?

Yes. Nuts grow on trees, and peanuts, which grow on vines under the ground, are legumes. The misnomer originated because a peanut's shell was considered nutlike and its fleshy inside not unlike a fresh green pea, hence the name "pea-nut."

While peanuts and peanut butter are now standard household foods, this wasn't the case in the mid-1800s. The peanut hadn't been in America long, having traveled from South America first to Europe (where it wasn't well received), then to the Orient and Africa, before reaching the American colonists, who considered it fit only for animals and the very poor. Slaves in the South knew better, having brought *nguba* ("peanut") vines with them from Africa, hence the peanut's nickname, "goober." Though peanuts were used to feed hungry soldiers during the Civil War (they even roasted and made "coffee" out of them), they were still considered a base food; peanut references, such as "peanut gallery" (the seats farthest from the action in theaters and fairs) and "working for peanuts," were denigrations until the turn of the century. Then, at the 1904 World's Fair, peanut butter was introduced as a health food for the elderly (children seemed to like it a lot more), and in 1906 two Italians living in Pennsylvania began a peanut-roasting business called Planter's Peanuts.

But perhaps the biggest boon to the little bean's popularity was a scientist named George Washington Carver, who dedicated his life to educating the public about the health-giving properties and versatility of the humble peanut. In his lifetime (1864–1943), this black agronomist from the Tuskegee Institute in Alabama invented and patented over three hundred peanut products, including peanut butter, mayonnaise, cheese, chili sauce, shampoo, shaving cream, axle grease, and shoe polish.

IS IT DANGEROUS TO EAT RAW EGG YOLKS?

In 1989, after a spate of outbreaks of salmonella, potentially lethal food bacteria traceable to raw egg yolks, people were warned to eat egg yolks only after thorough cooking. Cookbooks and cooking magazines were discouraged from printing recipes that contained uncooked yolks (such as hollandaise and eggnog), and recipe testers began revising like mad. Although concern is founded, hysteria is not. Fear of salmonella is easily ameliorated by taking several precautions.

While it is estimated that 40 percent of chickens are contaminated with salmonella, not necessarily all of the 40 percent actually carry the bacteria. (One estimate, given by the Egg Nutrition Center, is that one in ten thousand eggs is tainted.) To avoid all possibility of contamination, take these precautions: Discard eggs that are cracked, as salmonella grows tenfold per hour at room temperature. Store eggs in the refrigerator, and keep dishes that contain eggs, like mayonnaise, well chilled. Salmonella is killed at 160 degrees Fahrenheit, or when eggs are pasteurized, which means keeping them at 140 degrees for three minutes. Yolks can then be used with complete confidence in recipes that require no further cooking.

Acids are also assumed to kill salmonella, though there has never been a definitive statement issued by the FDA corroborating this. Theoretically, lemon juice and vinegar added to raw yolks kill any salmonella bacteria within ten minutes, so mix yolks and acidic ingredients first and allow them to stand while you make dressings that include raw egg yolks, such as Caesar salad dressing and mayonnaise.

IS THERE ANY DIFFERENCE BETWEEN BROWN EGGS AND WHITE EGGS?
Just the color of the shell. Brown eggs and white eggs are laid by different breeds of hen. Any nutritional and taste differences between eggs are determined not by shell color, but by what the hens eat and the conditions in which they are raised.

WHAT ARE SHIRRED EGGS?
Shirred eggs are baked eggs, cooked in buttered ramekins until just set. They are often topped with bread crumbs, spinach, mushrooms, or cheese.

Eggs may be easily shirred in the microwave, though they won't form any lovely crustiness. Simply butter a ramekin (small glass dish), break the egg into it, and prick the yolk carefully once or twice with a toothpick or sharp knife. Cover loosely, and cook at 100 percent for one minute.

WHERE DID EGGS BENEDICT COME FROM?
Delmonico's Restaurant, in New York City. The story goes that in the late 1920s two of the famed restaurant's patrons, Mr. and Mrs. LeGrand Benedict, complained there was nothing new on the lunch menu. Some possibilities were discussed, and the result—toasted English muffin halves topped with slices of Canadian bacon, poached eggs, and a dollop of hollandaise sauce—was named in the Benedicts' honor.

WHAT IS A *CROQUE-MONSIEUR*?

Croque-monsieur (from the French word *croquant,* meaning "crisp") is the staple of every French café. It is a sandwich made of crustless bread, filled with Gruyère cheese and a slice of ham, grilled in butter, or pressed between a special sandwich-grilling iron made for this purpose. Adding a fried egg to the sandwich makes it a *croque-madame.*

WHAT IS CRÈME FRAÎCHE?

Crème fraîche is pasteurized cream to which a lactic bacteria culture has been added. The result is a thick, tangy cream not unlike sour cream in taste, but much more velvety. And, unlike sour cream, which curdles when heated, crème fraîche can be mixed easily into hot liquids. It is divine spooned over fruits and berries, and plopped on savory and sweet foods, like baked potatoes and rich desserts.

While crème fraîche is an inexpensive staple in France, in America it tends to be hard to find and unnecessarily expensive, especially when making it at home is so simple. Combine one cup of whipping cream with one tablespoon of buttermilk in a glass container. Let the mixture stand at room temperature until very thick, between eight and twenty-four hours. Stir well, cover, and refrigerate. It will last up to ten days.

WHAT MAKES CREAM SOUR?

Like crème fraîche, sour cream is made from pasteurized cream treated with lactic acid. It often also contains a stabilizing agent, like rennet or gelatin, to help keep it creamy. It has no relation to *sour milk,* which is unpasteurized milk that has aged and turned sour as a result of naturally occurring lactic acid bacteria. Therefore, the pasteurized milk in your refrigerator will never turn into sour milk (a staple of many prepasteurization recipes, when soured milk products lent both taste and leavening properties) simply into spoiled milk.

If you have an old recipe that calls for sour milk, substitute buttermilk.

What is buttermilk?

Originally, buttermilk was what remained in the milk churn after fresh milk had been left to "clabber" (allowed to stand until it was somewhat sour). The fat in the milk would float to the top, becoming butter. This was removed and the rest of the milk rechurned. It would be slightly sour and flecked with golden butter particles.

Today, buttermilk is simply whole (or skim) milk soured by a culture. Sometimes bits of butter are added to give the look of authentic, old-timey buttermilk. Nutritionally, it is comparable to whole (or skim) milk. It is slightly sour and a boon to many baked goods, especially biscuits and pancakes. It is also suitable for drinking, though this seems to be an acquired taste. It tastes a lot like thin yogurt and may be substituted, cup for cup, for the same.

What is clotted cream?

Also called Devonshire cream, as it is the specialty of Devonshire, England, clotted cream is an incredibly rich unpasteurized cream product that defies comparison. I tasted it for the first time as a teenager, when my mother brought four small glass jars of it from London. I promptly ate three and only reluctantly allowed the family to consume the fourth.

While I believe I dug into this semisolid, ivory-colored divinity with my fingers, it is traditionally served as part of a "cream tea," spread on scones, or spooned atop fruits and desserts. In America, it is available in specialty shops and some supermarkets. Because it is made from unpasteurized milk, which is hard to find, it is difficult to duplicate at home.

If you find yourself in possession of some unpasteurized milk, the process is worth a try. Heat the milk, without boiling, until a semisolid circle forms on the top. Remove the mixture from the heat and allow to cool, whereupon the top will turn yellow and crusty, and the cream beneath thick and creamy.

While I have tried this once, with satisfactory results, it did not approach that first clotted cream experience.

WHAT IS FRESH CHEESE?

A self-explanatory term, fresh cheese is cheese that has not been ripened or aged. It is simply milk that is allowed to thicken, sometimes with the addition of bacteria, or with rennet or gelatin, until the milk separates into semisolid curds and liquid whey. After the whey is drained off (to varying degrees, depending on the variety of cheese), the curds are shaped. Examples of fresh cheese include cottage cheese, cream cheese, and fresh mozzarella.

WHAT IS POT CHEESE?

Pot cheese is the same as cottage cheese, except that more of the whey is drained off, resulting in a thicker, richer product with the consistency of a ricotta cheese. When pot cheese is molded, it goes by the name *farmer cheese*.

WHAT IS CHANTILLY?

Chantilly (named for the château de Chantilly, the house of a seventeenth-century nobleman known for its fine cuisine) is the French name for fresh cream whipped to the consistency of soft, whipped cream. Unsweetened, chantilly is used in savory preparations, such as *poulet à la chantilly* (chicken with cream); sweetened, it accompanies desserts.

WHAT'S THE DIFFERENCE BETWEEN LIGHT AND DARK BROWN SUGAR, AND CAN THEY BE USED INTERCHANGEABLY?

The addition of molasses, a by-product of the sugar-making process, is what makes sugar brown and moist. Light brown sugar contains less molasses and therefore has a more subtle flavor. Almost without exception, light and dark brown sugar may be substituted for each other, cup for cup, with the understanding that dark brown sugar will impart a somewhat more intense flavor.

HOW DO YOU KEEP BROWN SUGAR FROM GETTING HARD?

Because air robs brown sugar of moisture, the best way to keep it soft is to store it airtight. Buying brown sugar in plastic bags helps. If the sugar does become hard, try one of the following: (1) Place a piece of apple in the sugar bag or box, and seal it tight. In one to two days, the sugar will leech moisture from the apple and soften. Remove the apple and store the sugar in an airtight container. (2) Put the loose sugar in a baking pan alongside an ovenproof cup of water. Cover the pan, and bake at 200 degrees Fahrenheit for twenty minutes, until softened. (3) You can also try softening sugar in the microwave. Place the sugar and a slice of apple in a microwave-safe dish and microwave for twenty seconds. Break up the sugar, allow it to cool, and use it as soon as possible, since sugar softened in both the oven and the microwave becomes hard again rather quickly.

WHAT IS CASTOR SUGAR?

Castor (or caster) sugar is superfine sugar, most commonly used in Great Britain. The British also enjoy two types of other sweeteners not ordinarily found in the United States: Demerara sugar and golden syrup.

Demerara sugar is a dry, crystalline light brown sugar from Guyana. It is used like white sugar and is of identical sweetness. Golden syrup is a very light treacle (the British term for molasses) that has the consistency of thick corn syrup. The color is clear and golden, and the taste subtly sweet and toasty, quite unlike any other syrup on the market. The most popular brand of golden syrup is Lyle's, which has recently found its way onto American supermarket shelves, either bottled or in lovely green tins emboldened by a crowned golden lion.

How is maple sugar made?

Pure maple syrup (what the Native Americans called "sweet water") is tapped from maple trees in Canada, New York, and Vermont during a very short (four to six weeks) season in early spring. This sap is boiled and the water content allowed to evaporate, until the syrup becomes thick and quite sweet. It's a long process, taking between twenty and fifty gallons of sap to make one gallon of syrup. Boiled until almost all the liquid evaporates, the syrup becomes *maple sugar,* which is nearly twice as sweet as white sugar.

Commercially made pancake syrup contains 2 percent or less of real maple syrup, and is usually made of corn syrup with artificial maple flavoring.

What is the difference between molasses and sorghum?

Molasses is a by-product of the sugar-making process. After the sugar cane or sugar beets have been refined, what's left is a blackish-brown liquid. *Light molasses* comes from the first boiling of this liquid, *dark molasses* (which has a stronger, smokier taste) from the second. *Blackstrap molasses* comes from the third boiling, and is somewhat bitter, but prized for its health-giving properties, namely its high iron content (3.2 milligrams per tablespoon). Whether molasses is unsulfered or sulfured depends entirely on whether sulfur has been used in the refining process; unsulfered molasses tends to be a bit lighter and clearer than sulfured.

Sorghum is made from a grass of the same name and is processed much like molasses. The tastes are similar, with sorghum perhaps a bit stronger. They may be substituted, cup for cup, for each other, provided the cook finds the taste suitable.

WHAT IS MALT?

Malt is made from barley that is sprouted, roasted, and ground. This powder is used in the making of beer and spirits (primarily scotch) and malt vinegar. If the powdered malt is soaked in water, heated, and liquefied, the result is *malt extract,* a heavy syrup that is used as a sweetener. Dried and mixed with sugar and dried milk, malt extract becomes *malted milk powder,* the toasty-sweet stuff we stir into milk and ice-cream drinks. Malt tablets are also available in some pharmacies and are used as a dietary supplement rich in niacin and B-vitamins.

WHAT IS MARZIPAN?

Marzipan, a confectionery paste made of ground almonds, sugar, and egg whites, is either eaten as is (usually molded into tiny fruit shapes and dipped in colored sugar) or is used for flavoring and decorating cakes and pastries. Though Arabs brought marzipan to Europe, the name is an anglicization of the Italian *marzapane,* originally meaning a "sweet box" and its contents.

WHAT'S A MOTHER OF VINEGAR?

A mother of vinegar is a ghostly looking glob that forms in wine that's been left to sit too long. Don't throw it away, as this apparition is in fact what makes vinegar.

The bacterium (*Mycoderma aceti*) found in wine, when heated to between 59 degrees and 86 degrees, will begin to grow a mother. This often happens completely by accident, when a bottle of wine (or vinegar, which can grow its own mother) is exposed to warmth for a prolonged period of time.

To make vinegar, a mother must be transferred to a clean bottle or crock, to which wine (white, red, or champagne) is added. After several weeks, this wine will have turned to vinegar, at which point the mother must be transferred and reused, or discarded, as left unchecked the mother will continue to swell until she completely fills the vessel.

WHAT IS THE DIFFERENCE BETWEEN SACCHARIN AND ASPARTAME?

Saccharin is a synthetically produced, noncaloric sweetener five hundred times sweeter than sugar. Chemically, it breaks down to $C_7H_5NO_3S$, which translates to benzosulfimide gluside. It was discovered in the 1880s, apparently by accident, by a researcher at Johns Hopkins University. Several studies have shown saccharin to be carcinogenic.

Aspartame, known popularly by its brand name, NutraSweet, was introduced in the 1980s. A synthesis of the amino acids L-aspartic acid and L-phenylalanine, it is 180 times sweeter than sugar. It loses its sweetening powers when heated, but has, for the most part, replaced saccharin as the artificial sweetener of choice in cold, sugar-free beverages. It is not, however, recommended for use by pregnant women, those with preexisting pigmented melanoma (a type of cancer), or for people suffering from PKU (phenylketonuria, an inherited disease).

Claims that artificial sweeteners aid in the fight against obesity have been repeatedly discredited. It seems the body, tasting this artificial "sugar," anticipates sugar's effects. When these fail to occur, the body begins to crave sugar and calories, stimulating the desire to eat. Hence, any calories saved by choosing, say, a diet drink, are usually made up for later in the day by actual food.

WHAT IS FOOD COLORING MADE FROM, AND IS IT SAFE?
Artificial food coloring, the liquid tints we buy in the market in tiny plastic bottles, is made from various oils. Minuscule amounts are needed to color foods. Natural food colorings, which are less readily available, are derived from plants, vegetables, and insects. These colors tend to be weaker and less stable. Both come under the intense scrutiny of the Food and Drug Administration and are considered safe.

WHAT SORTS OF FLOWERS ARE EDIBLE?
The flowers of many plants, fruits, and vegetables are indeed edible. Most commonly eaten are squash and zucchini blossoms, which can be dipped in seasoned flour and lightly fried. Nasturtiums and pansies are seen more and more in salads, and violets have long been prized for cake decorating, either candied (dipped in a simple sugar syrup and crystallized) or au natural. Some flowers are used as herbs (lavender, lovage), others eaten as greens (dandelion, mustard flowers), and some brewed into tea (chamomile). Other edible flowers include arugula flowers, borage, calandula, chive flowers, daisies (petals only), geraniums, hollyhocks, honeysuckle, marigolds, rose petals, and violas.

Before chomping up the garden, consult a book on horticulture.

ARE THERE CERTAIN FOODS THAT SHOULD NOT BE PUT IN STERLING SILVER? CAN YOU WASH STERLING SILVER IN THE DISHWASHER?

Any food that contains sulfur, like eggs or sulfured molasses, will cause silver to tarnish. While this will not hurt the silver, it will require that it be repolished. One food that can irreparably damage silver is salt, which can pit sterling silver permanently. For this reason, silver salt shakers should be emptied after each use.

Sterling silver may be washed in the dishwasher, provided it is not washed with stainless steel, which can cause sterling silver to discolor. Many owners of fine silver also insist on clearing the plates and utensils themselves, to avoid accidental dumping of an heirloom fork into the trash.

WHAT IS THE WORLD'S MOST EXPENSIVE FOOD?

Fresh truffles are about $480 a pound, and the spice saffron sells for about $600 a pound. Beluga caviar, however, tips the scales at upwards of $800 per pound. The prices are three very good reasons these wonderful foods are enjoyed in very small quantities.

Barr, Ann, and Paul Levy. *The Official Foodie Handbook: Be Modern—Worship Food*. New York: Arbor House, 1984.

Birmingham, Frederic A., ed. *Esquire Drink Book*. New York: Harper & Brothers, 1956.

Bruno, Pasquale, Jr. *The Ultimate Pizza*. Chicago: Contemporary Books, 1995.

Burum, Linda. *A Guide to Ethnic Food in Los Angeles*. New York: HarperCollins, 1992.

Clayton, Bernard. *Bernard Clayton's New Complete Book of Breads*. New York: Simon and Shuster, 1987.

Conran, Terence, and Caroline Conran. *Conran Cookbook*. New York: Weathervane Books, 1980.

Craig, Diana. *A Miscellany of Cooks' Wisdom*. Philadelphia: Running Press, 1992.

David, Elizabeth. *English Bread and Yeast Cookery*. New York: Viking, 1980.

Drury, John. *Rare and Well Done*. Chicago: Quadrangle Books, 1966.

Evans, Travers Moncure, and David Greene. *The Meat Book*. New York: Charles Scribner's Sons, 1973.

Fisher, M. F. K. *The Art of Eating*. New York: Vintage Books, 1976.

Fussell, Betty. *I Hear America Cooking*. New York: Viking Penguin, 1986.

Green, Jonathon, ed. *Consuming Passions*. New York: Fawcett Columbine, 1985.

Hazan, Marcella. *More Classic Italian Cooking*. New York: Random House, 1978.

Herbst, Sharon Tyler. *Food Lover's Companion*. New York: Barron's, 1995.

Hillman, Howard. *Kitchen Science*. Revised edition. Boston: Houghton Mifflin Company, 1989.

Jaffrey, Madhur. *An Invitation to Indian Cooking*. New York: Vintage Books, 1973.

Kafka, Barbara. *Microwave Gourmet*. New York: William Morrow and Company, 1987.

Lang, Jenifer Harvey, ed. *Larousse Gastronomique*. New York: Crown Publishers, 1988.

Lobel, Leon, and Stanley Lobel. *The Lobel Brothers Complete Guide to Meat*. Philadelphia: Running Press, 1990.

Loomis, Susan Herrmann. *The Great American Seafood Cookbook*. New York: Workman Publishing, 1988.

McGee, Harold. *The Curious Cook*. San Francisco: North Point Press, 1990.

Miller, Mark. *Coyote Cafe*. Berkeley: Ten Speed Press, 1989.

Nathan, Joan. *Jewish Cooking in America*. New York: Alfred A. Knopf, 1994.

O'Neill, Molly. *New York Cookbook*. New York: Workman Publishing, 1992.

Panati, Charles. *Extraordinary Origins of Everyday Things*. New York: Harper & Row, 1987.

Rolnick, Harry. *The Complete Book of Coffee*. Hong Kong: Melitta, 1982.

Roden, Claudia. *Coffee, A Connoisseur's Companion*. New York: Random House, 1994.

Rombauer, Irma S., and Marion Rombauer Becker. *The Joy of Cooking*. New York: New American Library, 1964.

Root, Waverly, and Richard de Rochemont. *Eating in America*. Hopewell, New Jersey: The Ecco Press, 1981.

Root, Waverly. *Food*. New York: Simon & Schuster, 1980.

Russo, Julee, and Sheila Lukins. *The New Basics*. New York: Workman Publishing, 1989.

St. Pierre, Brian. *A Perfect Glass of Wine*. San Francisco: Chronicle Books, 1996.

In every corner of the world, on every subject under the sun, Penguin represents quality and variety—the very best in publishing today.

For complete information about books available from Penguin—including Puffins, Penguin Classics, and Arkana—and how to order them, write to us at the appropriate address below. Please note that for copyright reasons the selection of books varies from country to country.

In the United Kingdom: Please write to *Dept. JC, Penguin Books Ltd, FREEPOST, West Drayton, Middlesex UB7 0BR.*

If you have any difficulty in obtaining a title, please send your order with the correct money, plus ten percent for postage and packaging, to *P.O. Box No. 11, West Drayton, Middlesex UB7 0BR*

In the United States: Please write to *Consumer Sales, Penguin USA, P.O. Box 999, Dept. 17109, Bergenfield, New Jersey 07621-0120.* Visa and MasterCard holders call 1-800-253-6476 to order all Penguin titles

In Canada: Please write to *Penguin Books Canada Ltd, 10 Alcorn Avenue, Suite 300, Toronto, Ontario M4V 3B2*

In Australia: Please write to *Penguin Books Australia Ltd, P.O. Box 257, Ringwood, Victoria 3134*

In New Zealand: Please write to *Penguin Books (NZ) Ltd, Private Bag 102902, North Shore Mail Centre, Auckland 10*

In India: Please write to *Penguin Books India Pvt Ltd, 706 Eros Apartments, 56 Nehru Place, New Delhi 110 019*

In the Netherlands: Please write to *Penguin Books Netherlands bv, Postbus 3507, NL-1001 AH Amsterdam*

In Germany: Please write to *Penguin Books Deutschland GmbH, Metzlerstrasse 26, 60594 Frankfurt am Main*

In Spain: Please write to *Penguin Books S.A., Bravo Murillo 19, 1° B, 28015 Madrid*

In Italy: Please write to *Penguin Italia s.r.l., Via Felice Casati 20, I-20124 Milano*

In France: Please write to *Penguin France S.A., 17 rue Lejeune, F–31000 Toulouse*

In Japan: Please write to *Penguin Books Japan, Ishikiribashi Building, 2–5–4, Suido, Bunkyo-ku, Tokyo 112*

In Greece: Please write to *Penguin Hellas Ltd, Dimocritou 3, GR–106 71 Athens*

In South Africa: Please write to *Longman Penguin Southern Africa (Pty) Ltd, Private Bag X08, Bertsham 2013*